Charles Derber is one of our most astute and eloquent social critics…His political analysis is persuasive and is enlivened by graceful prose.

Howard Zinn, *From GREED TO GREEN*

In this lucid and informed study, Charles Derber breaks through the necessary illusions and shows how the United States is being turned into a "sociopathic society."

Noam Chomsky, *From SOCIOPATHIC SOCIETY*

"This book is crucial for understanding the recent transformations of American populism and politics, with the second coming of Trumpism. Trump wins support by presenting himself as a populist, which means in order to understand Trump and his appeal, it is necessary to understand populism and its evolution. Despite Trump's claim to embody the interests of the common citizen against contemptuous 'elitists,' he has surrounded himself by corporate oligarchs, often billionaires, who have cut taxes for the very rich as they slash services upon which the vast majority depend. Derber proposes this can only be countered by a genuine left-wing populism which offers programs that truly guarantee a viable standard of living for people who are legitimately anxious and insecure. Derber's contrast of far-right populism with a positive left-leaning populism offers a distinctive perspective on populism itself, and makes clear what needs to be done to defeat far-right populism. This is a book that will give hope in the midst of dark times!"

Yale R. Magrass, *Chancellor Professor of Sociology and Anthropology, University of Massachusetts-Dartmouth*

"This text offers a clear and concise framework that can help students and the general public make sense of the present political moment. The book builds on social movement literature to make a case that we need such social justice movements to be at the forefront of a new left positivism that can counter the negative positivism of the right. Part of what is captivating about this text is that it applies a fresh new frame to a set of factors that are being hotly contested among pundits and intellectuals trying to make sense of the moment. As well, the text shows that we already have the tools we need to build this positive populist movement because we've already done this at other points in our past."

Adam Saltsman, *Associate Professor & Acting Chair, Department of Urban Studies, Worcester University*

"There have been numerous texts published on the subject of right-wing populism and the Trump presidency in the last eight years. However, I believe that this book provides a new and unique perspective that hasn't really been addressed in those works. The juxtaposition of left-wing versus right-wing populism in this book is a novel approach to the subject that would inform both scholarship and activism. The presentation of a potential positive populism that is rooted in democracy provides a potent and useful model for understanding mobilization on the left and a critical ground for generating hope for a way out of the current dark times."

Stanislav Vysotsky, *Associate Professor of Sociology, University of the Fraser Valley*

"We are living through unprecedented times, causing a great deal of generalized anxiety. Across a broad array of social movements – for immigration, climate and environmental justice, health equity, educational justice, and housing/economic organizing – people are looking for fresh analysis and strategies. This book really answers that call, and Derber's style of writing is intelligent and insightful while also being accessible to public audiences. I believe this book will have wide appeal as it is such a timely contribution, importantly presenting sociological and political economic analyses of our current political moment. And while this political turn seems extreme and unparalleled, this book lends historical analysis to dissect what is happening, what predated this moment, and what is needed to protect the commons and preserve human rights."

Shelley White, *Associate Professor of Global Public Health, Boston College*

"In this clear and well-argued analysis Charles Derber rescues the long-suppressed story of America's experience with populism. Debunking the dominant narrative which describes populism as inherently demagogic, right-wing and supportive of authoritarianism, he recalls that populists were important players on the left in four phases of American history: abolitionism, the 1890s uprising against the Robber Barons, the New Deal labor movements and in the 1960s the movement for civil rights and against the Vietnam War. While hard economic times generate popular anger on both left and right against political and corporate elites Derber argues that Donald Trump's attack on globalisation and his use of tariffs apparently to encourage investors to support American workers are a smoke screen. Behind it, Trump offers the billionaire class lucrative government contracts and big tax breaks while also cutting crucial social programs for workers. The Democratic Party has become too embedded in identity politics to oppose Trump effectively. It needs to emphasise economic and class issues. Political optimism is scarce these days but Derber makes a powerful case that populism of the left has a broader base in American society than the mainstream media usually suggests. His book deserves to become a key text for uniting community organisers and activists of all kinds."

Jonathan Steele, *former chief foreign correspondent for The Guardian*

"If you want to learn about the history of progressive populism and its phony populist opposition, this is the book for you. If you also want to learn what you can do about Trumpism now, this is the book for you."

Ralph Nader

"*Fighting Oligarchy* disentangles the central confusion of our times over how to address the falling living standards for most Americans. Corporate-backed right-wing populism will fail to address the real drivers of extreme inequality, stagnant wages and rising costs, and billionaire power grabs. As Charles Derber writes in this illuminating book, the only path forward is a progressive left populism, with a program to challenge billionaire oligarchy and corporate power."

Chuck Collins, *Institute for Policy Studies, co-editor, Inequality.org and author of* Burned by Billionaires: How Concentrated Wealth and Power are Ruining Our Lives and Planet

Fighting Oligarchy

This book offers a new analysis of why Trump's Far Right populism helped him win the Presidency twice, and how it enshrined a corporate establishment that he claimed to run against. Charles Derber presents a counter history of positive left populism and argues that populist parties gain power in eras of hard times for working people while mainstream parties lose voter support as they defend the existing system.

Fighting Oligarchy: How Positive Populism Can Reclaim America makes the unorthodox case that only a left-leaning positive populist movement is likely to defeat Trump and his corporate regime. Derber highlights the core principles of resistance to build a new and sustainable US democracy.

Charles Derber is professor of sociology at Boston College, USA. He is the author of 30 books, most recently *Dying for Capitalism* (Routledge, 2023) *Who Owns Democracy* (Routledge, 2024) and *Bonfire* (Routledge, 2025).

Universalizing Resistance Series
Edited by Charles Derber and Suren Moodliar

The modern social sciences began in the late 19th century when capitalism was establishing itself as the dominant global system. Social science began as a terrifying awakening: that a militarized, globalizing capitalism was creating the greatest revolution in history, penetrating every part of society with the passions of self-interest and profit and breaking down community and the common good. The universalizing of the market promised universal prosperity but delivered an intertwined sociopathic system of money-making, militarism and environmental destruction now threatening the survival of all life itself.

In the 21st century, only a universalized resistance to this now fully universalized matrix of money, militarism and me-firstism can save humanity. History shows that people can join together under nearly impossible odds to create movements against tyranny for the common good. But when the world faces a universalizing system of madness and extinction, it takes new forms of resistance moving Copyright Material – Provided by Taylor & Francis beyond the "silo" movements for social justice that have emerged notably in the US in recent decades: single-issue movements separated by issue, race, gender, social class, nation and geography. The story of what universalized movements look like, how they are beginning to be organized, how they "intersect" with each other against the reigning system of power, and how they can grow fast enough to save humanity is the purpose of this series.

The series is publishing works by leading thinkers and activists developing the theory and practice of universalizing resistance. The books are written to engage professors, students, activists and organizers, and citizens who recognize the desperate urgency of a universalizing resistance that can mobilize the general population to build a new global society preserving life with justice.

Fighting Oligarchy
How Positive Populism Can Reclaim America
Charles Derber

For more information about this series, please visit: https://www.routledge.com/Universalizing-Resistance/book-series/RESIST

Fighting Oligarchy

How Positive Populism Can Reclaim America

Charles Derber

Routledge
Taylor & Francis Group

NEW YORK AND LONDON

Designed cover image: Jay Yates, Unsplash

First published 2026
by Routledge
605 Third Avenue, New York, NY 10158

and by Routledge
4 Park Square, Milton Park, Abingdon, Oxon, OX14 4RN

*Routledge is an imprint of the Taylor & Francis Group, an informa
business*

For Product Safety Concerns and Information please contact our EU
representative GPSR@taylorandfrancis.com. Taylor & Francis Verlag
GmbH, Kaufingerstraße 24, 80331 München, Germany.

ISBN: 978-1-041-11998-2 (hbk)
ISBN: 978-1-041-11997-5 (pbk)
ISBN: 978-1-003-66257-0 (ebk)

DOI: 10.4324/9781003662570

Typeset in Sabon
by KnowledgeWorks Global Ltd.

Contents

Introduction

The Two Faces of Populism: Tyranny and Democracy

Populism is a tradition that rejects mainstream politics supporting the existing system. It champions a new politics of "the people" fighting the ruling Establishment to secure a genuine democracy. In current hard times, mainstream parties will face growing rejection by the voters, making populist parties major players in the future. The US has long had two very different forms of populist politics and movements. They are the actors most likely to deeply change the current ruling system but lead in entirely different directions.

The Establishment in the US is a corporate regime ruling in the name of the people. While it permits a veneer of democracy, with some important civil liberties, it is marked by authoritarian hierarchies both in the economy and the government. Its power elite includes leading CEOs and the wealthiest Americans in the billionaire class, the military-industrial complex, and top echelons of the Executive branch of government. The "people" are everyone else: all poor and working Americans, including those called "middle class," across all race, gender and nationality groups.

Far-Right and Left populism – the two populisms discussed in this book – identify different establishments and different concepts of the people. But both are major forces in hard times. Far-Right negative populism – an authoritarian movement posing a deep threat to even the veneer of democracy – cannot easily be defeated without a Left-leaning positive populism that fights for democracy in the economy and politics, aiming to create a post-oligarchic America.

One of these two populisms is destined to rule much of the future, both in the US and the rest of the world. This book tells the story of how to defeat the ruling Far-Right regime, at this writing governed by Donald Trump as head of the world's most powerful corporate oligarchy. Ironically, this regime came to power riding the strength of classic anti-corporate Far-Right populist language offered by Trump himself. It's a language that US workers have strongly responded to – when strongly offered. But even many culturally conservative workers reject Trump when he betrays his promise to drain the corporate and big money swamp, moving instead to support a progressive populism.

Trump shook the country in three presidential campaigns with the fury of his populist rhetoric. He railed against corporations outsourcing the jobs

DOI: 10.4324/9781003662570-1

of American workers. He launched a thunderous attack on "globalism" and "global elites" – both economic and cultural – that he said were destroying America and its workers.

Trump promised a populist revolution. Back in 2016, when two US corporations, Carrier and United Technologies, were planning to send hundreds of US jobs to Mexico, Trump famously said:

> *"Companies are not going to leave the United States anymore without consequences. Not going to happen. It's not going to happen, I'll tell you right now," Trump said.*[1]

The "consequences" included Trump withdrawing government contracts from companies outsourcing jobs, taking away tax breaks and repeatedly threatening "globalists" who should be replaced by "patriots." As detailed in Chapter 3, Trump began his second term with a blitz of major tariffs against Canada, Mexico and China, creating a trade war threatening the global economy. Trump unleashed his "Liberation Day" on April 1, 2025, which created tariffs of 20% or more on much of the world. In the name of his populism, Trump made clear he was prepared in his second term not only to use steep tariffs but also to take the necessary new power at home to jam through his entire agenda, including autocratic control over the judiciary, the military, the media, and a compliant Congress. His tariffs remain a core part of his America First strategy, bullying the entire world and ordinary Americans who face stomach-churning economic uncertainty and decline.

In the first few weeks and months after his reelection, Trump was already purging prosecutors in the Justice Department, unconstitutionally freezing massive spending bills previously signed into law, and hiring Elon Musk at the new Department of Government Efficiency (DOGE) as the "shadow president" to fire tens of thousands of civil servants and deport millions of immigrants. In the spirit of Project 2025, OMB Director, Russell Vought, Elon Musk and Trump sought to abolish multiple government agencies and initiate "wholesale removal" of virtually *all* government regulations, saying this was the best chance ever to shrink government to an absolute minimum:

> *"If it's not possible now, it'll never be possible. This is our shot," he said. "This is the best hand of cards we're ever going to have. And if we don't take advantage of this best hand of cards, it's never going to happen."*[2]

This would open up education, health care, and numerous other public goods to private companies, who would reap massive new profits from a takeover of public life. But it was all carried out in the name of a populist war to protect American workers from government bureaucracy and globalist cultural elites. Trump's heavy reliance on Project 2025 made clear a fundamental truth: *Trump's agenda was to cut the US government to the bone, a revolutionary agenda crafted since Trump's first term and making clear that Trump's populism, paradoxically, was explicitly and centrally designed to expand the profits and power of the world's wealthiest corporate oligarchy.*

Musk's "chainsaw" was used to destroy government curbs on corporate wealth and power. Trump aimed to reduce public spending on health, education and other public goods, freeing up trillions of dollars in tax cuts mainly for the billionaire Establishment he had railed against in his populist campaign. He also shredded environmental, labor and regulations on companies, as part of his war on government, while opening the door to massive corruption and sweetheart deals, enriching himself and his fellow corporate elites. To move beyond the constitution, he was declaring national emergencies of trade and national security while bringing billionaire oligarchs to join him in the Oval Office and openly run America. This created a true emergency: a life-and-death assault on ordinary working people in the name of a populist crusade to save workers and the nation.

While Trump's anti-corporate populism was mainly rhetoric, his expansive use of big tariffs endangered growth and threatened many small businesses, while alarming some bigger ones. It protected the ruling corporate oligarchy in the long term, but his tariffs did begin to change the global ways they exercised power and gain profit. Trump aimed to shift the existing "allied" paradigm of global trade – empowering and profiting major corporations in all developed nations – to a "unilateralist" or nationalist approach. Trump calls his new model "America First," prioritizing American corporations over foreign companies – and over workers around the world.

Trump claimed he was fixing serious problems created by corporate globalization and deindustrialization in America. Those problems are, indeed, painfully real. We urgently need a positive populism that will work to solve them, helping the US working class being devastated by Trumpism.

Trump's campaign included genuine nationalist populists such as Far-Right firebrand Steve Bannon. Bannon rages at the corporate and cultural elites exploiting and abandoning American workers through their self-enriching globalist strategies. He sees Trump reflecting his own populist fever:

> *So that's really Trump's version of populism. It's both cultural and economic, but it's really a push against an established order that's truly globalist in nature and has really lost touch with the American people, with the working class and lower middle class in this country. They are the backbone of the country.*[3]

While Trump does not share Bannon's pro-worker version of populism, he has his own Far-Right populist impulses that worry many corporate elites. Corporate legitimacy depends on maintaining a veneer of democracy and civil liberties, so some business elites worried about his impulses toward dictatorship. They are also wary of his tariffs and anti-globalist initiatives, bringing steep economic downturns; corporate elites rushed to his office in the first 100 days of his second term to tell Trump his tariffs would wreck their companies, "empty their shelves," and crash the economy. (Kelby Vera, "Top Trio of CEOs Warn Trump Tariffs Will Empty Store Shelves," Huff-Post, April 23, 2025, huffpost.com) But they were attracted to his war on government and his promise to eliminate regulation of business. Most of all, they loved his effort to radically reduce corporate taxes and abolish unions.

Bannon opened a window to the public of the tensions within Trump world between anti-globalist Far-Right populists like Bannon and the corporate leaders who see him cementing their own control of America and the world. Corporate elites could take comfort in the second term when Trump appointed billionaires like Scott Bessent as his Secretary of the Treasury and Howard Lutnick as his Secretary of Commerce, with Bessent seen as an influential Wall Street "adult in the room" who would rein in Trump's populist impulses.

Within a 100 days of his second term, Trump began a Far-Right populist revolution, much of it driven by and for corporate interests. In the name of populism, Trump offered his corporate oligarchs virtually everything they wanted: shredding major regulations on big companies, cutting corporate taxes, making unions un-constitutional, ending consumer and environmental protection by defunding both the Consumer Finance Protection Board and the Environmental Protection Agency, abolishing the Education Department, Labor Department, Head-Start and America-Corps, trying to defund, sue or withdraw licenses from legacy mass media, including CBS, ABC, cable TV news such as CNN and MSNBC, and national public radio (NPR) and public broadcasting (PBS), and massively cutting or abolishing crucial government agencies and the social spending – including parts of Social Security, Medicare and Medicaid – that workers who voted for him depend on.

The courts and public pushed back, with varying success, on many of these policies, leading Trump to become more dicratorial. Trump believed his populist revolution required using authoritarian approaches – led by a strongman like himself prepared to employ illegal or unconstitutional measures whenever necessary, including attacks like January 6 and rejecting election results as "rigged," as well as kidnapping and deporting innocent Americans and seeking to defund opponents, including the Democratic Party.

As in other Far-Right authoritarian regimes such as Hungary and Turkey, where presidents such as Viktor Orban and Recep Erdogan have turned themselves into Far-Right dictators who stay partly within the law and leave many people feeling safe, Trump's Far-Right populism can be seen as a form of "fascism-lite." It does not shoot millions of protesters dead on the street nor strip most people of all rights; certain "zones of legal abyss," where rights are eliminated, co-exist with "zones of legality" where rights and normal courts continue to operate. (Amanda Taub, "The Frightening Precedents of Trump's 'Legal Abyss,'" NYTimes, May 3, 2025, nytimes.com)

But by being embedded in a continuing thin veneer of democracy, Trump's authoritarian populism actually is more dangerous to workers, citizens and human rights – and can endure longer. We urgently need a democratic positive populist movement and an anti-oligarchic populist Democratic Party mobilizing millions of voters and protesters with long-term vision and commitment. How to do that is the central subject of this work. It is the only way to save ordinary working people and the nation from oligarchic control and create toward an enduring and genuine democracy.

Far-Right and Left Populist Traditions Co-Exist in the US

Trumpism is today's version of Far-Right populism in the US and, at this writing, is in political ascendancy and sweeping away the hegemony of mainstream American politics. Left-leaning populist movements, led by labor, climate and anti-war social movements, are helping lead "resistance" movements to oligarchy and authoritarianism. Both forms of populism use the language of rule of the people – the language of democracy – against the Establishment to galvanize voters and win power.

While they share forms of anti-corporate and "pro-worker" rhetoric, and both aim to "shake up the system," the two populisms are in deep conflict with each other and have completely different political agendas. Nonetheless, both represent the decisive political forces likely to contend for power as mainstream and Establishment Parties fail to solve long-term systemic problems and crises, leading to their rejection by the majority of voters. Both emerge in response to the rise of unchecked corporate power and the failure of real democracy.

Far-Right populism, despite its populist rhetoric, supports policies that empower and enrich the corporate state with authoritarian leaders. In the US, it divides the working class by race and religion, based on Christian Nationalist notions that the only "true people" of the nation are white Christians. This is mixed in with anti-immigrant fervor in the name of protecting the "true people" and workers of America. These divisions keep the poor and working people from uniting to fight the ruling power, all in the name of protecting them. White Christian Nationalism has a long US history, traditionally arguing that only a "strongman" can conquer evil enemies at home and abroad. It is inherently authoritarian.

Trump has moved the nation full-throttle into a militant, authoritarian white Christian nationalism. In *The Flag and the Cross: White Christian Nationalism and the Threat to American Democracy*, Phillip Gorski argues that Trump has decisively abandoned multiracial democracy to install a white Christian nationalism that only a mobilized US public can now reverse.

Trump's agenda is a racialized and deeply politicized Christianity, growing out of the long history of the interdependent evolution of nationalism, racism and capitalism in America. Fifty-eight per cent of Americans identify as Christian. A very small but influential and activist Christian minority, as studied by Pew and other pollsters, fit the general criteria of Christian nationalism. (Andrew Mangan, "Americans overstate Trump's win. Plus Is Christian Nationalism Popular?," Daily Kos, Feb. 9, 2025, dailykos.com) This is combined with a broader Far-Right corporate aim to revoke much of the New Deal and 20th-century secular labor and democratic reforms. Whether this move back toward the original Robber Baron era – and the larger Trumpist Far-Right populist movement in America succeeds – is a central question of this book, and I argue that the answer will depend on the prospects of Left populist politics to remain positive and gain mass support.

Left-leaning populism defines and defends democracy in the populist language of rule by the people. Building and deepening democracy is the heart of its existence and purpose. Liberal and left populist policies seek to unify the working class across all races and ethnicities to advance economic and political democracy, aiming to gain power by mobilizing workers to fight corporate regimes for justice and democracy. Positive populism fights not just to defeat Trump but for a transformed populist nation. Like Far-Right populism, Left populism has its own deep history in the US, but it is not well-known to the public, partly because the Far Right and the mainstream have ignored or denounced it as un-American and ill-suited to American politics. The discrediting of Left populism, largely out of favor in the current Democratic Party, has allowed Far-Right populism to surge with total support in the Republican Party.

Both forms of populism tend to gain power in prolonged hard times, when most working people are facing economic struggles, whether depressions or long periods of job insecurity and decline in solidarity. Both seek to win the support and active participation of workers in the name of changing the system. But while they can gain support from some of the same voters, as when Bernie Sanders and Donald Trump both won significant numbers of working-class voters in their 2016 presidential primary races, they tend to define each other as part of the "elites" or Establishment that must be overthrown. They share deep anger toward the existing system but differ radically both in their view of solutions and the value of democracy.

Negative vs. Positive Populism: Beware the Negative but Not All Populism Is Negative

Negative populism, especially on the Far Right, tends toward authoritarianism, corporate oligarchy and social division by race, gender and religions, leading toward violence. Positive populism seeks economic and political democracy by trying to build a unified working class with strong solidarity across race, gender and religion to fight corporate power. Far-Right populism is almost always negative in the ways just described, even though, as in the case of Trumpism, it claims to be unifying and speaking for and with "the true people" against the Establishment, while empowering Trump himself as a strongman to protect them. Liberal and Left populism, while rejecting the negative elements of racial, gender and religious division, can succumb to its own forms of negative populism. This includes tendencies toward educational elitism, cancel culture, political correctness, siloed identity politics pitting different minorities against white workers, and periodic authoritarianism and violence.

Nonetheless, while Left movements can succumb to negative populism, they can also sustain powerful positive populism. The mainstream has worked to give populism of all forms a negative connotation as "authoritarian," "tyrannical" or "violent." Mainstream parties have been successful through most of U.S. history in discrediting all populism, construing populist leaders as demagogues stirring up a storm of emotional rage and fear to support their own power. In this light, populism is nothing but a movement toward mob rule, where an autocratic leader gains and keeps power by playing to the worst instincts of ordinary people.

This image of populism has weakened public awareness and the crucial importance of forms of populism that are not demagogic, violent or moblike. But while many in the public have been indoctrinated with the idea that populism is inherently demagogic, positive populism exists – and is central to changing a ruling system. Positive populism, which has a long and important history in the US, rejects authoritarianism and oligarchy and seeks to overcome division by race, religion or ethnicity, and end their own forms of political correctness while embracing non-violence. It aims to build social relations and resistance to corporate power across the working classes. Positive populists were important players in abolitionism, the 1890s populist uprising against the Robber Barons, the New Deal labor movements, the 1960s civil rights and anti-war movements, and are again rising in emerging labor, peace and pro-democracy movements today.

I argue in this book that the most important forces to defeat Trumpist Far-Right populism are Left-leaning populist movements with a long history in the US and now showing new forms of life. They involve coalitions between industrial workers and a growing number of students and educated post-industrial workers organizing to challenge corporate oligarchy and the war system. But they need to build a much larger social justice coalition of movements challenging not only corporate power and militarism but also racism, sexism, climate change and authoritarianism, many led by women and people of color. To defeat Trump and Far-Right populism also requires that they build ties with large sectors of the Democratic Party, moving it toward the positive populism – and an agenda to move beyond oligarchy- that it has largely abandoned.

With Trump in the White House, Far-Right populism rules the nation and Left populism is weak. But we document here extensive and startling public opinion data showing that pluralities – and in some instances – supermajorities of the US public share Left populist views of the malignancy of our corporate Establishment. Polls suggest that millions of Americans, including many who voted for Trump, appear receptive to a politics challenging corporate power and the war system. Sectors of the public who voted for Trump could swing against him when the corporate oligarchy he cemented into power goes against his promises and further reduces wages or raises prices. But there is no guarantee that the positive populists who could defeat him will win over a potentially receptive majority, including disenchanted Trumpists and culturally conservative workers who are the plurality of all American workers.

During the Trump years, positive populists will aim to create major national opposition – in the public square and in the courts – and will likely build early opposition in their strongest bases at the local, state and regional levels. These will be crucial launching pads, serving as models both for resistance and new policy as they work toward regaining power in upcoming national struggles and elections. Populism, like the people's rule or democracy it champions, always starts at home, rooted in the social relations and the building of solidarity and caring spreading among family, friends, neighborhood, locality and civic organizations. When successful, it leads toward solidarity and collective action in the workplace, community and social movements, as well as real democracy in our politics.

The aim of positive populism is a peaceful revolution toward an economy that puts ordinary workers in democratic control of companies, the economy, and the nation. It wields non-violence to end the war system. It fights for a real democracy that puts the people in control of their own governments and society. Most of all, it spreads caring justice, radical empathy and love as the foundational principles for the economy, the nation, and the world. Bernie Sanders, probably the most influential economic populist in US politics, says it clearly:

> I believe...we are in this together. These are not just words. The truth is on some level when you hurt, when your children hurt, I hurt. And when my kids hurt, you hurt. And it's very easy to turn our backs on kids who are hungry or veterans who are sleeping out on the street and we can develop a psyche, a psychology which says, 'I don't have to worry about them, all I'm going to worry about is myself, I need to make another five million dollars.' But I believe what human nature is about is that everybody impacts everybody else...in all kinds of ways that we can't even understand. It's beyond intellect. It's a spiritual, emotional thing. So I believe that when we do the right thing, when we try to treat people with respect and dignity, when we say that that child who is hungry is my child, I think we are more human when we do that... That is my religion. That's what I believe in.[4]

Hard Times Are the Seedbed of Populism

Populism is the successful politics of hard times, though it can emerge in affluent eras as well. By its nature, populism attacks the system or Establishment as unjust and in desperate need of democratic change. In hard times, this attack on the system resonates with the majority of people suffering serious socio-economic problems. Such difficulties can arise from stomach-churning economic recessions and depressions, but they often take the form of long periods of gradual decline, both in economic well-being and social relations or solidarity, as well as in the erosion of national democracy.

Sustained suffering and oppression tend to intensify the appeal of populist movements. They offer a voice and solidarity for people to express their grievances, and reinforce the view that their suffering is "systemic," that is, hard-wired into the existing socio-economic and political order. This view is embraced by both Left and Right populism, and both have gained more power historically when hard times have been sustained over long periods.

Persistent hard times in recent decades were created by President Reagan in his neoliberal revolution and have been institutionalized over the last several decades. While Trump catastrophically increased hard times, earlier corporate policies fueled by Reagan created the foundation for the economic, social and political crises that create deep insecurity and fear among American working people. This has created political instability and rejection of mainstream parties, with much of the public today looking for solutions offered by populists on either the Right or the Left. Populist parties will emerge as the most important contenders for power as the existing capitalist system is unable to repair its deep economic, environmental, sociocultural, military and authoritarian political crises.

This is not to say that populist politics always succeeds in hard times. Often it fails, and mainstream parties supporting the Establishment continue to rule. Nor does it suggest that hard times are the only time that populism emerges and can win. Affluence can also breed populism, particularly among young people and the professional-managerial class (PMC). Only historical analysis of particular periods will help explain why populism emerges and why it succeeds or fails, winning democracy or losing it further, both in hard times and good times.

Far-Right Populism Such as Trumpism Makes People's Lives Worse: Why Have Millions Embraced It?

Trumpism is putting in place economic, social, environmental and authoritarian policies that will do serious long-term damage to millions of people. Those disproportionately affected are the working-class voters who voted for Trump. Why did they embrace him?

There are at least six different explanations of Trump's large working-class base, fleshed out in Chapter 3. One is the intensity of the hard times for working Americans who felt that Trump expressed their grievances and rage at the system. The second is the abandonment of populism by liberals and the Democratic Party in favor of a form of identity politics that did not challenge the corporate system and pitted elements of the working class against each other. A third is the complicity of liberals in sustaining a system of educational credentials and cultural hierarchy that reinforced the feeling of insecurity and low status among many non-college working people. A fourth is the history of racism and other social divisions in the US that makes Far-Right populist White Christian rage familiar and appealing to millions of Americans. A fifth is the inherent attraction of Far-Right populist rhetoric to working Americans who gain a major sense of relative social worth when defined as "true Americans" and given rights and social esteem denied to other groups in the nation and world. Far-Right populism, crucially, builds new social relations and communities among people who feel abandoned and discredited. Sixth, the Far-Right promises a strongman ruler powerful enough to defeat the ruling Establishment and to protect the "true people" of the great nation. Its machismo intensely binds a fearful people to a leader perceived as so tough that he can protect the people from every enemy at home and abroad. This all bleeds into Trump's defining Far-Right assault on democracy, saying repeatedly, "I alone can solve your problems," leading to a cult of the great leader and an irresistible seduction of authoritarianism.

The Way to Defeat Far-Right Populism Is to Embrace Positive Populism

Since we face sustained hard times, politics without strong populist elements is unlikely to succeed. Mainstream parties are eroding and collapsing throughout much of the world as global economic, environmental and sociocultural problems intensify. In multiple countries, as occurred during the 1930s, this is leading toward the rise of Far-Right populist or fascist parties throughout much of Europe as well as in the US and in large parts of the Global South. In the 1930s, Left-leaning parties and movements failed to build a powerful populist coalition to counter the fascist Far Right and transform the failing capitalism of their eras.

There are strong arguments that the same failure is taking place across a wide spectrum of liberal and Left movements in the US and much of Europe today. Liberal ruling parties, viewed as complicit in economic and social decline, are facing revolts from their voters. Left movements, facing repression and demonization from corporate elites, are fragmented and weak, often succumbing to their own negative populism and facing democratic crises.

While I discuss Far-Right populism at some length, I also look intensively at the history and future prospects of a Left-leaning positive populist coalition and agenda. I examine historical moments like the 1890s populist revolt against the Robber Barons, analyzing where they succeeded and why they ultimately failed. I tell the stories of a succession of 20th- and 21st-century Left populist movements, from the anti-war movement of World War I to the New Deal labor movements to the 1960s civil rights and anti-war student movements to the 21st-century Occupy movement and more recent revived labor and anti-war movements, exploring both how they won the populist democratic victories they did and why so many failed.

We are far from a cohesive and powerful movement stopping Trumpism in the US today. But there are elements of a new populist Left-leaning coalition that could gain substantial power as the destructive impact of Trump's corporate oligarchic policies – blatantly contradicting the populist rhetoric he advanced in his campaigns – are experienced by millions of Americans. The elements of this emerging positive populist coalition include revived labor struggles seeking to defend the very existence of unions as well as organize newly threatened working-class constituencies in manufacturing, retail, agriculture, public health, government and the huge service sector. Other rising populist forces include organizations like the Poor People's Campaign, seeking to mobilize 80 million poor people to vote. Its founder and leader, Rev. William Barber, is often seen as the Martin Luther King of today. Barber calls for a "fusion coalition" of the working class, the poor and the civil rights movement that has been the foundation of all his organizing movements and the heart of any future Left-populist movement that can change the country.

In a fusion coalition, our most directly affected members would always speak to the issue closest to their own heart. But they would never speak alone. When workers spoke up for the right to organize and engage in collective bargaining, the civil rights community would be there with them. And when civil rights leaders petitioned for the expansion of voting rights for people of color, white workers would stand with them. Again.[5]

The younger generations have also always been important to Left-populist movements. Anti-war students, who are budding members of the rapidly growing "PMC" are becoming a new major part of the post-industrial labor force. Sociologists in the 20th century, including Alvin Gouldner and myself, developed an analysis of the PMC as an important new class formation. The PMC is increasingly being absorbed into the working class as professional employees are subject to managerial and corporate control, though they continue to have some distinct economic interests and cultural values that can make them antagonistic to non-college workers. But they are now also playing a critical new role in the development of Left-leaning positive populism.

As capitalism develops into "post-industrialism," it helps create a new educated and more professionalized labor force. The PMC has diverse sectors, but many have historically been critical of capitalism itself and have sometimes built major coalitions with the old industrial labor force, as in the New Deal. Today, growing corporate control of universities is leading populist labor leaders like Shawn Fain, president of the United Auto Workers, to organize students and adjunct faculty in increasingly corporatized universities into unions. He is embracing their anti-war politics while they are embracing a stronger identity as newly proletarianized workers in the corporate-controlled knowledge economy. This lays the groundwork for a new populist coalition between professional workers and non-college industrial workers, now beginning to organize and plant the seeds of working together against the corporate oligarchy and its war system.

Fain lambasted both university administrations and the Biden Administration for supporting the Gaza war as he was organizing both students and workers in the fight against militarized capitalism spreading on campus:

> *United Auto Workers (UAW) President Shawn Fain lambasted the mass arrests of pro-Palestinian protesters on college campuses across the country, while emphasizing the union's call for a cease-fire in the Israel-Hamas war in Gaza.*
>
> *"The UAW will never support the mass arrest or intimidation of those exercising their right to protest, strike, or speak out against injustice," Fain wrote Wednesday on the social platform X. "Our union has been calling for a ceasefire for six months. This war is wrong, and this response against students and academic workers, many of them UAW members, is wrong."*[6]

Fain's anti-war stance is a crucial new chapter in American politics. Fain is clear he intends to put full union force into both the organizing drives on universities and the anti-war movement:

> *Should the university decide to curtail the right to participate in protected, concerted activity; discriminate against union members or political viewpoints; and create or allow threats to members' health and safety, among others, UAW 4811 members will take any and all actions necessary to enforce our rights.*[7]

Meanwhile, Leftist politicians in the Progressive Caucus and the "Squad" of the Democratic Party, such as Bernie Sanders and New York Congressional Representative, Alexandria Ocasio Cortez (AOC), are calling for a populist Democratic Party. They want to unite with the new labor and anti-war populist social movements in fighting big corporations and authoritarianism to build a sustainable American democracy. Many Democratic Progressives, like Connecticut Democratic Senator, Chris Murphy, and former Ohio Democratic Senator, Sherrod Brown, are also labor-friendly populists. After the 2024 defeat by Trump, the Democratic Party and the social justice movements are in a divisive and crucial debate about the political path forward.

This book, in part, is a response to that debate. In the light of Trump's 2024 reelection, a major Democratic faction argues the Democratic Party has grown too Left-wing and must moderate to win a larger section of the public. They want to win over middle-of-the-road centrists and anti-Trumpist Republicans. They reject populism, arguing that the 2024 Democratic defeat was due to errors in messaging strategy – not in the message itself. This was largely the position taken by Kamala Harris and the Democratic Party – and remains a mainstream powerful tradition in the Party.

Another major Democratic faction argues that the Democratic Party can only succeed by winning back the working-class base that it had during the New Deal. This group is working in the spirit of Tom Frank, author of the influential book, *What's the Matter with Kansas*:

Progressivism without populism is like a car without fuel – it might look like it's moving, but it's really just coasting.[8]

Frank knows enough history – and has seen the result of a Left populist vacuum in Kansas – to know a crucial truth. A Democratic Party without populism is a recipe for Far-Right populist rule. Bernie Sanders, AOC, and a growing labor-friendly and anti-corporate group of activists inside the Democratic Party argue passionately for a Left-leaning positive populism. They believe it must involve the Democratic Party, but needs to build a mass grassroots movement that is crucial to defeating Trumpism and overthrowing corporate rule. Faiz Shakir, a former campaign manager for Bernie Sanders ran unsuccessfully in 2025 to be Chair of the Democratic National Committee (DNC), arguing that the Democratic Party now should do everything with the aim of "building power for the working-class." (Joan Greve, "The Democrats to elect new chair as party grapples with how to rebuild after 2024 losses," The Guardian, Jan. 31, 2025, theguardian. com) The young Gen Z leader of the US anti-gun violence movement, David Hogg, who briefly became vice-chair of the DNC in February, 2025, says he will bring "uncomfortable truths" to the Democratic Party, which must become transformed as the party of youth and workers. (Tessa Stuart, "David Hogg Knows Why Democrats Lost Young Voters," Rolling Stone, Jan. 31, 2025, rollingstone.com)

The birth of a labor movement that is also anti-war in the early 2020s is absolutely crucial in beginning to build a new positive populist resistance movement. It has the potential to help build a populist coalition of students and other young people with unionized workers, professional employees and labor leaders, as well as with people of color and women, who are among the most vulnerable targets of Far-Right populism and embrace most strongly the key populist values of solidarity and community. All these forces create new ties among people who are increasingly vulnerable and alone, building the solidarity at work and in social movements essential to making systemic and democratic change.

Those moderate Democrats opposing transformative positive populists argue that the "radicalism" of Left populists like Bernie Sanders and AOC will turn off millions of culturally conservative workers. They raise a concern central to this book. Populist populism is transformative, and needs to unify ordinary working Americans of diverse religions, ethnicities and cultural values. In today's divisive culture wars, this means speaking to and winning over culturally conservative workers as well as progressive ones.

This will require a major change in the culture of contemporary liberalism and sectors of the Left, who must resist historic tendencies toward ideological purity, cancel culture, and political correctness, all now tied to contemporary Democratic Party identity politics. A positive populism is infused by empathy for and dialogue with those with different cultural and religious values. It can bridge those differences only with a radical culture of compassion and community while offering transformative class-based economic changes uniting working people across current cultural divides. This transformative fight for a regime change at home is the essential mission both for the Democratic Party and for positive populist social movements in the Trump era. It is the only way to defeat Trumpism and prevent a new authoritarian takeover in the future.

Democrats, both liberal and radical, have contributed to the problems caused by the culture wars.

The only way to win over the great majority of working Americans is to fight hard for the economic transformations in all workers' interests, not just those who share your position in current cultural wars. This requires a truly positive populism, a class politics that rejects political correctness, cancel culture, siloed identity politics and other negative forces that drive away many conservative working-class voters. It fights for a public goods economy and social democracy serving the public and defending all workers' well-being, but recognizes the need for a government that is both democratic and efficient, accountable to and run by ordinary people who feel invisible today to politicians and bureaucrats in Washington, D.C.

Bernie Sanders speaks powerfully to the need for a Democratic Party that goes beyond resistance to a positive agenda for ending the power of the oligarchs. He notes that Elon Musk, while leading the cuts of worker programs for DOGE, had more personal wealth than 53% of all Americans. Musk gave Trump $159 million in his reelection campaign but gained several billion in wealth from government contracts in the first 100 days of Trump's second term.

To deal with Musk and the entire oligarchy, a positive populist movement – in coalition with a new positive populist Democratic Party moving beyond the Carter, Clinton and Obama years – must push for a national wealth tax, ending Citizens United and dark money allowing oligarchs to buy candidates, and a change in corporate charters mandating corporations to operate in the public interest. Positive populism also fights for a liveable minimum wage, free universal health care and college education, and other forms of social democracy that have worked successfully in Europe and are the best way both to win support from working-class voters and oppose Trump. Both defeating Trump and embracing a new regime change at home can only come from a positive populist Democratic Party aligned with social movements leading not back to the "normalcy" of the pre-Trump years but forward to a post-oligarchic America.

These Left-leaning populist forces grow in resistance to Trump nationally and will succeed only as they fight to limit corporate giveaways and tax breaks, preserve unions and social safety nets, end big money in politics, end corporate corruption, and curb climate change and war, serving the interest of all workers while also seeking to create democracy that Trumpism is shredding. But until Trump is out of the White House, there are obvious limits to their ability to protect "the people" and defeat oligarchy at the national level. Nonetheless, regional, state and local Democrats will have a surprisingly strong opportunity not only to resist but also to pass models of positive populism legislation to curb corporate wealth and power, and protect workers, the environment and democracy. And we shall see that national positive populist resistance has also scaled up in Trump's second term, with hundreds of thousands of people protesting against oligarchy on the streets. A central theme of this book is showing why and how the Democratic Party must join them and reject the return to "normalcy," helping lead the protesters and the nation with a transformative positive populist agenda.

Because of the Left's vulnerabilities to negative populism and the failure that it breeds, we need a new perspective on how to build and sustain a positive populist coalition and resist authoritarianism under Trump in his second term and beyond. I draw from history and recent lessons about the need for a class politics targeting the corporate oligarchy that Trump has put front and center in his regime and that is leading his authoritarian assault on the rule of law. Its members include Trump's closest officials and advisors, from Elon Musk and his Silicon Valley billionaire "bros," to the other billionaires in his cabinet and those in his inner circle of aides in the White House and Far-Right media. I then move from how to resist to how to build a new post-oligarchic agenda that can attract Americans from both parties, as well as Independent, as shown in surveys of American voters.

I conclude this book with a brief summary of regime-change politics and "ten commandments" or ten principles of positive populism, which draws heavily on the lessons of Martin Luther King, still arguably the most important positive populist in American history, as well as crucial lessons from the New Deal. King tried to unite populist civil rights, anti-war and labor movements – and more broadly unite blue-collar workers with the rising and increasingly proletarianized students and young highly educated workers. King came to believe it was essential to challenge militarized capitalism and fight for a multiracial democracy both in the economy and the political system. He made clear that building nonviolent solidarity and community activism at local levels and throughout an authoritarian South was the heartbeat of positive populism. And he focused on the crucial importance of uniting the civil rights movement with the working class and labor movement as central:

> *As I have said many times, and believe with all my heart, the coalition that can have the greatest impact in the struggle for human dignity here in America is that of the Negro and the forces of labor, because their fortunes are so closely intertwined.*[9]

The New Deal never succeeded in fully creating the civil rights-labor rights struggle central to King's vision. But it created its own form of populist regime change at home based on an early coalition of industrial labor with a PMC helping shape a new public goods economy – an early American version of working-class politics and European social democracy. I draw on some of my own experiences in these movements as well as the broader history and global political analysis of Far-Right and Left populist politics sweeping through much of the world today. The aim is to overcome Trumpism and his corporate oligarchy and enact a democratic revolution truly of, by and for the people.

Notes

1 Jacob Parmuk and Chrstine Wang, "After Carrier gets incentives to keep some jobs in US, others can't leave 'without consequences' CNBC," Dec. 1, 2016, cnbc.com
2 Robert Tait, "Musk intensifies government spending attack with push to cut all regulations," *The Guardian*, Feb. 4, 2025, theguardian.com
3 Ross Douthat, "Steve Bannon on 'Broligarchs vs Populism,'" *NYT*, Jan. 31, 2025, nytimes.com.
4 "Bernie Sanders, post on Facebook, Bernie Sanders," Facebook, 2018.
5 Barber, cited in Berkeley Talks Transcripts: William J. Barber II, "Forward Together," April 14, 2019, news.berkeley.edu. See also William Barber, "The Third Reconstruction: How a Moral Movement Is Overcoming the Politics of Division and Fear," Boston: Beacon Press, 2016.
6 "UAW chief slams mass arrests of pro-Palestinian solutions on college campuses," The Hill, May 1, 2024, thehill.com
7 UAW 4811 wrote in a statement, UAW chief slams mass arrests of pro-Palestinian solutions on college campuses," The Hill, May 1, 2024, thehill.com
8 Top 30 quotes of Tom Frank, bookery.app
9 MLK, "MLK championed civil rights and unions," AFL-CIO, no date, aflcio.org

1 Hard Times
When Populism Wins

We Are in Sustained Hard Times for Ordinary People

We face institutionalized hard times in the coming era, with the existing capitalist system, even before the Trump era, unable to solve the crises it has created in the economy, the environment and the war system. These polycrises are inflamed by new economic crises sparked by Trump's tariffs and trade wars. Trump also intensified the breakdown of social relations in civil society, deep corporate corruption of Establishment political parties and government, militarization of policing in US cities, mass illegal deportation of immigrants, and the unraveling of democracy itself.

The current era of hard times, foreshadowed in the stagflation of the Carter years and oil shocks of the late 1970s, was institutionalized in the Reagan revolution. Reagan ushered in neoliberal capitalism and a modern corporate oligarchy. He created a second Gilded Age that has bred populism, as did the first 1890s Gilded Age.

Hard times most often involve crises in the economic security and social relations of working people. It can involve severe depression, as in the 1930s, or deep recessions, as in the 2008 financial crisis. Trump has created unprecedented economic uncertainty and extreme market shock, not seen in modern times. It is accompanied by decline in social cohesion, rising prices and growing immigrant, environmental and constitutional crises. These crises all breed populist attitudes involving anger toward corporations, support for workers and openness to a broad political agenda of tax reform and social democratic reforms for labor, enhancing wages and access to affordable health care, education and housing.

Hard Times Breed Supermajorities of Populist Views

Multiple economic indicators, polling data and stories, such as public reaction to Luigi Mangioni's killing of a health insurance CEO, document the experience of hard times and suggest how they can fuel public populist reaction. Even before the horrific economic and political crises in the Trump era, neoliberal market policies and failures in mainstream Establishment

DOI: 10.4324/9781003662570-2

parties were breeding rapid and fierce populist anger at the corporate Establishment. These data contradict many prevailing assumptions about the values and politics of the US public, with public views historically aligned with populism and becoming more so after Trump first took power in 2016.

The polling data are unequivocal. The Pew Research Center summarizes findings from a 2023 poll, even before the second-term Trump crisis:

Anti-corporate sentiment in US is now widespread in both parties....
When it comes to the decisions made by members of Congress, large
shares of Americans say major donors, lobbyists and special interests
have too much influence.

By contrast, just 9% of adults say the people in lawmakers' districts
have too much influence; that compares with 70% who say the people
in their districts have too little influence (19% say they have about the
right amount).

Pew reports that only 25% of Americans believe that large corporations have a positive effect on the way things are going. *A supermajority of 71% of the US public say that large corporations have a negative effect on the country.*

Gallup found that the public's distrust of big corporations extends now to banks:

Gallup has been polling Americans on their confidence in various
institutions — including banks — since before the 1980s. While a ma-
jority of Americans once said they had a "great deal" or "quite a lot" of
confidence in banks, that changed dramatically after the 2008 financial
crisis. In 2007, 41 percent of Americans expressed substantial confi-
dence in banks; by 2009, just 22 percent did. While this level crawled
back up to 38 percent in 2020, it has since fallen again and never
reached the consistently high levels of the mid-'90s and early 2000s.

Pew, Gallup and other major polling firms all report striking historical data indicating that distrust and disapproval of big companies and big banks have been growing for several decades. The decline accelerates in economic downturns like the financial crisis of 2008, when public support for big companies and banks sharply declined. This reinforces the idea that populist anti-Establishment sentiment spikes in hard times. The rise of populist public attitudes has been relatively continuous since 1980 when the Reagan revolution embraced globalization and crushed unions, institutionalizing decades of hard times.

There are many other polling findings hinting at anti-corporate majorities or supermajorities of Americans. A Navigator Research poll in 2024 asked

Americans who they blamed for the high taxes they pay. The vast majority of Americans overwhelmingly blamed the rich and did not blame the poor.

As Tax Day Approaches, the Vast Majority of Americans Blame the Rich for the Taxes They Pay, Not Poor Americans

Bipartisan majorities and majorities across racial groups say "rich Americans and big corporations who pay less than their fair share" are more responsible for the amount of taxes they pay.

Who do you think is more responsible for the amount of taxes that you pay?

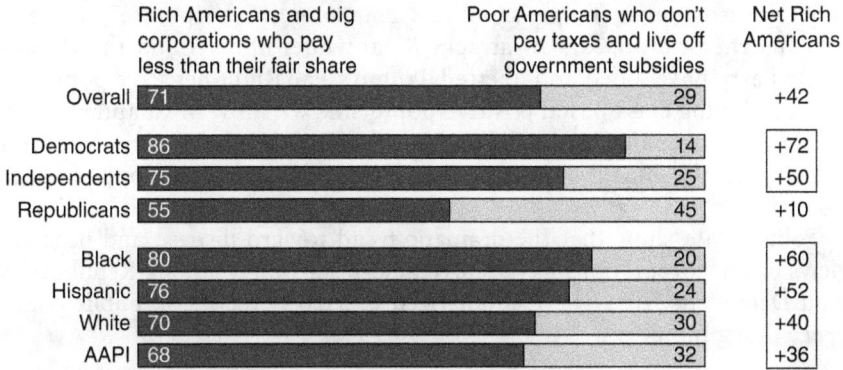

	Rich Americans and big corporations who pay less than their fair share	Poor Americans who don't pay taxes and live off government subsidies	Net Rich Americans
Overall	71	29	+42
Democrats	86	14	+72
Independents	75	25	+50
Republicans	55	45	+10
Black	80	20	+60
Hispanic	76	24	+52
White	70	30	+40
AAPI	68	32	+36

Nationwide survey of 1,000 registered voters conducted March 7-March 11, 2024. **Navigator.**
For more info, visit navigatorresearch.org.

Figure 1.1 Americans blame the rich, not the poor, for high taxes.

Navigator summarizes its research as follows:

By an overwhelming margin, people believe the rich and big corporations who pay less than their fair share in taxes are more responsible for the amount of taxes they pay than poor Americans who don't pay taxes. 71 percent say they view "rich Americans and big corporations who pay less than their fair share" as more responsible for the amount of taxes they pay compared to just 29 percent who say they blame "poor Americans who don't pay taxes and live off government subsidies" more. Majorities across party lines blame the rich and big corporations more than poor Americans, including 86 percent of Democrats, 75 percent of independents, and 55 percent of Republicans.[1]

This is another sign of a dramatic bipartisan rise in anger at big companies and the rich. Traditionally, Americans blame "welfare queens" and the poor for their taxes. But the data suggest that a bipartisan majority are now rejecting this classic argument. Instead, they are pinning the blame squarely on the corporations themselves and their success in avoiding paying high taxes.

The populist anger fueled by the hard times of a failing neoliberal corporate order has been most successfully politically captured by Trumpism, with Trump's attack on globalizing and outsourcing companies reaching a bipartisan audience. This reflects the dramatic rise in populist anger, from both Right and Left, toward big corporations and banks. It is helping create a hidden populist plurality – by some polling measures already a significant majority – that could drastically upend the fate of both Trump and the nation.

Trump's populist rhetoric has resonated with working-class voters, despite the irony that Trump's policies empower the corporate oligarchy that his rhetoric appears to attack. Meanwhile, liberals and the Democratic Party have aided and abetted Trump's Far Right negative populism by abandoning class-based positive populism. We show in Chapter 5 how the Harris campaign exemplified liberal embrace of the corporate and military Establishment at a time when Trump was capturing public anger against it.

Polling data show that the dramatic trend toward distrust and negative views of big corporations has occurred more startlingly among Republicans than Democrats. As Gallup summarized in a 2023 report on public confidence in big business:

> After nearly a half century when Republicans routinely viewed big business in a more positive than negative light, their perspective shifted to being more skeptical of it in 2021 and remains that way in 2023.
>
> A record-low 18% of Republicans now say they have a "great deal" or "quite a lot" of confidence in big business, whereas nearly twice as many — 35% — report having "very little" or no confidence in it. Another 45% offer restrained support, expressing "some" confidence...
>
> Before 2021, the only other years that Republicans' assessments of big business tilted clearly negative were 1981 (-11) and 2009 (-12), amid two of the worst recessions the U.S. has experienced since Gallup began tracking Americans' confidence in institutions in 1973.

While public support for big companies and banks has been declining, support for labor unions has been rising dramatically. This hints that disapproval of the corporate Establishment is linked to populist views supporting labor activism. Data from Gallup indicate that:

> Seventy-one percent of Americans now approve of labor unions. Although statistically similar to last year's 68%, it is up from 64% before the pandemic and is the highest Gallup has recorded on this measure since 1965.

Gallup: Decline in Disapproval of Unions

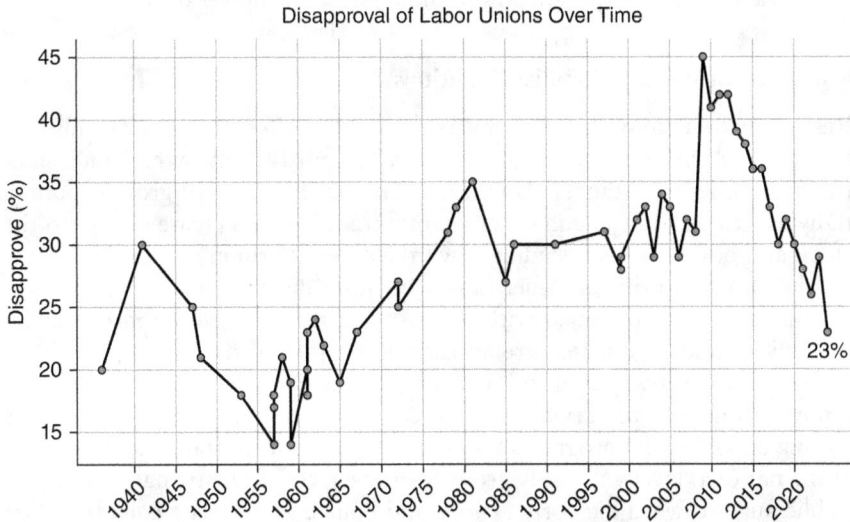

Disapproval of Labor Unions Over Time

Figure 1.2 Americans strongly approve of labor unions.

Data courtesy of Gallup. Graphic produced by the U.S. Department of Labor.

Commentators on the Gallup polling data observe that:

> *A recent Gallup poll revealed that disapproval of labor unions has fallen to 23%, the lowest level in 57 years, while support for unions has reached 70% — just one point below the highest level recorded since 1965. These statistics suggest a shift in public attitudes toward organized labor, and it's important to consider what this means for workers and their interests.*
>
> *This low point in union disapproval is noteworthy at a time when discussions around workers' rights, fair wages and workplace conditions are once again gaining prominence. The Gallup poll's findings suggest that more Americans, particularly younger workers, are recognizing the role unions play in providing them a voice in their workplace to advocate for these issues. This aligns with other reports that highlight increasing public support for unions across various sectors, potentially reflecting a broader call for stronger protections for workers.[2]*

Again, the same trends exist, as we show later, among Republican voters and Democrats. This suggests that Trump's populist campaign rhetoric could come into conflict with his rule by corporate oligarchy, with Trump rejecting even anti-trust actions that could end the corporate monopolies his own voters strongly oppose. The clash between Trump's rhetoric and governing policy will likely decrease his public support, especially among those who voted for

Trump because of his populist rhetoric and almost all of whom, according to polls, want to curb corporate power and increase the power of workers.

Prospects for Positive Populist Coalitions

Resistance to Trumpism will grow as the public suffers the shock of his corporate oligarchy consolidating power in a Trumpist regime, which intensifies the hard times of ordinary Americans. The hard times will grow exponentially as Trump's tariffs and other chaotic trade policies create shocks to the stock and bond markets, leading toward a severe "Trump-cession."

The supermajority of Americans who now disapprove of big corporations and banks, combined with the growing majority who approve of labor unions and organizing, are an early indication of rising prospects for a Left-leaning positive populism. As Trump offers the billionaire class big government contracts and tax breaks that contradict his populist rhetoric, while cutting crucial social programs for workers, populist resistance to Trumpism at the national level will likely grow. Moreover, the dramatic national rise in public anger toward big corporations and banks, as well as a corresponding national support for labor organizing, began to emerge early on in Trump's second term to challenge Trump's extreme Far-Right policies.

As long as Trump is in the White House, there will be limits to positive Left-leaning populists' ability to pass new national laws and change the country. Far-Right populism will tend to have the upper hand. But the strong anti-corporate and pro-labor public views documented in the polls, as well as Trump's wildly unconstitutional and corrupt attacks on popular government programs and workers, will become major sources of Left-leaning populism in blue regions, states and localities, as well as at the national level. In the last chapter, I show that new populists will rise in many anti-Trump states, cities and towns as centers of resistance, and many state and local governments will pass Left-leaning populist measures supporting labor, health care, the environment and social services, as well as pro-democracy measures to protect the rule of law.

Resistance will also rise at the national level – and has already led to massive "hands-of," No Kings Day and other big national protests in the first six months of Trump's second term. Trump's blatant snatching of innocent people off the street and deporting them, his militarization of domestic policing in LA, Washington DC and other cities, his defunding of the most essential regulatory agencies and social safety nets, and his melding of his own new executive power with the power of his broader corporate oligarchy inevitably gave rise to public outrage and mass fear and protest. New labor and anti-war movements among students and industrial workers as well as professional employees, are rising and finding support in the Left of the Democratic Party from Bernie Sanders and the Progressive Democratic Caucus. They are trying to build new coalitions of industrial workers, poor people, young people, minorities, women, students, professional service employees and climate activists into a new pro-democracy and positive populist resistance movement. We show the need for moving beyond siloed identity politics to class politics that can shift the Democratic Party away from its Establishment agenda toward positive populism. This can build the rising mass resistance to Trump's authoritarianism and move the nation beyond the ruling oligarchs.

The mainstream Democratic Party which remains aligned with the corporate and war system may prevail in some short-term elections but will increasingly fail. In polls taken two weeks after Trump's reelection, as he issued a flood of tariffs, a majority of Americans said they felt the Democratic Party was not responding to their priorities; they criticized the Democrats for focusing on social issues like gender and LGBTQ rather than the cost of living, inflation, higher wages, billionaire wealth and tax avoidance and other bread-and-butter populist issues. (Jeremey Peters, Ruth Igielnik, and Lisa Lehrer, "Many Americans Say the Democratic Party Does Not Share Their Priorities," NY Times, Feb. 2, 2025, nytimimes.com) While Left-leaning populist coalitions will face many hurdles, they are the best hope for defeating Trumpism and moving toward positive economic and political system change.

Their best prospects will emerge when they not only resist Trump but also move affirmatively toward a post-oligarchic America. Resistance needs to be linked to a new, transformative agenda that the anti-corporate and pro-worker majorities of voters documented in this chapter strongly need and can support. This means key measures to limit the wealth and power of corporate elites.

These include major wealth taxes on the uber-rich and strict curbs on the money they can donate to candidates. This requires overthrowing of Citizens United and other recent Supreme Court decisions swamping elections with billions of dollars of dark money flowing to corporate candidates and into K Street dens of corporate lobbyists. It also means a comprehensive social democratic agenda supporting programs to help workers, including a livable minimum wage, stronger job security, access to free health care, education, a clean environment and affordable housing and other positive populist programs that have long been enshrined in many European social democracies, such as Denmark, Sweden and Germany. They are so popular in Europe that even Far-Right parties in these nations are afraid to try to take them away.

The polling documented in this chapter shows that ordinary American workers are not different than their European peers. They desperate need a government and nation listening to their voices. The want to crack down on corporations and oligarchs who are stealing them blind and burning down their jobs and democracy.

Notes

1 navigator.com, March 11, 2024.
2 Emily Peck, "Labor union disapproval hits a 57 year low," Axios, Aug. 28, 2024, axios.com

2 Far-Right Populism
The Appeal of the Dark Side

The Far Right Has Long Riled Up Its Brand of Populist Anti-Establishment Rage in America

In this chapter, we review the dramatic history of Far-Right populist movements in the US. We tell the story of why and how they have emerged and evolved through so many eras, often gaining millions of supporters. They have used a variety of forms of nativist or hyper-nationalist, anti-Establishment discourse to capture the rage and fervor of a predominantly working-class and white Christian Nationalist base opposing a fantastical array of enemies: a Communist cadre of Jewish, Rockefeller and other pillars of the global Establishment running a "New World Order." In practice, Far-Right populists divide the working classes, making collective resistance impossible in the name of protecting them.

Trumpism is hardly new. The public voted for it in 2016 and 2024, partly because it draws on so many earlier Far-Right populist traditions going back to the beginning of the country. At the same time, each stage of Far-Right populist development is different. While there are shared themes – involving nativism, racism, nationalism, "America First" and authoritarianism – they have different concepts of who is the Establishment, both globally and at home, and what it means to attack it.

They also tend to offer different views of "the people." The power they succeed in mobilizing ranges from being a fringe sector of the Republican Party to taking the entire party over, as Trump did. What they all tend to share is the view that you need an authoritarian leader or strongman to defeat the corrupt Establishment and protect the "true people" of the nation from Satanic enemies, both abroad and at home.

Trumpism is the most powerful Far-Right populist regime in modern US history. In early America, the Far-Right populist movement that ran the Confederacy and the Southern Jim Crow Democratic Party was also extremely strong. Trump has embraced much of that Southern Democratic Far-Right populism as well as Far-Right Republican extremist groups and ideas emerging in the mid-20th-century Republican Party. He has amalgamated them into a ruling party. He ran for office promising to shake up and take down

DOI: 10.4324/9781003662570-3

the US and the global corporate Establishments, claiming to be a populist who would "drain the swamp" and raise up the "forgotten worker." This was his rhetoric; the way he governed is another story altogether.

The Narratives of Far-Right Populism

Like all populists, Far-Right populist movements have championed "the people" against the ruling US and global Establishment. Their definition of the Establishment includes global Communist, Jewish or other conspiratorial internationalist regimes running the world, as well as Communist and Wall Street powers that dominate both the world and America itself. They also frequently assail foreign powers, calling themselves isolationists and America Firsters, protecting the true people of the nation from global conspiracists.

The many earlier US Far-Right populist movements that attack Wall Street and global banking interests as dominant and evil are not well known, though they are broadly in line with Trump's own attack on globalism. Remarkably, Far-Right populism often attacks Wall Street as Marxist. This is a peculiar but long-standing element of US Far-Right populism, surfacing in the 1930s America First movement, in the McCarthy era, and in the White Christian nationalist movement allying with Ronald Reagan.

Far-Right populists historically have defined "the people" as white Christian Americans who are being unfairly stripped of resources and status not only by monied and monopolistic corporations but also by Marxist elites in government who align with minorities and immigrants – the alien "enemies at home" – to steal resources rightfully belonging to the true Americans. Interestingly, Far-Right populists often describe both big corporations and much of the government as Marxist and "globalist." Their most consistent narrative is promoting "America First" nationalism that protects "true Americans" against both global Communism and global banks and corporations, many foreign and "Jewish," complicit in a New World Order.

Far-Right populism typically identifies not only conspiratorial global Communist and financial powers that make up the global Establishment but also "the enemy at home," a favorite Trump line. Historically, Far-Right populists place blame for the country's deep problems not only on the global Establishment but also on the people in the US who are "poisoning the blood" of the country and destroying it. White Christian nationalism typifies this kind of populism, identifying enemies who are immigrants, Muslims and other non-Christians and, implicitly, a large spectrum of non-white citizens. The role of racial division has always been central to Far-Right populism, a dominant theme throughout US history. It unites poor and working white people with "patriotic" local white business leaders, claiming to protect them against those threatening the nation and poisoning its blood.

Far-Right populism feeds emotionally and politically on intense fear, hate and violence that it uses to attract its base – the "true people" – while also to consolidate its own authoritarian power. In this respect, Far-Right populism is, by nature, negative and destructive. It always rules through division, hate and violence, seeking a strongman with authoritarian power essential to destroying enemies at home and abroad.

Such strong and authoritarian leaders are seen as essential to overthrowing a cabal of anti-American elites and saving the nation. The list of enemies varies – and is both long and contradictory. It often includes some of the biggest capitalist global banks and corporations, along with Communists and the global Marxist Left; the Far-Right "enemies list" also includes the UN, as well as gays, feminists, Jews, Freemasons and atheists.

Far-Right populists promise to overthrow alien or Marxist economic and cultural elites who dominate the US Establishment and what Trump calls the "deep state" of "big government." They promise to overthrow the power of the federal government and its Marxist bureaucratic civil servants, as well as the foreign companies and sectors of "globalist" American corporations or banks, historically viewed as controlled by Jews and "a new world order." They promise to return power to the "true Americans," typically defined as white Christians, white working people and white "patriotic" business and political leaders working in and for the nation.

The working class is divided by race, gender, and religion, unable to unite against class enemies. Their only true allies are those sharing their blood, religion and culture. Their only real enemies are foreigners, non-Christians and Marxist "globalists" abroad, usually seen as tightly linked to "enemies within" – including American Marxists, minority groups and immigrants in the US. Their only savior is an authoritarian American leader. This is Trumpism, but it's a very old Far-Right populist ideology.

Four Eras of Far-Right Populism

The history of Far-Right populism can be broken into several main stages after the Civil War. Until the 1930s, American Far-Right populists were mainly linked to the Southern Democratic Party. But since the New Deal, they have found their home mainly on the Far-Right of the Republican Party. We look briefly at the hard times breeding support for populism in each stage, the different and evolving discourses and stories Far-Right populists used to win over millions of supporters in each stage, how they built a large base in their era and how they ultimately failed before a new Far-Right populist movement emerged. The most important stages preceding Trump are:

> *Democrats are America's earliest Far Right Populists: From the Confederacy to the 1920s, Populism begins as a Southern challenge to Northern capitalism*
> *Father Coughlin, Huey Long, and American Firsters: Far Right Populists in the 1930s and 1940s*
> *From McCarthy to Goldwater: Anti-Communists and Populist John Birchers Bring Far Right Populism to the GOP*

Reagan and Robertson: Republican Far Righters of Christian Nationalism Join and Clash in the Reagan Revolution

Trumpism borrows elements from all of them, but also created his own unique amalgam. It threatens to be more powerful and destructive than any of the others.

The Democratic Party Invents American Far-Right Populism: The Populist Seedbed in the South

In the age of Trump, we identify Far-Right populism with the Republican Party. But the Democratic Party founded American Far-Right populism and embodied it for at least 150 years. Starting in the slave South at the birth of the nation, the Democratic Party ruled as a racist Far-Right populist regime until the Civil War.

Many historians see President Andrew Jackson as the first US populist head of state, a Democratic Party leader who was called the "People's president." Jackson attacked government elites and financial powers and dis-established the Second Bank of the US (a central bank) in the name of protecting the ordinary hardworking American farmer, laborer or pioneer, true white and Christian Americans. He said in classic populist spirit that "it is to be regretted that the rich and powerful too often bend the acts of government to their selfish interests." At the same time, his Far-Right populism spilled out in his lifelong role as a militant slave owner and slave trader – and in his brutal violence against Native Americans as he expanded the nation and his presidential authority in his own version of Manifest Destiny and "America First."

Jackson gives us a very early glimpse into where Trump is headed, as J.D. Vance hinted in a 2021 podcast:

> "I think that what Trump should, like — if I was giving him one piece of advice, [is] fire every single mid-level bureaucrat, every civil servant in the administrative state," Vance said at the time. "Replace them with our people. And when the courts — because you will get taken to court — and when the courts stop you, stand before the country like Andrew Jackson did and say, 'The chief justice has made his ruling. Now let him enforce it.'"
> Jackson supposedly said that quote after he evicted Cherokee Indians from northern Georgia, despite the Supreme Court determining in 1834 that they owned the region.[1]

Like Jackson indicated early in his second term, Trump believes that even the Supreme Court has no authority to challenge his executive power. Jackson was foreshadowing in his early Far-Right populism the most dangerous element of Trumpism. And Vice President J.D. Vance is clearly ready to back Trump up in any such constitutional showdown.

Jackson, an iconic president symbolizing Far-Right Democratic Party populism, prefigured Trump in other important ways that illuminate how deep in history Trumpism runs. Jackson, like Trump, ran as an anti-Establishment champion of ordinary people. He is still perceived by many Americans as the earliest great presidential champion of "the people." As one commentator notes about Jackson, making explicit the parallels to Trump:

> *He (Jackson) preached about helping the common man. As the first president not part of the founding elite, he rode a populist insurgency to political victories in the 1820s and 1830s. The populism he espoused held that westward expansion meant more chances for "the common man" to participate in national affairs. He considered himself one.*[2]

Like Trump, Jackson attacked financial oligarchs, central banks and government elites, all in the name of turning the country back from US and foreign big banks to ordinary people. He persuaded many ordinary Americans and historians that he was the true original fighter for the white Christian ordinary folk, seeking to destroy the rising power elites that seemed very similar to the elites Trump vilifies as his own populist enemies. (Harry L. Watson, "Andrew Jackson's Populism," Tennessee Historical Quarterly, Vol. 76. No. 3, Fall, 2017, pp. 218–239.)

Jackson also prefigured Trump with his nationalist and expansionist foreign policy he claimed would be the salvation of the people. This involved the embrace of a "sovereignist" agenda for enriching America by conquering the foreigners that stood in the way of America's needs for land, resource and territories. Such policy meant taking the land of Native Americans as well as putting in his sights land owned by Mexico; Mexican territory was invaded and taken over by Presidents such as James Polk, emulating Jackson's territorial expansion by taking Texas in the name of Manifest Destiny. Trump hung Polk's picture in the Oval Office in his second term. (David E. Sanger, Greenland? Canada? The Canal? The Mystery Behind Manifest Destiny. NY Times, April 29, 2025, nytimes.com; Jack Bicknell, "Andrew Jackson: Man of the People," The Daily Economy, Aug. 13, 2022, thedailyeconomy.org)

Jackson was a general and became a war hero in the aftermath of the 1812 war against Britain, when he destroyed the British army in 1815 and became known for his power and "tenacity." He was no stranger to war and brutal conquest. Jackson is well known for his founding role in the infamous "Trail of Tears," where the US launched a horrific attack on Native Americans to displace them from their ancestral lands and take ownership of them. The Trail of Tears began with the 1830 Indian Removal Act, championed by Jackson, which ordered the forced displacement of Native Americans living east of the Mississippi River – from Georgia and North Caroline to Tennessee – across the Mississippi to Oklahoma and beyond. The Indian

Removal Act uprooted more than 60,000 Native Americans – including Cherokee, Chickasaw, Seminole and Creed tribes – from their native lands through treaties and military force. The nature and scale of destruction was horrific. (The Gilder Lehrman Institute of American History, "The Trail of Tears," History Resources, no date, gilderlehrman.org)

Jackson championed the idea that America had the right to take over whatever territories that "savages" and other foreigners occupied. Jackson's early form of American populism – conquest for the good of the American people – against those seen as inferior and standing in the way of American prosperity would become the guidebook for many future US presidents, with Trump among his greatest admirers and emulators.

When Trump first became president in 2017, he hung Jackson's photograph in the Oval Office. Frequently praising Jackson, Trump called him "an amazing figure in American history – very unique in so many ways." (Olivia Waxman, 5 Things to Know About the President Whose Portrait Donald Chose for the Oval Office, Time, Jan. 25, 2017, time.com)

Jackson and Trump both ruled in the spirit of "America First," to destroy all the enemies of the people at home and abroad. Trump's attacks on immigrants have striking parallels with Jackson's deportation and purging of Native Americans. At home, the Establishment enemies of both Jackson and Trump were central bankers and "globalist" corporate or cultural elites. Abroad, it was foreign peoples and nations treating America unfairly. Both Jackson and Trump claimed they were the voice of the people against the elites, and both believed in a strong executive with imperial presidential powers.

After Reconstruction, when the North retreated from its occupation of the South in 1876, the Jim Crow Democratic Party immediately inaugurated its second long stage of Far-Right populism, most ruthlessly in the South but spreading across the West, Midwest, and other sectors of the country. Jim Crow continued as the defining feature of the Democratic Party until LBJ signed the 1965 Voting Rights Act, ushering in the beginnings of multiracial democracy. Democrats' Far-Right populism's long reign in America helps explain the title of historian Heather Cox Richardson's important book, *How the South Won the Civil War.*

The Confederacy graphically illustrated why Far-Right populism became entrenched in America. In the name of defending morality and "the people," it could appeal to millions of white workers, providing them a religious and conservative cultural lifeline in desperate times. And it provided the argument for the South's challenge to the Northern capitalist Establishment, offering deeply moral arguments for the expansion of the South and its breakaway from the evils of monied and dirty Northern corporate rule. It's long legacy, running deep in the American bloodstream, helps explain why Trump's Far-Right populism resonates so deeply with millions of Americans. As a politics of white Christian nationalism and authoritarianism, Trumpism in many ways is reviving America's earliest political traditions, claiming to represent America's earliest vision of republican governance, championing the working people and "patriotic" local or domestic business against foreign and "globalist" elites.

One of the secrets of the Democrats' long reliance on Far-Right populism was captured in Nancy Isenberg's best-seller, *White Trash*. Far-Right populism gained mass support among the Southern "White Trash," because it offered them a way to redefine themselves not as garbage but as enjoying relative economic privilege. They were morally superior beings.

Economically, white trash folks were poor, hardly embodiments of privilege. Coming from England, they had long been part of a class of the dispossessed, lacking land and stable incomes. This poverty continued when they migrated to the US South. But compared to slaves, they suddenly found themselves enjoying a new status. Being poor carries a different meaning when one is better off than millions of other people. The pain of poverty is softened when you compare your fate with people who have no rights to property, civil rights or freedom.

White trash workers were not only economically better off than the slaves but were culturally viewed as part of the noble race, sharing the whiteness that the Southern culture defined as the essence of divinity and God's blessing. The pain of poverty is always experienced partly in the context of one's position in the moral hierarchy and status system. Claims about moral status are at the heart of the populist appeal to working people.

The concept of relative worth or status is always central to populism because it speaks to the deepest needs of people. One's view of oneself – as well as of the world – depends on where you sit in the moral status hierarchy. Populism offers working people the eternal solace that, whatever their economic situation, they are blessed with the most important of gifts: human worth and value. It means everything to the soul that there are others clearly inferior to you. The Far-Right populism of the Southern Democrats meant that white trash compared themselves favorably every day with Black slaves who had no dignity or worth. Trumpist populism today offers a new form of this relative "social worth" to hard-pressed white workers and "white trash" today, using the fire and violence of anti-immigrant and racial authoritarian politics to bring a sense of relative worth to insecure white workers.

But the early Southern Democratic Party was populist because it served a second broader purpose. It offered the South a way to defend their people against the evil Northern capitalist Establishment. This defense of people against the Establishment is always the essence of populism. The Southern Democrats' Far-Right populism was a crusade against the rising American capitalist Establishment that would take power nationally after the Civil War in the age of the Robber Barons.

The South, like most feudal social orders, was built around a moral order that Southern elites defined as Godly. Defining an evil system as moral is the essence of what I have called "immoral morality." The South was a classic immoral moral regime, utilizing Far-Right populist moral arguments to defend the evil of slavery and challenge the corrupt Northern capitalist Establishment preparing to attack them. In this instance, a regional Establishment in the South would exploit an unusual form of populism to attack another immoral moral Establishment that was going to destroy it and replace it.

The Confederacy was an intensely moralistic regime – and it utilized all its moral weapons to attack the Northern capitalism Establishment. Indeed, Southern Democrats' volley of moral assaults on Northern capitalism turned into an all-out spiritual war, underlying the Civil War. It laid the groundwork for the later Republican Far-Right populists, including Trump, challenging the US and global Establishment.

The Democratic Southern populists defined the "wage-slavery" of Northern capitalism as a far greater economic evil than their own slave system. Northern workers were not sheltered, fed and taken care of like Southern slaves. When workers in the North got too old to work, the bosses felt no responsibility for them, letting them go hungry as they aged. Southerners, in contrast, fed and housed their slave children and workers and provided for them after they were too old to work. As South Carolina Senator John Calhoun famously said, "slavery is a positive good," pointing to the care offered to ill or old slaves:

> *look at the sick, and the old and infirm slave, on one hand, in the midst of his family and friends, under the kind superintending care of his master and mistress, and compare it with the forlorn and wretched condition of the (Northern unemployed) pauper in the poorhouse.*[3]

Calhoun wrote that Northern capitalism is based on a cruel class struggle:

> *a conflict between labor and capital. the condition of society in the South exempts us from the disorders and dangers resulting from this conflict; and which explains why it is that the political condition of the slaveholding States has been so much more stable and quiet than that of the North.*[4]

Southerners made a classic populist assault on the Northern capitalist Establishment as driven only by profit and greed rather than the Southern system, which was based on a sense of divinely chosen order, in which people were cared for through their lives by natural superiors who rejected greed for nobility.

This was part of a much broader vision of the South as a society based on God and traditional values, where families and communities respected their women, raised their children in Godly ways, and lived a life based on religion and eternal morality. Wrapped in this intense morality, the South attacked the Northern capitalist Establishment as immoral. It was driven by money and greed rather than nobility and manners. It cultivated an unceasing and narcissistic competition for upward mobility rather than the calm self-acceptance of one's place as defined at birth. The South was a region ruled by honor and glory, but Northern capitalism cared little for honor, focusing only on making money. South Carolina Senator John Calhoun, as noted above, famously compared the kindness of slave owners with the cruelty of Northern business.

After the Civil War, Northern capitalism became the national Establishment. But Far-Right populism continued to be ingrained in the Democratic Party after the end of Reconstruction and the 1876 withdrawal of Northern forces from the South. The Democratic Party resurfaced as the Jim Crow party of the South and parts of the West and Midwest. For the next 50 years, it would continue to be the main Far-Right Populist Party and force in the US.

The populist elements of Jim Crow in the Democratic South after the Civil War and the end of Reconstruction were similar to those in the Confederacy. On the one hand, Democrats attracted white working-class people by enforcing racist segregation that favored whites economically and culturally over Blacks. They launched a new round of moral and economic attacks on the national Northern capitalist Establishment. In films like *Birth of a Nation*, presenting the slave South as a paradise of honor and nobility, Southern Democrats redoubled their critique of Northern corporate regimes as morally bankrupt. Birth of the Nation could be shown adoringly in Woodrow Wilson's White House, with Wilson still a fervent Southern Democrat who supported Calhoun's notion of a noble and Godly South. Far-Right militias like the Ku Klux Klan, whom Wilson supported, made sure Blacks were kept in their place while allowing Southern Democratic populists to attack both Wall Street and the New Deal Establishment. It was a magical formula to build the Southern populist base of white workers and support authoritarian and neo-fascist movements.

Father Coughlin and Huey Long: America Firsters and Populist Authoritarians in the 1930s and 1940s

The Great Depression of the 1930s, the worst and longest economic crisis in the US, fueled both Far-Right and Left-leaning populism. This is hardly surprising since hard times are almost always a catalyst of populism. The Far-Right and Left populisms of the 1930s were very different, but they were both political efforts to win over the support of desperate workers by targeting the Gilded Age corporate Establishment – created in the 1890s and presided over by three corporate Presidents in the 1920s – that caused the Depression and did nothing to help the workers. Trumpist rhetoric today incorporates elements of both the Far-Right and Left populists of this era, particularly the rhetoric of military non-intervention. Here, we focus mainly on the Far-Right populism rising in the Great Depression, discussing Left New Deal populism later.

The Far-Right populism of the 1930s is known primarily for its principal goal of keeping the US out of World War II and maintaining neutrality between Nazi Germany and the Communist Soviet Union. As with Trump, the position of non-intervention in a major foreign war is often part of Far-Right populism, and it was central as World War II loomed. But while the military is clearly a part of the US Establishment, as seen by both Right and Left populists, Far-Right populists are not typically critics of militarism itself but of particular wars. In the 1930s, America Firsters and the German-American Bund, both Nazi sympathizers, focused their populism on keeping the US out of the war. They were not only sympathetic or explicit members of the Nazi party, but defined US entry into war against Germany as an economic and moral disaster, with most believing that the Soviet Union was a far greater threat. At the same time, they wanted America to have a strong military presence in both the Atlantic and Pacific theatres, so they were hardly pacifists and mainly focused on how to defend nationalist American interests first, above all else.

Some "American Firsters" were US conservative "sovereignists" who fiercely opposed the League of Nations in the 1920s and any form of world government. But the "sovereignists," much like the American Firsters and, like Trump today, were not complete isolationists and sought more US power in parts of the world seen as essential to the glory of America and an America First vision.

Many leading America Firsters, including their most influential spokespeople, Charles Lindbergh and Henry Ford, openly supported Hitler and authoritarianism. Lindbergh, in a 1939 essay in Readers Digest on the white race, wrote that white Europeans and Americans needed to band together to protect their "blood."

We can have peace and security only so long as we band together to preserve that most priceless possession, our inheritance of European blood, only so long as we guard ourselves against attack by foreign armies and dilution by foreign races.[233]

(wiii)

This was typical America First racist language, echoing Hitler and usually attacking Jews, with his overt anti-Semitism a staple of Far-Right populism. But America Firsters' support for Hitler told a much larger and less familiar story about Far-Right populists. The war was diverting the nation from its much larger urgent needs: to overthrow the Establishment that had driven the US into the worst economic disaster of its history, while also curbing the Soviet Union. Democratic capitalism did not serve the suffering American people; that would take a strongman who could take on US and global Jewish and other internationalist financial houses and big corporations that were leading America into the hands of an internationalist Communist conspiracy.

While America Firsters focused singularly on keeping the US out of World War II, their ideology and agenda included a broader Far-Right critique of Wall Street and the American Establishment. While many 1930s Far-Right populists, such as Henry Ford, were rich capitalists – evoking Trump's current band of wealthy Far-Right billionaires – some were openly contemptuous of even the veneer of capitalist democracy. They advocated replacing the existing system with some variant of authoritarianism and American fascism, which they claimed would be good for both American business and workers.

We focus first in this section on Father Charles Coughlin, a neo-Nazi American sympathizer tied to populist Far-Right American Firsters; we then look at Huey Long, a different type of populist who was an authoritarian demagogue evocative of Trump today. Coughlin, a Catholic priest, was famous for his radio broadcasts in the 1930s listened to by millions in the US – reaching one of every four Americans; he was the Rush Limbaugh of that era. He used radio to turn the Far Right against globalist capitalism and against war with Hitler, as he eventually argued that fascism might be the best way to save America and its workers.

Father Coughlin was an iconic cultural symbol of 1930s Far-Right populism. His radio success made him the voice of the movement. While he was increasingly anti-Semitic and was viewed by many as pro-Nazi, lambasting war against Hitler as a boondoggle for US banks and ultimately embracing American fascism, he claimed to be fighting for the American worker against the American corporate Establishment. Coughlin had initially supported FDR and the New Deal, but by 1934 he attacked FDR as too friendly with bankers and too ready for a globalist war at odds with a nationalist program to defend America and its desperate workers. Coughlin created a new political organization called the National Union for Social Justice, calling for nationalization of railroads and other key industries, taxation of the rich, protection of workers and loosening of credit and the money supply by predatory banks, all while opposing the US war on Hitler and ending the scourge of globalist financial internationalism with a nationalist America First agenda.

In 1935, Coughlin summarized his political philosophy as follows:

> *I have dedicated my life to fight against the heinous rottenness of modern capitalism because it robs the laborer of this world's goods. But blow for blow, I shall strike against Communism, because it robs us of the next world's happiness.*

This highlights the contradictions of Far-Right populism. It is populist because it attacks the corporate Establishment. But while it uses the rhetoric of protecting the worker, it is as hostile to socialism and Communism as it is friendly to fascism and to social hierarchy. The workers cannot protect themselves; as Coughlin's thought evolved, he concluded they needed a dictator to do it.

In the early 1930s, Coughlin strongly supported New Deal style government regulation and guarantees of a minimum wage and maximum hours. In 1930, he had said on his radio:

We have lived to see the day that modern Shylocks have grown fat and wealthy, praised and deified, because they have perpetuated the ancient crime of usury under the modern racket of statesmanship.[89]

Coughlin's critique of the capitalist Establishment never flagged in its anger against big corporations and "Shylock" Jewish bankers as enemies of human rights and social welfare; moreover, the modern capitalist system really couldn't be salvaged in anything like its current form. He sounds almost Marxist in his critique that:

social justice should replace the practices of modern capitalism; that the doctrine of exploitation should be relegated to the same graveyard where rots the corpse of feudalism, that the theory of exploitation should take its place with the theory of slavery

Coughlin's populist rage was directed mainly at the bankers, arguing that J.P. Morgan and his banking industry, allied with Jewish global banks, have gained "control over industry" and that the banking industry "gained control over capitalism" and now is a tiny cabal;

a small group of individuals, of parasites who did not produce but who lived upon the labors of others, this control of money which enabled them, in days of prosperity, to grow fat upon interest and, in the days of depression, to grow fatter upon confiscations...

And at their head are the global "princes of high finance," mostly Jews who are running wars and global enterprises to fill their own coffers and bankrupt their own workers and nations. He names names:

the Rothschilds in Europe, the Lazzeres in France, the Warburgs, the Kuhn-Loebs, the Morgans and the rest of that wrecking crew of internationalists whose god is gold and whose emblem is the red shield of exploitation–these men I shall oppose until my dying days

Coughlin's Far-Right populism denounced this mainly Jewish financial globalist Establishment as contemptuous of the average man, referring, as Trump does today, to "the forgotten worker." Coughlin rails that the bankers are barely aware of ordinary workers, who are truly "forgotten." He lambasts them for their elitism and devaluing of the very people they make their fortunes from:

> *the so-called average man, the man who barters the labor of his hands for the means of his livelihood. As far as all practical purposes are concerned he is your inferior in the intellectual order and in the social order.*
>
> *I know how you valuate the common man in the scales of actuality–the actualities of life. You deem him to be the plaything of impulse, the toy of emotion.*[5]

But while Coughlin praises ordinary workers' skills with their hands and contributions by their labor, he veers from a Left-leaning populism by shifting from the New Deal to the idea that he knows the bankers embrace: an authoritarian regime that can make America great again.

Coughlin, himself, moves toward this version of the Far-Right populist philosophy: only a strongman can ultimately save the workers and the bankers themselves from the just rage of the ordinary worker, whose fair earnings have been stolen from him. Without the strongman, without Hitler or his American counterpart, heads will roll, as did, Coughlin notes, those of Louis XVI and Antoinette – and justly so!

Coughlin's Far-Right populism, rooted in his view of an evil financial and Jewish-dominated Establishment destroying the nation and its good Christian people, led toward fascist solutions for the worker. By the mid-1930s, Coughlin was making public statements favorable to rising European fascist leaders like Franco, Mussolini and Hitler. Harvard political scientists Steven Levitsky and Daniel Ziblatt write that Coughlin became "openly antidemocratic and questioning the value of elections." A New York Times reporter in Berlin reported in 1938 said that Coughlin has become "the German hero in America for the moment," making clear that Nazism was the best defensive front against Bolshevism as well as the best deal for workers. (wiki)

By the late 1930s, Coughlin had leaned into rebuilding America as its own form of fascist state, with a strongman who could take down both the ruling Establishment and restore the dignity of the nation and its great Christian working class. Had Coughlin seen Trump in action, he might have celebrated him as the Great Leader who could do the job. His overt fascism was an extreme form of the authoritarianism that emerged in almost all US Far-Right populist movements.

A second famous 1930s populist, Huey Long, is particularly relevant today because many now see him as a Donald Trump of his time. The Louisiana governor was a pugnacious, Southern populist with unabashed authoritarian impulses, using violence against his political opponents and leading many to call him "Louisiana's Hitler." A Southern Democratic populist rather than

Republican, he attacked the capitalist Establishment but also the New Deal Administration.

Governor Long melded Far-Right and Left populism, an amalgam of contradictions. He critiqued corporate power and could sound like a Left populist, indeed, more ideologically Leftist than FDR and, in this sense, very different from Trump. But he was dedicated to saving capitalism, and he ruled as a bully and a quasi-dictator in the spirit of traditional Far-Right populism. He evoked Donald Trump's anti-democratic and autocratic style of governance more than any other 1930s leader.

Many historians rightly see Long as sharing Left populist views of the extreme evils of US and global capitalism. He was a Southern Democrat who had a searing critique of the US corporate Establishment. It was more than just rhetoric; he believed that a strongman leader like himself, committed to mass distribution of wealth to the working classes, was the solution to saving workers during the Depression and ending abuse of corporate power. He was willing to carry through on a working-class agenda that Trump promised but never remotely delivered. At the same time, he was as ruthlessly authoritarian in his politics as Trump, talking and ruling like a Mafia boss, breaking or manipulating election laws and voting schemes to defeat those opposing him, and generally using corruption to consolidate his power.

Long was not a classic Far-Right Southern Democratic populist; in fact, he was among the least racist of Southern leaders in Jim Crow states. He didn't attack Jim Crow or dismantle segregation, but he delivered to Blacks in his state more education and economic support than his Southern Far-Right peers. He didn't blame Blacks for white workers' problems as much as he blamed the white corporate Establishment and, to some degree, the Jewish international bankers.

Indeed, his "Share the Wealth" plan in 1934 was a genuine challenge to the white financial Establishment, as well as to the New Deal, promoting truly massive federal spending, a wealth tax and major wealth redistribution. The Left populist spirit of these proposals took shape in "Share the Wealth" clubs that garnered millions of working-class supporters, who participated locally in grassroots labor education and activism.

Long did share key elements of Far-Right Southern Far-Right populism, including his fierce nationalism and authoritarianism, that aligned him with American Firsters. He opposed foreign intervention in a war against Hitler, much like other American Firsters. He was a conservative nationalist leaning toward isolationism. He saw foreign wars as largely the playthings of US oil companies and bankers, saying that oil companies and Wall Street controlled US foreign policy. (wiki)

Long was also, like Trump, passionate about tariffs. He wanted people to call him a "tariff Democrat." Republican presidents like William McKinlay and Teddy Roosevelt had long viewed tariffs as essential to protect Northern business, while Southerners wanted low tariffs to sell their cotton cheaply abroad. As a "tariff Democrat," Long was enthusiastic about tariffs as a populist symbol of economic and political nationalism, rejecting the global economic order he saw dominated by big business. Like Trump, he also saw tariffs as a crucial populist solution to protecting jobs at home.

While many commentators at the time called him the American Hitler, Long did not embrace Nazi Germany, though he hated the Communists more than the Nazis. But his populist authoritarianism was his brand, with bullying, threats and dubiously constitutional power grabs occurring as frequently as Trump's own brazen anti-democratic power grabs. Long reveled, as Trump does, in winning over people who like tough talk with his threats and extreme bullying language. Huey reveled in his nasty, boastful and authoritarian tricks and style.

> They say they don't like my methods. Well, I don't like them either. I really don't like to have to do things the way I do. I'd much rather get up before the legislature and say, 'Now this is a good law and it's for the benefit of the people, and I'd like you to vote for it in the interest of the public welfare.' Only I know that laws ain't made that way. You've got to fight fire with fire.
> — Huey Long (T. Harry Williams, Huey Long, p. 748)
> I'd rather violate every one of the damn conventions and see my bills passed, than sit back in my office, all nice and proper, and watch 'em die.
> — Huey Long on lobbying state legislators (Williams, p. 298)
> You sometimes fight fire with fire. The end justifies the means. I would do it some other way if there was time or if it wasn't necessary to do it this way.
> — Huey Long (Williams, p. 749)
> Everything I did, I've had to do with one hand, because I've had to fight with the other.
> — Huey Long to wife, Rose (Williams, p. 749)
> Always take the offensive — the defensive ain't worth a damn.
> — Huey Long
> I can frighten or buy ninety-nine out of every one hundred men.
> — Huey Long (Williams, p. 751)
> I used to get things done by saying please. Now I dynamite 'em out of my path
>   (All quotes from "Huey Long in his own words," hueylong.com)

People close to Huey said that he saw himself not as America's Hitler but as the reincarnation of Napoleon Bonaparte. His populism was a fierce fight to protect and empower workers, with delusional authoritarian ambitions. It is hard to think of a populist who integrated so many contradictory features of Left and Right populism. After the Great Depression and World War II, the two populisms again began to distinguish themselves from each other more clearly, with Far-Right populism diving deep into the Republican Party and embracing more authoritarianism. Left populists moved from the center to the Left fringe of the New Deal, seeking to build economic as well as political democracy. Many Leftist Populists, after the New Deal, gave up on the Democratic Party and tried to build autonomous social movements and third parties.

Senator Joseph Mccarthy's Red Scare and Populist John Birchers Delivered Southern Populism to the GOP in the 1960s

After World War II, the Cold War between the US and the Soviet Union took center stage in the US and much of the world. Anti-Communism became the core ideology of the Center and Right in the US, championed also by Harry Truman. Anti-Communism was bipartisan, reflected in the war fever and militarism sweeping both political parties. It became central to mainstream politics.

But the Far Right of the 1950s and 1960s developed its own distinctive paranoid and extreme populist anti-Communism. Starting with the Red Scare of the McCarthy era in the early 1950s, it became part of a broader conspiratorial nationalist and anti-globalist Far-Right worldview flourishing in movements like the 1960s John Birch Society. It saw the international "Communist Threat" as a movement toward a One World Government promoted by a wild assortment of heavily Jewish global banks and powerful and secret cabals of corporate globalists with liberal or Marxist sympathies, linked at home with Communist Democrats, anti-American Black civil rights movement activists, and counter-cultural immoral beatniks rioting on the streets.

The 1950s and 1960s Far-Right populists – starting with McCarthy – embraced the nationalism of America Firsters and saw a rising international Establishment of powerful Jewish global banking houses, Communist states, and international bodies like the UN. Resisting this global cosmopolitan elite – and its subversive Communist allies among elites in the US itself – became the main agenda of McCarthy Far-Right US populism. McCarthy lasted only five years on the national scene, but his influence helped inspire the John Birch Society and Barry Goldwater, both uniting the fire of McCarthy's anti-Communism with elements of Southern Democratic Far-Right populism after the Democrats began to reject their long disgraceful, racist, anti-democratic Jim Crow heritage.

His anti-Communism per se did not make McCarthy a Far-Right populist. But McCarthyism had a few key elements that were part of a long populist tradition and have led many Americans today to compare McCarthy and Trump. This goes beyond the fact that Roy Cohn, the chief counsel for McCarthy during his famous hearings on Communists in the Army, was one of Trump's main mentors. Cohn was known for his vicious slurs and lies, accusing and threatening to prosecute everyone from leading Hollywood directors to top generals to intelligence figures in the FBI and CIA to President Eisenhower himself as a Communist. Trump is said to have learned from Cohn how to bully, threaten and prosecute everyone against him as traitors. Cohn taught Trump to "attack, attack, attack," deny everything, and always claim victory. (YouTube, "What Donald Trump Learned From Roy Cohn," CNN, Sept 1, 2016, YouTube)

For McCarthy and Cohn, you were either a Communist or a "true American." This is a recurrent sign of Far-Right populism. It differentiates the public into the "true Americans" versus the "Commies" or some other form of "un-Americans." As with Trump, the prosecutorial zeal of McCarthy created a climate of fear in the country. Anybody, even Eisenhower, could be called Communist and anti-American. Painting with such a broad brush always creates a national climate of threat and intimidation, a rule by fear, usually led by a strongman, to purge the nation of un-American influence and terrorize dissenters.

Moreover, while this is a less explicit element in McCarthy, his Red Scare was part of a strategy to assail a dangerous and powerful Establishment – both global and American. Unlike most Far-Right populists discussed thus far, McCarthy did not explicitly use the populist language of an evil ruling US corporate Establishment – made up of bankers, Wall Street or the Jews – unless they were individuals who were openly Communist or tied to them. His populist style, though, did incorporate a view that the Communist global regime and its fellow travelers on the home front – mainly liberals, New Dealers, Leftists and academics, writers or civil rights and peace activists – were all cultural cosmopolitans and, implicitly, a danger to the country.

McCarthy essentially built an anti-Communist populist coalition united by:

> opposition to internationalism, particularly the United Nations; opposition to social welfare provisions, particularly the various programs established by the New Deal; and opposition to efforts to reduce inequalities in the social structure of the United States.[67]
>
> (wiki mccarthisym)

Anyone in government, including the State Department or Pentagon, and anyone inside or outside government supporting the New Deal, foreign aid, the UN, or international trade agreements and globalizing corporate influences, could be targeted by McCarthy. Part of his power was his ability to define, with large public support, almost anybody as Communist or anti-American. In a foreshadowing of the Trumpist era, even public health could be branded as a Communist threat, with McCarthy ginning up anger against government overreach or scientific incursions on freedom:

> One focus of popular McCarthyism concerned the provision of public health services, particularly vaccination, mental health care services,

and fluoridation, all of which were denounced by some to be communist plots to poison or brainwash the American people. Such viewpoints led to collisions between McCarthyite radicals and supporters of public-health programs, most notably in the case of the Alaska Mental Health Bill controversy of 1956.[68]

(wiki macarthism)

This foreshadowed the Trumpist anti-vax populism that became part of a broader attack on public health led by JFK Jr. and others deeply skeptical of science and public health, especially vaccines. McCarthy tacitly extended his singular fury against the Communist Threat into a populist hate of big government, science, urban life, higher education, liberalism and global cosmopolitanism linked to a Communist world order.

Donald Trump, the anti-global populist, 70 years later, did much the same, and not just in his crusade against vaccines and public health. Trumpism is a new era of McCarthyism, borrowing not only from the mob-style bullying and fear-mongering of Roy Cohn but also McCarthy's own attack on globalism and internationalism as a sign of anti-Americanism.

The line between McCarthyite Far-Right populism and Trumpism is rapidly fading.

McCarthy had an intense but relatively short run of power, disgraced after five years when he attacked President Eisenhower in 1954 as a Communist. McCarthy was dead by 1957, but his movement was reincarnated in the John Birch Society in 1958 by Robert Welch, a businessman who left the liberal ivy campuses where he studied to start a candy business. His Junior Mints and Pom-Poms became hugely popular, a popularity that his John Birch Society (the JBS) never quite achieved. The Birchers were named after John Birch, an early 20th-century missionary in China who was religious, extremely conservative and passionately anti-Communist. The John Birch Society never became as much a subject of popular culture in the early 1960s as did Junior Mints. But Welch, a big fan of McCarthy, would succeed in taking McCarthy's anti-Communism and transforming it through the JBS into a full-scale Far-Right populist movement that launched an invasion of the Republican Party under Barry Goldwater in the 1964 election. The Birchers were critical in shifting Far-Right populism from its long home in the Southern Democratic Party to its new home in the Republican Party, now gaining remarkable ascendancy under Trump and the transformation of the Republican Party into MAGA.

McCarthy, as discussed above, focused centrally on anti-Communism and did not embed it fully in the classic populist politics of an evil "Establishment" against "the people." Welch and the JBS were obsessed with anti-Communism, but they built a broader analysis of a "One World Government," a malignant global Establishment and the US elites who were promoting globalization and free trade agreements as part of it – all conspiring to undermine the prosperity and culture of "true Americans." The JBS opposed NAFTA, CAFTA (the Central

American Free Trade Agreement), the FTAA (Free Trade of the Americas Agreement) and many other free trade agreements. Left populists would later take up the same challenge to free trade agreements, but with different arguments.

Nonetheless, the Bircher opposition to free trade and globalization has now become dogma in Trumpist rhetoric, and, for many of the same nationalist and anti-collectivist reasons. It was tied to hatred of globalist financial and banking houses and contempt for cosmopolitan culture that would lure hard-working US farmers and industrial workers to reject great American traditional culture. The One World Government would undermine the traditional family, forcing acceptance of equal rights for women. It would breed interracial marriages. And it would create pressure to send their kids to liberal universities where global cosmopolitanism of coastal cultural elites would turn them into Communists. It would fuel moral degeneracy, long a central focus of Far Right and fascist movements. This became an obsessive focus of the Birchers, an inevitable consequence of global economic and cultural elites' war against "the people" down on the farm.

The Birchers hated any form of "world government" as a form of "collectivism." It was anti-American and incompatible with national sovereignty and identity, as well as traditional American values. Birchers trained their sights on the UN as a stalking ground for world government and the takeover of the US by a global Establishment. They went back to the Freemason movement of Europeans, whom the Birchers saw as part of an ancient "illuminati" European tradition seeking a collectivist, all-powerful world government. In 1966, Welch wrote that the Illuminati are still working to promote an evil globalization and world order, with:

> *grandiose dreams of overthrowing all existing human institutions, and of rising out of the resting chaos as the all-powerful rulers of a 'new order' of civilization.*[6]

This hatred of globalism and an evil world-government global Establishment helped shape the increasing populist politics of the Birchers. In the early 1960s, the Birchers created an organization, Populist America, signaling their new explicit commitment to Far-Right populism.

This all grew as well out of the anti-Communism of the America Firsters and McCarthyism, and it also had roots in nationalist economics and growing discontent of the populist Right with Eisenhower. Ike symbolized disastrous economic and political internationalism to the rising anti-Ike Far Right. Welch had grown up assuming that Robert Taft's conservative corporate Republicanism would take over the Republican Party and implement its nationalist America First roots. Instead, Eisenhower, as seen by Welch and other Far-Right populists, was taking the Republican Party deep into a new global regime, both militarily with NATO and economically with free trade and global economic agreements and investments across the world. Ike had surrendered to Rockefeller and his global designs. What had happened to the paradise of Taft, a Republican truly committed to America First and the sacred principle of nationalism?

Here, we see another variant of Far-Right populism, in which two competing Establishments come into conflict. The Birchers launched all-out war on One World Government and an evil collectivist global Establishment, one that was tied to Wall Street and the Established East Coast US financial elites. A schism was emerging in American capitalism between East Coast global finance and heartland industrialists. Far-Right populism began to take sides with the Birchers and "Main Street not Wall Street." As the Birchers framed it, they were:

the men of Main Street, not Wall Street which Eisenhower represented.
They were the everyday men and women who were concerned about
where they country was headed.[7]

They saw Eisenhower as aligned with globalists and Wall Street rather than ordinary people, a classic Far-Right populist theme. They attacked Wall Street, Rockefeller interests, the globalist Council on Foreign Relations and the biggest banks.

But they were not, as populist rhetoric might suggest, fighting for democracy. Welch and the Birchers did not believe in democracy – indeed, they associated with fringe violent Far-Right militias that were neofascist or extreme racists. The Birchers embraced a version of Southern Far-Right populism based on states' rights and White Christian Nationalism. The Birchers rejected the global Establishment but believed "the people" could only be protected not by the people themselves but by America First nationalist elites and anti-Communist strongmen.

Who could step into those shoes? The perfect candidate of the time emerged, Barry Goldwater, who ran as the Republican candidate for president in 1964. Goldwater represented the Far-Right forces gathering in the GOP to oppose the globalism and "liberal values" of Eisenhower, Wall Street and the Rockefeller-funded Council on Foreign Relations. Indeed, while he was not a Bircher, he is most famous for his defense of the Birchers to mainstream Republicans, claiming

extremism in the defense of liberty is no vice.

This defense of the Birchers not only defined Goldwater's place in history but also reflected an earthquake in US politics and US populism. Goldwater was defeated in a landslide by LBJ, but he had already begun a major shift in the ideology, elites and base of the Republican Party. As LBJ and the Democrats were signing the 1965 Voting Rights Act, creating the first primitive version of the US as a multiracial democracy, Southern Democrats were bolting out of the Democratic Party into the new Southern and Western Party of Goldwater. Cowboy capitalists from Texan oil were beginning to encroach on Wall Street financial capitalists as Goldwater began to usher in a new Republican Party.

Goldwater could open the gates, but didn't last long enough to make a revolution toward a new Far-Right populist GOP. The first steps in that direction would be made by Nixon and Reagan – and then consummated in full force by Trump.

The shift in the Republican Party is intertwined with the shift of Far-Right populism from the Democrats to the Republicans in the modern era. Indeed, White Christian Nationalism, at the very heart of Far-Right populism, had rested comfortably in the Southern Democratic Party for 150 years, since the founding of the nation. But Goldwater, spurred by Far-Right groups like the Birchers and responding to the emerging rivalry in the US corporate Establishment between Wall Street and Southern cowboy capitalists, will be remembered as the man who helped turn Far-Right White Christian Nationalism into an ideology of the Republican rather than the Democratic Party.

Trumpism was the latest and most consequential stage, making the GOP the new political house of Far-Right populist threats to democracy. As historians reckon with the rise of Trumpism and the shift of the Southern strategy from Democrats to Republicans, they will have to dust off the footnotes of books documenting the Birchers and their authoritarian legacy. A very small group of Birchers still lives on today, flourishing mostly in Southern conservative states like Texas; they not surprisingly see a new reason to take hope, expressed by one Bircher preacher in Houston in 2016:

> *"We must teach our children their heritage…. We've slowly forgotten our principles." But there is a powerful reason to rejoice…a reason for renewed optimism: God has sent America a new, powerful leader. He's a good man, a moral man. God has delivered Donald J. Trump to save the United States of America.*[8]

One current Bircher noted:

> *The Society's ideas, once on the fringe, are increasingly commonplace in today's Republican Party. And where Birchers once looked upon national Republican leaders as mortal enemies, the ones I met in Texas see an ally in the president. "All of us here voted for Trump," "And we're optimistic about what he will do."*[9]

Pat Robertson and Pat Buchanan vs. Ronald Reagan? Populism for and against the New World Order

It took only 16 years from the time that Goldwater introduced Southern Far-Right populism into the GOP for it to become part of its core agenda, transforming not just the Republican Party but America in the Reagan revolution. Even earlier, in 1968 and 1972, Richard Nixon had begun to rely on the "Southern strategy." Turning against the young Leftist civil rights activists and anti-Vietnam War protesters all over the streets in 1968, Nixon realized that he could win over to the GOP a "silent majority" of ordinary patriotic and religious farmers and workers in the South and across much of the West and Midwest, who didn't like the civil rights movement led by Martin Luther King or the Vietnam War but hated the atheist "anti-American" student activists even more. Nixon was not a true populist, but he exploited the core Far-Right populist strategy to divide the nation between the "true Americans," – the white working people of the "Silent Majority" – and the enemy within who were attacking their jobs, patriotism and basic values. These enemies at home were Black civil rights activists attacking everything white and the white student hippies and activists who were attacking everything American, especially its brave soldiers and wars. The "silent majority" worked and paid taxes; the activists had a lot of sex and went to schools paid for by the silent majority's taxes. Nixon's Southern Strategy was the first stage in applying Goldwater's lessons to an evolving Republican Party, which was turning into a 21st-century form of the 19th-century Far-Right Southern Democratic Party that helped found the nation.

But the real rise of Far-Right poulism, as it began to redefine the Republican Party, grew dramatically stronger with Ronald Reagan. As historians and conservative thinkers such as Max Boot highlight, Reagan was a forerunner of Trump in many respects, including his Christian nationalist and racialized politics. (David Smith, "Did Reagan pave the way for Trump? 'You can trace the linkages,' says biographer," The Guardian, Sept. 21, 2024, theguardian. com) White Christian Nationalism became a central part of the Reagan coalition, mobilizing a new Christian Far-Right populist coalition close to the heart of Republican grassroots power.

Television preacher and savvy political organizer, Pat Robertson, who founded the Christian Broadcasting Network and the Christian Coalition, became arguably the most important figure bringing White Christian Nationalism and Far-Right populism into Republican politics in the Nixon and Reagan eras. Seen by many as a direct heir of populists like Huey Long and Charles Coughlin, Robertson helped lead a Far-Right populist attack on a "satanic" and anti-Christian "New World Order" of huge global banks and a cultural war against Christianity and the spiritual foundations of civilization.

Robertson's New World Order portrayed globalization today as the latest and most advanced stage of a dangerous centuries-old plot to subject the world to a collectivist and Godless global dictatorship. As with the Birchers and Huey Long, Robertson believed ancient European secret societies promoting a secular world order of free peoples discussed earlier – including the Illuminati and the Freemasons – helped inspire and unite a vast array of liberal, corporate, financial and communist secular anti-Christian elites into a global coalition to create a satanic world government. Like the Birchers, he attacked Wall Street, the Trilateral Commission, the Rockefellers and their Council on Foreign Relations as part of a concerted effort to build a Godless world government, linking global banks to the forces of the anti-Christ. Like his Bircher predecessors, he argued this began with the Illuminati and

Freemasons seeking world government, who would turn in the 19th century to European bankers to suck the wealth out of the US through global investment schemes:

> *Later, the European economic powers [i.e., bankers, particularly the Rothschilds] began to see the wealth of North America as a great treasure, and some of them still wanted to get their tentacles into America's economy [note the "octopus" metaphor, a staple of anti-Semitic and anti-capitalist rhetoric]. They eventually did so not by force but by investing their money here, by sending people [i.e., Jewish bankers like Paul Warburg and Jacob Schiff], and by buying land. Europe could not defeat the United States by military force, but the European financiers knew that they could control the United States economy if they could saddle us with an American equivalent of the German Bundesbank or the Bank of England. [p. 61]*

Robertson saw these European financiers melding in the 20th century with the big American banking houses of Morgan and Rockefeller. Today's global Establishment, he argued, is a marriage of Rockefellers, the J.P. Morgan banks, the Federal Reserve, and policy centers including the Council on Foreign Relations and the Trilateral Commission. They are intimately tied to a global network of anti-Christian international forces banding together to destroy religion, undermine all traditional Christian values and destroy nationalism through global institutions like the UN.

Robertson's economic populism was embedded in a larger cultural populism building on America's founding Far-Right populism: Southern White Christian Nationalism. Robertson's populism was, first and foremost, a cultural politics attacking a rising anti-American and anti-Christian secular humanist Establishment. He blasted anti-AIDS gays fighting for gay marriage. He attacked anti-family and anti-abortion feminists who were being denounced by Bircher and super-Reagan ally, Phyllis Schlafly. Robertson also lambasted unpatriotic and immoral Marxist students protesting Reagan's policies in their secular classes, along with lazy hippies and bums in atheistic sanctuaries of Berkeley and San Francisco, symbols of American decadence.

But while Robertson is crucial to the story of US Far-Right GOP populism, he did not convert Reagan into an economic populist. Reagan became the most powerful architect of the rising 21st-century global corporate and banking Establishment that Robertson hated and fought. Nonetheless, Reagan saw the political virtues of bringing Robertson into his fold, a way to massively increase his appeal to culturally conservative white farmers and workers, whom Robertson could politically unite with Southern Evangelicals and mega-church pastors.

Despite Robertson's influence and the rise of Reagan's White Christian nationalist base, Reagan never became a populist. The Reagan Revolution empowered and institutionalized the global corporate and banking Establishment that the populists like Robertson despised. Reagan never attacked global corporations, banks or any big companies; they were the heart of his political movement. Reagan never attacked global corporations, banks or any big companies; they were the heart of his political movement.

But he found ways to keep Christian Coalition Far-Right populists as major figures in his coalition. As one pundit wryly noted, Reagan hugged his Far-Right Christian leaders so tight they couldn't breathe. He kept them close, too close to give them the breathing room to chart an independent course from the global banking and capitalist Establishment that Reagan embraced and populists like Buchanan genuinely hated.

Reagan was a consummate politician in this respect, integrating into his coalition Christian and corporate centers of power that were often at war with each other. And Robertson's complex relation with Reaganism should not disguise his power in genuinely reshaping the Republican Party.

At his death in 2023, CNN headlined that "without Pat Robertson there would be no Donald Trump." Like Robertson, Trump linked the evils of globalization to a Godless cosmopolitan culture of secular humanism and liberalism or Marxism – now taking on the new labels of "woke" and "DEI."

Robertson helped usher in an army of conservative populists in the late 20th century who would help remake the Republican Party. They are the prime force that opened the door to Trump's own Far-Right populism.

The most intriguing economic populist of the Nixon and Reagan era was Pat Buchanan, a conservative on fire against the corporate regime. Buchanan was a leading conservative pundit and political operative, working for both Presidents Nixon and Reagan, as well as running for president himself against George H.W. Bush in 1992. Because he helped reshape the 21st-century Republican Party toward the populism of Trump and MAGA, his story deserves its own attention.

Buchanan could have been confused with a Leftist Gilded Age populist in his unfettered attack on US corporations, banks and capitalism itself. At political rallies, Buchanan would say, "the peasants are coming with pitchforks." He argued that it was time for Wall Street to answer to Main Street. As the Wall Street Journal put it:

Mr. Buchanan has a distinctly nineteenth century view of the economy in which capitalism is dominated by robber barons who work with their lackeys in government to oppress workers.[10]

Alan Brinkley expanded on Buchanan's views as rooted directly in the Gilded Age populist revolution of the 1890s, when the modern capitalist Establishment took power:

Buchanan draws from powerful impulses in the American past. HIs rhetoric echoes the agrarian populism of the late nineteenth century with its harsh attacks on the railroads, corporations and banks, its suspicious of 'international finance,' and its deeper fears that in a new era and alien economy, individuals were losing control over their own fates[11]

Buchanan relentlessly skewered corporate executives as "corporate executioners." He rallied laid-off workers in Michigan, characterizing capitalism as the "law of the jungle." He told Bible Belt churchgoers, patriots on motorbikes and Evangelical churchgoers:

When go-go global capitalism is uprooting entire communities and families, I ask conservatives what it is we are trying to conserve.[12]

At the height of his popularity in the 1990s, Newsweek ran a story on "corporate hit men," splashing the words "Corporate Killers" in big blood-red letters on its cover.[13]

Buchanan combined his economic populism with cultural populism. He invented the phrase "silent majority" and worked in both the Nixon and Reagan presidencies to bring Christian conservative workers into the Republican Party. While raging against corporations and banks sending US workers' jobs abroad, he also gave a famous "culture war" speech in 1992, where he told the Republican Party there was now a "religious war" going on in the country that could destroy it. He made fiery speeches against immigration, abortion, multiculturalism and gay rights. His melding of conservative economic and cultural populism makes him, arguably, one of the figures historians will likely turn to as they analyze the rise of Trump and the transformation of the GOP into the ruling party of Far-Right populism.

Buchanan is an especially pivotal figure in the rise of Far-Right economic populism. His genuine challenge to mainstream Republican orthodoxy about the virtues of globalization and corporate capitalism highlighted and empowered the economic populism that ultimately influenced Donald Trump and his own headlining of anti-globalist economic populism. One could argue that Trumpism is the ultimate triumph of Buchanan's resurrection of a Far-Right strain of late 19th-century populism. Buchanan was among the most powerful figures to help shape the economic and cultural populism that would influence Trump himself, as well as the New Right represented by figures like J.D. Vance, who are the likely leaders destined to lead a Far-Right populist movement after Trump.

Notes

1. Paige Skinner, JD Vance Criticizes Judge after DOGE is Blocked from Treasury, *Huffington Post*, Feb. 9, 2025, huffpost.com
2. Olivia Waxman, 5 Things to Know about the President Whose Portrait Donald Chose for the Oval Office, *Time*, Jan. 25, 2017, time.com
3. John Calhoun, "Slavery a Positive Good," teachinggamericanhistory.org
4. John Calhoun, "Slavery a Positive Good," teachinggamericanhistory.org
5. ssa.go Charles Coughlin and the Search for Social Justice.
6. John Savage, "The John Birch Society is Back," Political, July 16, 2017, politico.com
7. NPR "The history of far-right populism, from the John Birch Society to Trumpism," wesa.fm.
8. John Savage, "The John Birch Society is Back," Politico, July 16, 2017, politico.com
9. John Savage, "The John Birch Society is Back," Political, July 16, 2017, politico.com
10. Alan Brinkley, in the Wall Street Journal, Feb. 22, 1996, cited in Derber, Corporation Nation, NY: St. Martins Press, p. 172.
11. Alan Brinkley "A Swaggering Tradition: Buchanan belongs to a long line of fiery populists who burn themselves out," *Newsweek*, March 4, 1996, pp. 28–29.
12. Buchanan, cited in Jason DeParle "Class is No Longer a Four Letter Word: The New York Times Magazine March 17, 1996, pp. 40 -43, See also Howard Fineman, "Extreme Measures," *Newsweek*, March 4, 1996, pp. 20–27.
13. Alan Brinkley "A Swaggering Tradition: Buchanan belongs to a long line of fiery populists who burn themselves out," *Newsweek*, March 4, 1996, pp. 28–29.

3 Trump's Trick

Populism with Billionaires

Trump's Grand Narrative

Trump won election and reelection by running as the "change" candidate against the Establishment in hard times. His rhetoric united the most important elements of earlier stages of classic Far-Right populism. Trump created a grand narrative to save the American working class from a globalist corporate regime outsourcing America's manufacturing jobs and run by "deep state" Leftist bureaucrats, a regime favoring the coastal liberal cultural elites who undermine traditional American values and sabotage Christianity. It would take a strongman to overthrow the Establishment, and Trump made clear that he personally would seize the necessary reins of power and force change, saying repeatedly, "I alone can fix it."

Trump was the first to unify an attack on the globalist international order, foreign companies and American elites that captured the entire Republican Party, rhetorically redefining it as a party of the working class and Christian nationalist values against the deep state and the alien Corporate and Cultural Globalists. Trump promised an "America First" policy that would once again make America the leader of global manufacturing and restore the security and pride of the "forgotten worker." In addition to bringing jobs home, he promised to use any means necessary – going well beyond traditional constitutional checks and balances – to purge aliens, immigrants and Marxist government elites that were in league with minorities and collaborating in the war on the American worker and "true Americans."

Trump's trick was to govern as the grand partner of the billionaire class that his populist Grand Narrative lambasted. He massively empowered the swamp that he had promised to drain. Yes his master rhetoric was pro-worker and populist, and his major "Liberation Day" tariff revolution began to change the neoliberal corporate globalization model, prioritizing US corporations over foreign ones. But his tariff and anti-globalization policies turned over greater power than ever to himself and to his oligarchic ruling regime.

Elon Musk, the richest and most powerful corporate billionaire in the world, emerged quickly after Trump's 2024 reelection as a "shadow

DOI: 10.4324/9781003662570-4

president," promising to help Trump cut more than a trillion dollars out of public programs like Medicaid, public health, public schools and environmental protections, all related to the purge of aliens and immigrants and vital to the well-being of all true and patriotic American workers. At the same time, Trump was seeking to end government regulations on corporations, eliminate unions and shut down the Labor Department and the National Labor Relations Board that made the rules protecting union organizers. Trump moved quickly to abolish or defund most other government agencies that could curb big business or reduce its profits. This radical and astonishing difference between Trumpist rhetoric and policy follows closely the script of earlier classic Far-Right populism.

Trump's Populist Rhetoric: What He Inherited and What He Invented

Trump followed in the steps of earlier Far-Right populists described in the last chapters but was distinctive from his predecessors in major ways. He was the first to take over the entire Republican Party and rebrand it in the fire of Far-Right populist discourse. That discourse blended anti-corporate Far-Right populism with white Christian nationalism to turn the GOP into a new authoritarian party. It had a working-class base but still served core corporate interests, with the oligarchy's power and profits as a central goal.

Trump's alignment of ruling forces was also novel. Trump succeeded in uniting dominant corporate elites with white Christian nationalists, an alliance that had been advanced before only by Ronald Reagan, who did not give the Christian Nationalists the same actual political and judicial power that Trump did. Nor did Reagan advance the anti-globalism and anti-war rhetoric of Trump. Quite the contrary.

In the rest of this chapter, I explore the distinctive features of Trump's populist rhetoric, the elements of populism that he carried into actual governance, the new power and authoritarianism of Christian nationalism, and the role of irrationality in Trump's base support. I offer a concluding assessment of Trump ruling in the name of populism while aligning unashamedly with the corporate establishment. Trump used every means possible – including unconstitutional schemes and declarations of emergency – to promote profits and the power of the corporate oligarchy and to enrich himself. I also show how the Democrats played a central role in aiding Trump's populist victory and new reign of authoritarian power.

The Success of an Illusion: Rhetoric vs. Policy

Trump's rhetoric incorporated classic Far-Right attacks on foreigners, aliens and "globalist" corporations and monopolies, claiming to save the "true Americans," mainly the white working class and Evangelical Christians.

The rhetoric was contradictorily tied to enriching and consolidating corporate oligarchy while defunding and slashing the safety nets and government regulations that workers depend on for survival.

In this section, we look at the new elements of Trump's populist discourse and policies. With much of it illusory rhetoric, Trump campaigned on and initially offered heavy reliance on tariffs and selective taxes to protect jobs and punish foreign companies or US globalists that outsource jobs, attacks on "woke" corporations that were capitulating to "Marxist" woke culture, punishment of foreign countries that didn't capitulate to territorial or other Trump demands, and promises to make America great again by restoring the US as the manufacturing mecca of the world. At the same time, Trump embraced other periodic Far-Right populist isolationist or "America First" themes against the FBI, CIA and military as well as against the "Marxist" civilian bureaucracy; he raged about foreign aid and domestic welfare that stole working people's taxes.

His authoritarian calls and policies to purge America of the immigrants and their liberal patrons in government led toward a police state. It built on $175 billion dollars for new Immigration and Customs Enforcement (ICE) police and nationwide internment camps holding millions of aliens for deportation. It led to Trump sending the military to help police major American cities. This requires looking carefully at what is new in Trump's populism and how much is a synthesis of long-standing Far-Right populist themes.

Trump's declarations of populism, while mainly expressed in his rhetoric rather than his governing policy, reflected some deep grievances in his own biography. He was a Queens realtor never accepted by the Manhattan capitalists and Wall Street elites. His anger toward the top tiers of the financial Establishment led Trump toward some traditional Far-Right populist ideology and policies, including attacks on outsourcing by global corporations, tariffs and taxes aimed at "woke" corporations, and efforts to end some wars and weaken NATO and the military-industrial complex. Moreover, Trump's own personal biography would also reinforce his populist authoritarianism embrace of becoming "a dictator on day one," and embody the strongman who would purge America of aliens and restore the country to the white Christian true Americans.

At the same time, the overall aim and effect of Trumpism was to shift more power than ever to the billionaires and corporate giants of Wall Street, Silicon Valley, and the US Corporate State. Pundits everywhere began to see Trumpism as making the US the most powerful version of the crony capitalism of other authoritarian states around the world. Moreover, the presence of scores of billionaires in Trump's inner circle, along with his work with them to destroy the constitutionality of unions and the very existence of regulations protecting working people, made clear the power of the anti-Establishment illusion. So, too, did Trump's "big beautiful" 2025 budget. It destroyed many of the regulations and social services essential to working people while redistributing more than 4 trillion dollars in tax to billionaires and slashing the corporate tax rate from 35% to 21%.

Never has a populist politics delivered so much power and money to a ruling corporate Establishment. Trump's populism would remove the veneer of capitalist democracy, making perfectly visible who really rules a capitalist state.

The Truth about Trump's Tariff Revolution and War on Government

In this section, we look at the deeper truth beneath two of Trump's most important economic agendas after his 2024 reelection as president. They have had enormous and catastrophic effects and are central to understanding the lies and hypocrisies of Trumpist self-proclaimed populism.

Both his tariff revolution after April 2, 2025, which Trump dubbed "Liberation Day," and his DOGE war on government were presented as populist salvations for the American working class. They would save US workers from the ills of corporate globalization and foreign nations exploiting America, as well as from the massive waste of their tax dollars in huge government spending. The problems of corporate globalization and deindustrialization were real enough; many progressives highly critical of Trump, including myself, were and remain deeply critical of the corporate globalization that Trump rhetorically assaults. But Trump's tariff revolution and war on government were anything but a populist assault on the corporate Establishment to save US workers.

Their intent and effect were largely the opposite: an overwhelming attack on ordinary workers and poor people that aimed to enrich the Oligarchic Establishment that Trump claimed he was attacking. Like all Far-Right populists, Trump claimed he was uniting the "true Americans" – mainly white workers and patriotic US corporations – against their common enemies both abroad and at home. He thereby disguised his brutal war at home against American workers.

The intensity of hard times has always been crucial to Trump's appeal – and Trump delivered a thunderous populist rhetorical message that spoke to the deep and real grievances of America's workers. Trump never delivered changes to the global corporate system that would curb the anti-worker power of America's biggest companies and banks. But enough of the rhetoric – and of his tariffs – survived to threaten the traditional corporate approach to "free trade." This helped sustain the loyalty of a sector of his working-class base who felt Trump was still the only US political leader fighting for them.

Since the end of the New Deal era and the rise of neoliberalism in the Reagan era, hard times have been pummeling working Americans in many different ways, creating long-term economic, social, environmental and political decline. With some of the successes of Biden's public investment policy, the

Democrats in 2024 celebrated their economic legislation as a sign that they were fulfilling their responsibilities as good stewards of the economy. But to non-college working-class voters of all races, this seemed delusional – as they struggled with insecure and low-paying jobs as well as unaffordable costs for groceries, rent, houses, health care, and education.

Trump ran as a self-proclaimed billionaire populist change agent who not only understood the hard times workers faced but also made them the center-piece of his campaign. Trump's anger and rage, which seemed so negative and destructive to Democrats, delivered exactly the emotional tone that working-class Americans were looking for. How could it be that any politicians could not understand the depth of their economic and social insecurity? How could they not make it central to their politics and agenda?

Trump claimed to be the voice of true Americans in the working class. And the emotional tone of his 2024 campaign message confirmed it. His thundering message of the need to blow up "the system" was exactly what working-class Americans felt. They were not part of the Establishment – and even though Trump was very wealthy – he also seemed not to be part of that system and sounded like he would take it down.

Trump's populist message gained credibility and built fervent support among his base for several reasons. First and most important, his populist rhetoric was specific – and threatened to rein in foreign and "globalist" companies to bring manufacturing jobs home for US workers. He also waged a classic Far-Right populist war against globalist government, the "new world order," destroying American sovereignty and greatness, which has always been part of the Far-Right message.

Trump's Tariff and Trade War

Trump called himself "tariff man," and I discuss his tariffs in detail here because they are at the heart of his economic agenda, a contradictory self-proclaimed populism, claiming to protect jobs in the US while enriching the corporate Establishment. Throughout his reelection campaign, he said how much he loved tariffs – his favorite word:

> *Former President Donald Trump waxed poetic about his love of tariffs again on Friday – including his love for the word itself.*
>
> *Speaking at a roundtable with voters in Auburn Hills, Michigan, the Republican presidential nominee said he thinks "tariff" is "the most beautiful word in the dictionary."*
>
> *"You have other words that are damn nice, like 'love,'" Trump said, while others in the room laughed. "But I tell you, I think it's more beautiful than 'love.'"*[1]

Trump said, "tariffs are the greatest things ever invented." (Sonam Sheth, "Trump can't stop talking about how much he loves tariffs," Oct. 18, 2024, newsweek.com) He promised he would use them as weapons to force American companies to create jobs at home and prevent foreign companies from selling Americans goods they made in China, Mexico or any other country. As reported in Reuters, in the Fall of 2024, Trump repeatedly threatened companies that didn't comply while rewarding them if they obeyed: threats that he soon delivered on as discussed shortly:

> *Companies that did not make their goods in the U.S., however, would face 'a very substantial tariff' when sending their products into the U.S., he said.*
>
> *On Monday, Trump said he would slap a 200% tariff on John Deere's imports into the U.S. if the agricultural equipment company moved production to Mexico as planned.*
>
> *Preserving and creating American manufacturing jobs by imposing expansive tariffs on friends and foes alike has become a central theme of Trump's economic message.*
>
> *Trump said he would reward U.S.-based manufacturers with tax breaks for research and development costs and the ability to write off the costs of heavy machinery in the first year.*
>
> *He repeated his promise to slash the corporate tax rate from 21% to 15% for companies that make their products in the U.S.*
>
> *Trump pledged to appoint a global manufacturing ambassador to convince foreign companies to move to the U.S. He also said he would create special low tax, low regulatory zones on federal lands for American-based manufacturers.*[2]

Tariffs might contradict Trump's promise to reduce prices, because they are paid by US consumers when American importers raise prices on the taxes they pay. *But tariffs are the perfect populist rhetoric. They symbolize a blunt, uncompromising strategy to punish US and foreign companies that are betraying US workers by selling anything not made by the American worker.*

This populist rhetoric was crucial to Trump's appeal to workers, part of the reason he kept returning to his tariff policies even as the courts began to declare them unconstitutional. By dwelling on tariffs, often saying they would be across the board and could go up to 50 or 100%, especially on goods imported from populist enemies like China, Trump was scoring points for Team USA. Most importantly, he was scoring political points for himself because there was no simpler or more emotionally powerful way to tell workers: I'm with you, 100%. And I'm going to go beyond the law when necessary to force the globalist companies and banks to get on board – and to attack foreign nations and companies, and to purge the immigrants and other aliens feeding off of the anti-American globalist regime that my America First will destroy.

After his reelection, Trump immediately began branding tariffs in a rhetorically populist way: to save US jobs and to force other countries to do what he wanted. Within a few weeks of being reelected president, Trump imposed 25% tariffs on most imports from Canada and Mexico, humiliating Canada by saying it needed to become America's 51st state, while telling Mexico that they could see much higher tariffs if they didn't keep US-bound asylum seekers and drug traffickers in Mexico. Trump bullied and humiliated Justin Trudeau, the Canadian Prime Minister who was leaving office. Trump also imposed much higher and escalating tariffs on China – thus putting tariffs on all three of the US's biggest trading partners, while also threatening European allies with tariffs as well as threatening tariffs on BRIC nations of Brazil, India and Russia if they tried to replace the dollar as the world's reserve currency. In the first few weeks of his campaign, this all led to retaliatory tariffs against the US by Canada, Mexico and China, threatening global markets and the stability of the global economy.

While Trump would soon try to stabilize the markets by pausing his tariffs and seeking to cut new deals with many of these countries, the threat to supply-side chains, price levels and global growth and stability, as well as relations with US allies, all remained high, even as the public and courts opposed and rejected them. The fact that Trump persisted at the length and level he did in the face of growing opposition was a sign that he was serious not only about tariffs but also about a new level of nationalist Far-Right populism that would take his presidency in uncharted directions.

Six months into his second term, Trump reignited his threat on scores of countries, including major trading allies, such as the EU, Mexico and Canada, with even higher tariffs, creating a new certainty of continuing market instability. As long as they remained in place, they created a very high probability of a serious economic downturn that might seriously hurt corporations as well as almost certainly cause major job-losses and price increases, badly hurting the workers who voted for him believing that his tariffs were a populist weapon to serve them.

In his first week, Trump also used tariffs as an imperial tool to force Denmark to sell Greenland to the US and to force Panama to turn the Panama Canal over to the US. Trump's call to the Danish Prime Minister was "horrendous":

> *Five current and former senior European officials briefed on the call said the conversation had gone very badly.*
>
> *They added that Trump had been aggressive and confrontational following the Danish prime minister's comments that the island was not for sale, despite her offer of more co-operation on military bases and mineral exploitation. "It was horrendous," said one of the people. Another added: "He was very firm. It was a cold shower. Before, it was hard to take it seriously. But I do think it is serious, and potentially very dangerous."….*
>
> *Many European officials had hoped his comments about seeking control of Greenland for "national security" reasons were a negotiating*

ploy to gain more influence over the NATO territory. Russia and China are both also jostling for position in the Arctic. But the call with Frederiksen has crushed such hopes, deepening the foreign policy crisis between the Nato allies. "The intent was very clear. They want it."

"The Danes are now in crisis mode," said one person briefed on the call. Another said: "The Danes are utterly freaked out by this." A former Danish official added: "It was a very tough conversation. He threatened specific measures against Denmark such as targeted tariffs."[3]

The populist appeal was partly the fury of the sheer bullying involved, using profane-laced rough language to humiliate the leaders of other countries far weaker, a longstanding strategy of empires to win over their citizens with pride in the power and glory of their nations. But Trump was also signaling that his nationalist approach was hardly a retreat from the rest of the world. Trump might be pulling back from economic and military alliances, but this was not a retreat from US global interests or US global corporate power. Rather than relying on existing trade rules or military alliances, Trump is acting, as discussed in Chapter 2, as a "sovereignist," in the early Far-Right spirit of Andrew Jackson and later 1930s "America First" populist leaders. There will still be expansionism in all the areas of the world that Trump deemed essential to US security and to US corporations whose wealth was central to that security.

Trump's Far-Right populism is not an abandonment of US national or corporate power. Rather, it is a break with American foreign allies and their corporations, relying on the sovereign strength of the US military and US corporations as the sole agents and beneficiaries of US power. Trump's "America First" model of global trade offers US corporations the added crucial virtue of helping to seduce US workers into a new pact with them. American corporations and their workers, in classic Far-Right populist terms, will now be allies against their common global enemies, with tariffs their shared weapon against the rest of the world.

When Trump came back into the White House on January 20, 2025, he brought with him billionaires who would serve as top advisors, including in key economic Cabinet posts such as Treasury Secretary Scott Bessent and Commerce Secretary Howard Lutnick. This signaled to corporate elites that Trump's new regime was not going to use the populist pitchforks to destroy their oligarchy – he would, in fact, give them more power and money than they ever could imagine, as his 2025 "big beautiful budget" would soon make absolutely clear. Nonetheless, not all corporate leaders were reassured. As in all administrations, there were different factions competing for Trump's ear. A number of Trump's corporate aides – and their allies in corporate media and in the corporate world itself – began to voice concerns about the tariffs pushing up prices and starting trade wars, with concerns about the effect of the tariffs on the US stock market as well as the global economy. After he slapped tariffs, even before Liberation Day, on Canada, Mexico and Trump, the chief economist at J.P. Morgan Chase said:

> *this weekend's actions challenge our underlying view that the Trump administration will strive to limit disruptive policies as it balances its desire to reduce engagement with the world with a commitment to support US businesses.*
> "*In short, the risk is that the policy mix is tilting (perhaps unintentionally) into a business-unfriendly stance.*"[4]

Trump made some conciliatory moves, first pausing his early tariffs on Mexico and Canada. This reflected the continuing power of corporate elites and global markets to put checks on Trump's delivery of his populist promises and fierce rhetoric. But hyper-nationalist and authoritarian Far-Right populists like Steve Bannon survived in Trump-world, and Trump himself was committed to his shift from the earlier "allied" globalist regime to his "unilateralist" America First one.

On Liberation Day, when the big tariffs came into force, Trump delivered on his promised tariffs both to protect US jobs and force countries to accept immigrants deported from the US. More US corporations grew fearful as the markets tanked and it seemed that Trump was becoming a genuine opponent of their global regime. In April 2025, a neoliberal corporate organization, the Liberty Justice Center, sued Trump representing five companies heavily dependent on trade and imports, arguing that Trump's tariffs exceeded his authority and violated international trade and US law. (Reuters and Guardian staff, "Trump administration sued over tariffs in US international trade court," The Guardian, April 14, 2025, theguardian.com) But while the threat of Trump's tariffs and trade wars were real – and were laying the ground for severe downturns or a new recession – the idea that Trump was becoming an anti-corporate populist was, again, an illusion, as he sought to empower and protect the US corporate oligarchs at the expense of foreign firms and nations and also most US workers.

Nonetheless, Trumpists such as Steve Bannon had long laid the groundwork for the corporate anxieties that were beginning to grow after Liberation Day. Bannon's populism, while representing a Far-Right authoritarianism deadly to immigrants, foreign companies and Leftists of all stripes, represented a potentially bad scenario for anxious US corporate elites. Bannon, who had been a central Trump advisor in his first term and was still a major ally in his second, voiced intense conservative anger and populism against the "globalist" corporate representatives of the Marxist New World Order.

Bannon was Trump's Pat Buchanan. He targeted especially the Silicon Valley "Broligarchs" – Mark Zuckerberg, David Sacks, Peter Thiele and other Tech titans – who were abandoning their traditional liberalism and flocking to Trump. Bannon may have helped create one of the few genuinely anti-corporate Trump initiatives in the FTC's antitrust action toward Google and

META, though CEOs like Zuckerberg stayed quietly in Trump's orbit. The "Broligarchs" wanted to help steer Trump toward their own vision of America First, one promoting corporate power and globalism.

Bannon, no longer in the White House, dissented from Musk and other "Broligarchs," speaking out about how liberals had totally failed to recognize Trump's true pro-worker populism:

> *...let's be brutally frank. Public intellectuals have done a horrible job because you haven't had the interest in really understanding what populism is.... It's just about Trump. And it's never about the core, where this springs from.*[5]

If Bannon, who had just served several months in jail, had persuaded Trump, corporate elites might have had reason to be fearful of certain measures. Bannon's populism was a missile partially aimed at the globalist oligarchy long ruling America, as well as at the deep state "Marxists" and alien immigrants poisoning American blood. He had launched a fierce and populist tirade against George Bush and the traditional Republican Establishment and some of the billionaires running Trump's second term, as well as against the Democratic Establishment embodied in Clinton and Obama, especially after the financial crisis of 2008. He argued, correctly, that both Bush and Obama helped underwrite the bailouts of the big banks that left the burden entirely on ordinary Americans, whose taxes paid for the bailout:

> *the damage that Bush did to the country, on so many different levels, in particular the financial crisis, which was not totally his fault but the fault of the established order. And the basic schmendrick (the American worker) underwrote all of that bailout and didn't get a bailout themselves. In fact, they got blown out of their equity, and they blamed it on African Americans and Hispanics that didn't have the income. But they (the globalist monied establishment) blew them all out of the equity of their homes and, by the way, kept the title to those homes, I might add, so they could resell it later. It's one of the greatest financial scandals in the history of this country. None of the crooks and the criminals that did this were ever held accountable.*
>
> *And when I say crooks and criminals, I mean the top accounting firms, the law firms, the entire establishment.... None of the elites in this country were ever held accountable for it. And that lit a fuse that went off on Nov. 8 and the early morning of Nov. 9 in 2016 with (the election of) President Trump. It was basically the forgotten man and woman's vengeance.*[6]

To hammer home his point, Bannon argues that Trumpism is winning because Trump is the only presidential leader, either Republican or Democratic, telling the workers that the bailouts and the larger global corporate system are being run entirely at their expense:

> *The entire postwar international rules-based order, all of it, Bretton Woods and all of it – the Pax Americana – it is all on the shoulders of the little guy. It gets down to the shoulders of the working class and the middle class....*

Bannon makes clear who is at fault, in addition to foreign companies and a new world order of globalizing finance and deep state Marxist bureaucrats:

> *The capitalists, because remember we're in a capitalist system, are always looking to drive labor costs down.*[7]

Bannon is embracing a historic version of Far-Right populism that is far more rhetorically critical of elements of capitalism than Trump's approach but fully aligns with Trump's authoritarianism. Bannon is an American fascist, in the tradition of Far-Right predecessors such as Father Coughlin and Henry Ford in the America First movement of the Hitler era. Trump and Bannon share the view that it will take extra-constitutional, dictatorial measures to change the "allied" corporate globalism to the nationalist America First model.

Trump offered just enough anti-globalist and pro-worker populist language, combined with his deportation of hundreds of thousands of immigrants supposedly living off the taxes paid by hard-working Americans, to keep the allegiance of much of the working class and win their longer-term support, even as he rules with and for his billionaire oligarchs. This support will be tested further as Trump's tariff and trade wars destabilize the economy and threate more severe downturns or a recession that will devastate American workers.

Trump's "big beautiful" budget, signed on July 4, 2025, made absolutely clear that Trump was fervently pro-corporate. He did share Bannon's elements of Far-Right populist cruelty and authoritarianism, since his budget directed an astonishing $175 billion to hire thousands of more ICE agents, build detention camps across America that could hold a million immigrants targeted each year for deportation; Trump's militarization of American policing added to the fascist element of traditional Far-Right populism discussed in the last chapter. But Trump's budget massively slashed the most important health care programs, including Medicaid and parts of Medicare, nutrition for poor kids and other crucial safety nets for low-income and other working Americans, all to deliver about 4 trillion dollars in tax cuts for the richest Americans and corporate elites over the next decade, including, as noted earlier, a permanent cut in the corporate tax rate from 36% to 21%. (Tax Policy

Center, 2025 Tax Cuts Tracker, Urban Institute and Brookings Institution, July 4, 2025, taxpolicycenter.org)

While rejecting populism and policies supporting working people, Trump's America First model does threaten US corporations in mostly unwitting or unintended ways. The economic downturn after "Liberation Day" led to loss in two days of more than 5 trillion dollars of US stock wealth. Continuing severe market declines in the following weeks and months scared many corporate leaders. A prolonged, deep recession – a very likely outcome of Trump's tariff and trade wars – seriously hurts the corporate bottom line.

Over time, though, these potential deep corporate losses are likely to be made up over time by all the ways Trump will restructure tariffs and trade, as well as deliver bailouts for Big Oil and Gas, Big Ag, Wall Street, and other severely affected companies. And the tariffs are just one part of a larger economic shift in America First non-trade changes in taxes, regulations and social spending that will massively benefit US corporations even during a major economic downturn.

The tax benefit is perhaps the most obvious. Trump's defining 2025 budget bill, as just noted, massively cut taxes on corporations and the wealthy, increasing US debt by at least 5.5 trillion dollars over the next decade, according to initial estimates of the Congressional Joint Committee on Taxation. (AP, "Senate approves Republican plan for trillions in tax breaks and spending cuts," The Guardian, April 5, 2025, theguardian.com) Most of the tax relief would go to billionaires and other super-wealthy oligarchs, with the 20% poorest Americans actually paying more taxes and losing income. The elimination of tax on tips, Trump's symbolic tax cut for workers, would expire in three years and go only to workers making less than $25,000 a year. The tax cuts on corporations and the richest American incomes are permanent. This was the most obvious way in which Trump's new agenda would actually enrich corporations in coming years. Trump had earlier made clear his position:

> *At one point during his address, Trump switched from president to historian. "In 1913, for reasons unknown to mankind, they established the income tax," he said, setting the stage for a sharp reduction in tariffs on foreign goods. "Citizens, rather than foreign countries, would start paying the money necessary to run our government."*[8]

Trump repeated that his model for America was the Gilded Age – 1870 to 1913 – when the US raised funds through tariffs rather than income taxes. Income taxes did not exist. The Gilded Age was a golden age for the Robber Barons, who became the nation's first billionaires while 90% of their workers were poor. Trump's long top priority, expressed as a businessman in the 1980s, has been to cut or eliminate income taxes, which he sees as mainly burdening the super-rich like himself.

Tariffs essentially are his way of raising massive amounts of money for the US government through a new consumer-paid massive sales tax, without relying on income taxes, seen by Trump as unfairly targeting the wealthy. Henceforth, tariffs – which Trump saw mistakenly as taxes on other nations rather than US consumers – would compensate corporations and corporate tycoons for any losses from new tariffs which some called the greatest tax cut on corporations in history. It would be ordinary Americans who would pay the real cost of the tariffs, with the Yale Budget Lab estimating that the Liberation Day tariffs would cost the average American household an average of $3800 a year. (AP, "Senate approves Republican plan for trillions in tax breaks and spending cuts," The Guardian, April 5, 2025, theguardian.com)

Beyond tax relief for his oligarchy, Trump claims he is helping US workers as well as US businesses by opening a new window for a renaissance of manufacturing in America. New manufacturing plants would be onshored along with most supply chains now operating profitably throughout the rest of the world. But this claim also involves deception and faulty logic. Manufacturing is becoming a smaller and smaller percentage of the US economy, and it is a sector increasingly automated and run by robots and AI rather than workers. Moreover, because it is impossible to predict how long and high any of Trump's tariffs would be, companies cannot have confidence that the investment in new plants taking several years to be built will still be profitable in the tariff regime when they became operational.

The same concerns will make it difficult to invest in new supply chains at home, which not only face uncertain future tariffs but are also extraordinarily difficult to replace from the scores of countries that currently have the technology, materials and labor that make them possible. And it would take major US investment in infrastructure, job training and technology – all essential new US industrial policy – to begin bring supply chain jobs and other manufacturing jobs back into America. Biden had begun to use such an approach. He created some smaller tariffs and began major investment in infrastructure, skills and cooperative relations with other nations that began to create chip production and other new jobs in America, while maintaining cooperation with other nations that also were experiencing deindustrialization and could partner with the US in responding to the very real cheap labor threat posed by some exporting countries like China and Vietnam.

But Trump is entirely unilateralist, and his tariff blitz is not strategically targeted or combined with industrial policy that creates jobs at home and a fairer trade system. In fact, Trump is cutting trillions in US spending, making it impossible to build the new jobs at home. Trump rejects the public spending and investment that his alleged worker-friendly populism requires both to skill the workforce and create the new technology at home. And he has refused to work with other deindustrializing nations, as trade expert Lori Wallach has highlighted, that would have created a resilient and cooperative trade bloc with the US to counter the real threat posed by deindustrialization and neoliberal trade policy. (Lori Wallach,

"The Tariffs We Want," Nation podcast with Jon Wiener, April 9, 2025, thenation.com)

All this meant that Trump's America First trade model that promises massive new manufacturing jobs and supply chains will assuredly fail. In fact, his tariffs and trade wars are more likely, as highlighted elsewhere in this book, to create economic downturns or even a recession intensifying the job insecurity and affordability crises already imperiling American workers. Moreover, Trump's dedicated war – launched in coordination with Elon Musk and Jeff Bezos to make unions unconstitutional – meant that any new manufacturing jobs would be low-paying and insecure. The populist gains for workers that Trump claimed were illusory, with workers paying for the tariffs and not getting the promised good jobs.

Meanwhile, the corporations will continue to get rewarded. Along with their trillion dollars in tax cuts, they will face less competition from foreign corporations at home, particularly from China; Trump had made clear that his tariffs were in large measure a way to protect the US and American corporations from Chinese competition, along with his America First foreign policy that seeks to take control of other foreign countries with essential resources or markets.

In addition, Trump offers to reduce tariffs for countries adopting corporate-friendly neoliberal policies empowering and enriching US corporations:

> *According to the April 2 executive order, Trump can unilaterally decide to lower the tariffs imposed on a country if it takes "significant steps to remedy non-reciprocal trade arrangements and align sufficiently with the United States on economic and national security matters."*
>
> *What constitutes a "significant step" isn't defined, but it certainly looks like an open invitation for governments to slash their tariffs and reverse policies to appease Trump and his billionaire buddies.*
>
> *For what exactly those policies may be, just look to the report Trump waved around at the beginning of his so-called "Liberation Day" tariff announcement speech in the Rose Garden.*
>
> *That document is a 400-page list of the policies that other countries have enacted – or are even considering enacting – that U.S. corporations don't like. It's the National Trade Estimates Report on Foreign Trade Barriers, an annual government report that has long been criticized as an inappropriate overreach to name and shame other countries' legitimate public interest policies. It's also a glimpse of the policies that Trump may seek to have destroyed in exchange for tariff relief.*
>
> *The policies targeted in this year's report include climate protections, including Canada's Clean Fuel Standard, the European Union's Deforestation-Free Supply Chain Regulation, and Japan's renewable energy incentives – all of which are aligned with global climate commitments.*

Public health regulations aimed at protecting consumers, preserving biodiversity, and preventing long-term health risks were also attacked. Employed by dozens of countries, these include bans, testing requirements, or even labeling policies on pesticides like Roundup's glyphosate, genetically engineered food, ractopamine in beef and pork, and heavy metals in cosmetics.

Regulations that promote competition in the digital ecosystem, laws that impose digital services taxes on Big Tech firms, place conditions for cross-border data transfers, promote fairness in the digital economy, and laws that regulate emerging technologies such as AI.[9]

Beyond all these ways that Trump's tariffs and trade war would help US corporations, many of which Trump implemented further in executive orders, trade deals and his "big, beautiful" budget, Trump also saw them as part of his strategy to weaken the dollar and thus reduce US imports while promoting US exports. Trump's unilateralist globalism might weaken trust in America and the dollar as the most reliable global reserve currency, an aim behind the tariffs explicitly advanced by his top trade advisors like Trade Secretary, Scott Bessent, and Stephen Miran, head of Trump's Council of Economic Advisors. (James Meadway, "Here's one key thing you should know about Trump's shock to the world: it could work," NY Times, April 7, 2025, nytimes.com)

A low or weak dollar would begin to end US trading deficits with other countries and the US status as a debtor nation, promoting US corporate exports and decreased imports from foreign companies. American workers would not be able to buy as many cheap goods abroad, but US companies could sell more abroad. A catastrophic decline in the faith and confidence of the US dollar and US Treasury bills could devastate both US workers and companies, creating huge economic destabilization and probably recession, but the companies would most likely be bailed out, as they were in the 2008 financial crisis.

As Ryan Harvey argues in his commentary on the article just cited above, Trump's unilateralist approach is in some ways a revised form of neoliberal globalism, providing a new set of mechanisms for ensuring that nations everywhere played by trade rules that were written to empower and enrich corporations long before Trump. (Ryan Harvey, "Commentary on Trump's Tariffs are Extremely Dumb, Just not for the Reasons You might Think," April 5, 2025, email: gtwaction@citizen.org) Foreign companies and nations – the new real target – will likely take a major hit, as will US workers and consumers. In the end, US companies could emerge as the major and only winners.

Trump's War on Government

As Trump began his tariff wars, his war on the federal government was already well on its way, led initially by Elon Musk at DOGE and later by

Musk's top aides as Musk's own popularity crumbled. Trump saw the government or his "deep state" as run by corrupt and globalist liberal political and cultural elites in the civil service bureaucracy. Echoing one of the main messages of Project 2025, Trump and Musk claimed federal bureaucrats – from top to bottom – were ripping off workers by taxing them to support not only waste and fraud but also to service the "woke" government agenda that was supporting immigrants, foreign aid and welfare for the undeserving at home.

The war on government, alongside his tariff campaign, became the main face of Trumpist populism. As the latest movement of Far-Right populism, Trumpism has always conceived government as the home of the Marxist, globalist elite. But it was not until his second term that Trump was able to find the means and personnel to defund and dismantle much of it.

Trump II was empowered by a more organized and well-funded "New Right," whose leaders and agenda represented the latest iteration of Far-Right populism. The New Right, which included think tanks and policy networks such as the Heritage Foundation, the Federalist Society, and right-wing thinkers such as JD Vance, had spent four years since the end of the first Trump term preparing the personnel and strategies to win the anti-government revolution. The plan was summarized in the Heritage Foundation's Project 2025 and would be implemented in Trump's second term by OMB Director, Russell Vought, an architect of Project 2025 who helped recruit JD Vance to write a foreword to its publication as a book.

The entire New Right ecosystem had been funded heavily by Vance's mentor, the Far-Right Silicon Valley billionaire, Peter Thiel, and by a growing sector of Big Tech and other corporate billionaires. They saw in Trump an ally to realize their dreams of absolute corporate power, as discussed in one illuminating public radio interview about the New Right:

CHAKRABARTI: *Okay, so tell me your view or what your reporting has found out about how much the kind of thinking of the New Right that Ian has been describing is finding support and acceleration within Silicon Valley.*

GIL DURAN: *Yeah, in my writing, I focus on how there's a dangerous ideology rising out of tech and Silicon Valley.*

It views democracy as an enemy, views dictatorship as preferable, and sees billionaires as the savior of humanity. And in 2024, they've made an alliance with the Republican party under Trump, which is also flirting with things like dictatorship, pro natalism, truth denial. And the idea of being able to seize government and turn it to their own ends.

And so in my writing, I focused on some different rising sort of cult beliefs, something called the network state, which would break up the nation states into much smaller territories run basically by corporate dictatorships and people like Curtis Yarvin, Peter Thiel, Mark Andreessen, Elon Musk are all at the center of these ideas.[10]

Drawing on the New Right's thinking and funding, Trump's achievement was to sell his war on government as a populist assault on the Establishment, even as it was designed and carried out by billionaire corporate elites. Elon Musk was the most visible "corporate populist," selling the idea that cutting a government of waste and fraud was a pro-worker revolution. Trump and Musk not only began firing tens of thousands of "woke" civil servants but abolished whole federal agencies. This opened the door to a corporate takeover of public goods like education and health care as well as the entire public sphere, bringing massive new government contracts and profits to companies like Musk's and Trump's own. But Trump sold it all as true populism for the people because it will allegedly reduce the tax burden on ordinary working people and free up capital for new jobs, securing the future of American workers.

This vision was institutionalized in the anti-worker and anti-government policy enshrined in Trump's defining second-term legislation of his "big beautiful" budget, signed on July 4, 2025. In the name of cutting taxes and the tyranny of the deep state and Marxist bureaucrats, it became the biggest redistribution of wealth in history from the poor and working classes to the corporate elites. It became famous for destroying much of Medicaid and cutting as much as $500 billion from Medicare, closing rural hospitals and shutting down clean energy subsidies. Trump did support parts of the government profitable to big companies: this included his trillion-dollar funding of the US military and his $175 billion building of anti-immigrant ICE police and prison detention camps, run for profit by big American companies.

As Trump was shutting down federal agencies, he was launching the biggest attack on American unions and workers in modern history. His array of attacks on labor was devastating:

Despite his vow to help coal miners, Trump halted enforcement of a regulation that protects miners from a debilitating, often deadly lung disease. He fired the chair of the National Labor Relations Board (NLRB), leaving the US's top labor watchdog without a quorum to protect workers from corporations' illegal anti-union tactics. Angering labor leaders, Trump stripped one million federal workers of their right to bargain collectively and tore up their union contracts.[11]

AFL-CIO president, Liz Shuler, attacked Trump's betrayal of workers:

"It's a big betrayal," Liz Shuler, president of the AFL-CIO, the main US labor federation, said. "We knew it would be bad, but we had no

idea how rapidly he would be doing these things. He is stripping away regulations that protect workers. His attacks on unions are coming fast and furious. He talks a good game of being for working people, but he's doing the absolute opposite."

"This is a government that is by, and for, the CEOs and billionaires," Shuler added.[12]

Many labor leaders and analysts share the consensual view that Trump is the most corporate-friendly and anti-union American president, even worse than Ronald Reagan, who was notorious for his anti-union crusade.

Reagan fired 11,345 air traffic controllers who went on strike, but the AFL-CIO's Shuler said that "pales in comparison" to Trump's ending collective bargaining for 1 million federal workers. "That's the largest single act of union-busting in our history," she said.

He is worse than Reagan when it comes to his approach to unions," said Julie Su, who was acting labor secretary under Biden. "We saw what Reagan did in the 1980s. That began a long decline in unionization. This president wants to make America non-union again. He's certainly trying to make the government non-union again."[13]

Heidi Shierholz, president of the labor-friendly American Economic Institute, said:

the "absolute scale of crushing unions" under Trump is "on a whole different scale from what we saw under Reagan. Trump is saying it's absolutely open season on union folks. He took an absolute chainsaw to the federal workforce. He's giving the green light to the private sector and local government to do the same."[14]

Trump's anti-immigrant crusade was also an economic war on working Americans, since hard-working immigrants who felt "hunted down" were too afraid to go to work on farms or construction sites, creating more intense supply-side crises in agriculture, housing and other economic sectors already suffering from affordability crises. Trump's attack on immigrants hit millions of American workers hard and personally, as they now found it even harder to pay for groceries or housing in shorter supply.

This war on government serving working Americans was the most brazen of Trump's populist tricks. He carried out an agenda developed by and for corporate elites in the name of saving true "patriotic" workers from America's corporate, globalist and Marxist Establishment. But while contradictory and absurd, it followed perfectly the long script of Far-Right populism discussed in the last chapter.

The war on government, like Trump's tariffs and anti-globalization discourse, was designed to unite US corporations with the US workers they were exploiting. Like tariffs, the war on government pitted both of them against shared enemies – in this case, domestic enemies – who were taking over the US government and ripping off "true" Americans. Trump had famously defined government as a "deep state" of alien Marxist coastal cultural elites, who ran the federal bureaucracy to dole out benefits to themselves and the "enemy at home." Using traditional Far-Right populist rhetoric, Trump painted these enemies as "frauds," free-riding on the "true" American worker. The "real" American worker, viewed as hard-working and mainly white Christian, was seeing his taxes ripped off by the "deep state" Leftist federal bureaucrats and the immigrants and lazy free-riding poor citizens supported by deep state programs.

Trump's war on government was the latest incarnation of traditional corporate rhetoric as well as long-standing Far-Right populist assault on government, with language highlighting "waste" and "fraud." The "waste" signaled that government was full of services that were unnecessary and inefficient; this corporate notion had long reigned in America, and there was enough real waste to sell it to the Trump base. The "fraud" cemented the Far-Right populist notion that those receiving deep state services – whether immigrants, poor people, Muslims or other non-Christians, the disabled, trans people, gays and ethnic aliens – were all imposters, fraudulent Americans lining up to grab the goodies created by hard-working true Americans. Their tax dollars were supporting those who did not want to work and were not entitled to American government benefits because they were not "true Americans." As we will show soon, the Democrats' identity politics, in the name of defending these groups, made it easier for Trump to attack them.

Trump's rhetoric – deeply rooted in the American bloodstream by the Far-Right populist movements discussed in Chapter 2 – gained power with voters and workers because of its long historical roots in US politics and discourse. As we show in the rest of this chapter, Trump gained more power than his Far-Right predecessors, in large part because the Democratic Party abandoned its own positive populism that spoke to the working classes.

Meanwhile, Trump connected on a fervent emotional level with his aggrieved base – and strongly united them. He cultivated a compelling image of such great strength, toughness and a natural ruling "strongman" that he seemed truly up to the job of taking on and beating the ruling Establishment. Finally, his embrace of Christian nationalism helped evoke a sense of his being touched by God, something resonating especially among his Evangelical base. The fact that he escaped assassination after being shot at and wounded at his 2024 campaign rally in Butler, Pennsylvania, increased the sense in his base that God was guiding Trump to lead America. All of this enhanced Trump's magic trick of using populist rhetoric to hold workers' support while empowering their bosses and the corporate system crushing them.

Six Conditions Leading to Trump's 2024 Reelection

In this section, we consider the stylistic and substantive factors just suggested in the paragraph above that led to Trump's disastrous win in the 2024 election. The American people and the Democratic Party now ignore these factors at their great peril.

The Democrats Abandon Positive Populism

The abandonment by the Democrats of their own form of populism that might have offered a systemic solution to hard-pressed Americans was a first and crucial factor explaining why white workers and Trump's base became so intensely wedded to Trump. The MAGA Republican Party, led by Trump, became the only major populist party. After the Reagan Revolution, which dismantled much of the New Deal, the Democrats joined in the demolition, with Bill Clinton calling for the end of the "age of Big Government" and inaugurating a "third way" centrist Democratic Party with no pretense of populist transformation of the corporate Establishment.

The Democratic Party's abandonment of Left populism opened the door to Trump's Far-Right populism and fueled the migration of the working class to MAGA Republicans. Obama largely continued Clinton's moderate or centrist approach, locking the Democratic Party into the "Bush Lite" of the post-New Deal Democrats. Kamala Harris's losing campaign to Trump in 2024 disastrously sustained the "Bush Lite" model, as she unified with anti-Trumpist super-hawkish Establishment Republicans like the Cheneys. Meanwhile, she repeatedly proclaimed that she was "a proud capitalist."

As the influential author, Thomas Frank has written, the Democratic Party's new liberalism has helped make it an elite party, a "party of college-graduates" and well-meaning professionals who have "largely dropped economic populism." (Thomas Frank, "The Elites Had It Coming," NY Times, Nov. 9, 2024, nytimes.com) The shift of the Democratic Party away from populism has been a suicidal gift to Trump.

In Chapter 5, we expand on this Democratic Party capitulation to the militarized capitalist Establishment in some depth. We need only note here two crucial ways in which it intensified Trump's appeal to his base. First, it signaled clearly to Americans, especially workers, that the Democrats were not going to be leading the charge against the billionaires and the corporate regime that was making them economically insecure, with precarious jobs and unaffordable groceries, rents and homes. For non-college working-class voters of all races, this eroded historical loyalty to the Democratic Party, as they looked for somebody who understood their economic desperation and might save them. As noted above, Trump promised them tariffs, breaking up monopolies, expulsion of immigrants who might take their jobs, lowering the deficit and controlling inflation, and reduction of taxes that would protect them from outsourcing and price gouging, making working-class economic plight his central 2024 campaign concern.

Democrats and Siloed Identity Politics

The Democrats' abandonment of New Deal labor-friendly populism – and the core Democratic Party identity politics that divided the working class into multiple racial, ethnic and religious silos competing for corporate crumbs – made Trump appear the only rational choice. White workers, in particular, stood to benefit from Trump, not only from his economic promises but also from his cultural assault on DEI and the broader identity politics of the Democratic Party. The Democrats' identity politics shifted the party from a concern with economic class to a focus on redeeming the cultural value and social worth of Blacks and women, while also tacitly asserting the superiority of its base of highly educated liberals over non-college workers.

Trump's Far-Right populism adroitly exploited this cultural politics. Trump played on a classical Far-Right populist view that higher education is just a form of dividing people into superior or inferior based on who is smarter and presumably has more merit. As Thomas Frank notes, the Democratic Party – full of college graduates and educated elites – has forgotten that credentialed knowledge is suspect in America and not a vehicle for Democrats to gain public support. (Frank, "The Elites Had It Coming," NY Times, Nov. 9, 2024, nytimes.com) The Democrats' abandonment of economic populism helped Trump exploit the long-standing cultural populism that makes cultural elites an easy target of the Far Right. And Trump didn't waste time. As we show shortly, he ripped into universities and cultural elites as the real enemies of working people – and the PMC's own celebration of credentialism and abandonment of workers gave Trump's cultural populism a huge part of the power that it has gained in attracting non-college workers.

The PMC and Democratic cultural uses of higher degrees and meritocracy melded with their DEI mantra to antagonize non-college white working people. With its focus on identity rather than class politics, Democrats were not only not saving workers economically but were accusing them of "white privilege," effectively blaming the working class for the nation's problems. At the same time, Trump's populism argued that the real blame lies on the Democrats' affirmative action and unfair favoritism toward minorities and immigrants, who were not "True Americans" as branded by his White Christian nationalism. Trump's working-class base could bask in the cultural sense of worth that his Far-Right populist rhetoric lavished on them. Trump thereby affirmed his base both by vindicating their own cultural conservatism while demonizing their economic rivals, whom he made clear, did not embody their own culturally chosen status or worth.

It's worth noting that Trump did follow through almost immediately on his reelection to get rid of DEI and affirmative action. This was his symbolic way of telling his white working-class base he hadn't been joking in his rhetoric. DEI and affirmative were among the first casualties of Trump's executive orders issued on the first day of his reelection. His briefing statement on the DEI executive order, January 22, 2025, reads:

- It terminates "diversity, equity, and inclusion" (DEI) discrimination in the federal workforce and in federal contracting and spending.

  - Federal hiring, promotions and performance reviews will reward individual initiative, skills, performance and hard work and not, under any circumstances, DEI-related factors, goals, policies, mandates or requirements.

- The order requires OMB to streamline the federal contracting process to enhance speed and efficiency, reduce costs and require federal contractors and subcontractors to comply with our civil rights laws.

  - It revokes Executive Order 11246 contracting criteria mandating affirmative action.
  - It bars the Office of Federal Contract Compliance Programs from pushing contractors to balance their workforce based on race, sex, gender identity, sexual preference or religion.
  - It requires simple and unmistakable affirmation that contractors will not engage in illegal discrimination, including illegal DEI.
- It directs all departments and agencies to take strong action to end private sector DEI discrimination, including civil compliance investigations.
- It mandates the Attorney General and the Secretary of Education issue joint guidance regarding the measures and practices required to comply with the Supreme Court's decision in Students for Fair Admissions vs. Harvard.

"Trump's briefing statement on the DEI executive order, January 22, 2025," AI overview[15]

Trump probably sealed the deal with a huge sector of his white working-class base with this order. It proved he would follow through with his Far-Right populist affirmation of one of his more important battles of his culture wars.

This would help build the power of his other populist cultural weapons discussed below.

Far-Right Populist Attacks on Educated Elites Resonate

The complicity of liberals and the Democratic Party in an educational hierarchy and elite credentialing system has further reduced the status of non-college workers, intensifying the appeal and resonance of Trump's Far-Right populist "culture wars." It helps Trump create an idea of "the Establishment" that not only includes global corporations but also the liberal Ivy universities, mainstream media, Hollywood and other "coastal elites" that many working-class people distrust. Trump's populist feeds on the rage against this cultural Establishment as much as against the ruling corporate oligarchy.

As jobs in post-industrial capitalism required more "knowledge-based" and scientific training, higher education expanded. Higher educational credentials became a necessity for many of the more well-paid and respected jobs in the new economy, such as those in Silicon Valley. Knowledge and credentials became a new source of stratification that put non-college workers at the bottom, and social worth was becoming even harder to gain if one not only had low wages but also lacked college or postgraduate credentials.

The PMC plays a contradictory role in this credentialing system, which is simultaneously economic and cultural. Professionals use credentials as a way to establish their own economic autonomy and turf. Professions created credentials to allow doctors, lawyers, engineers and other professionals to monopolize control and exercise authority, excluding others who claimed their own knowledge. But as professions began to get absorbed into post-industrial corporate settings, they were losing their autonomy, required to follow orders from on top just like non-college workers. The PMC could use their credentials to bargain for higher wages and better working conditions, even though they still earned social and cultural esteem as a meritocratic class of workers superior to non-college workers.

But as the PMC becomes more fully subordinated to high tech and other modern corporations, they are subject to increasing management control, much like their non-college fellow workers. As the PMC becomes part of the working class, it is a potential threat to corporate elites. A unification of the PMC with non-college workers is a recipe for a stronger labor movement, with professional employees, especially those in the public sector, now being among the most highly unionized members of the working class. The Service Employees International Union (SEIU), with two million members, many social service professionals, joined the AFL-CIO national labor federation in 2025, signaling growing union strength as professional and blue-collar workers unite.

The alignment between professional and non-college workers, though, is strained by cultural differences linked to education. The PMC tends toward a more liberal worldview, encouraged by higher education and its discourse of "critical thought." As noted above, the PMC has used higher education and credentials to assert its own worth and higher status over workers without higher degrees. It's in the interest of corporate elites to highlight these cultural differences, weakening the potential solidarity and strength of a growing bond between workers with different educational credentials.

Trump's Far-Right populism serves the very corporate Establishment that it rhetorically attacks by highlighting the cultural power embedded in higher education and the credential system. Trumpism attacks the university and education itself as the cauldron of "woke." Universities and even public schools become defined as the center of a cultural Establishment creating an anti-American secular culture of "Marxism" and "woke," which are attacking the foundations of the traditional culture valued by Trump's working-class and Evangelical base. After his reelection, Trump intensified almost immediately his war on universities as elite and anti-American.

For many years, Republicans portrayed colleges as bastions of leftism, awash in bias against conservatives and impervious to change.

With Donald J. Trump's victory to a second presidential term and a Congress potentially under unified G.O.P. control, Republicans are now poised to escalate their efforts to root out what they see as progressive ideology in higher education.

The return to power of Mr. Trump comes at a vulnerable moment for higher education. Universities have been under increasing pressure from lawmakers, while public confidence in colleges has fallen. Last year, two Ivy League presidents resigned following their widely panned performances before Congressional panels that grilled them about how they handled pro-Palestinian activists on their campuses. Other top university leaders have resigned amid criticism over protest responses.

Mr. Trump has said he thought that colleges needed to be reclaimed from "Marxist maniacs," and his running mate, JD Vance, has described universities as "the enemy."[16]

Universities found they have every reason to be concerned, as Trump launched into new wars, forcing universities to bend the knee to him, cutting off massive research funding, and demanding closure of "woke" and "Marxist" social, scientific and medical research. Here, Trump again was escalating traditional Far-Right populist and religious attacks on critical thinking and radical "anti-American" and "globalist" studies based on the secular Enlightenment rather than a patriotic "America First" system of white Christian values. This was all previewed even before Trump's 2024 reelection:

This is a moment of enormity for American higher education," said Lynn Pasquerella, president of the American Association of Colleges and Universities. "Many of President Trump's top advisers are the architects of Project 2025, which seeks to dismantle higher education, not reform it, and to replace what they perceive as woke Marxist ideology with their own conservative ideology.

Some items on Republicans' wish lists, like eliminating the Department of Education, will be challenging to achieve. But their plans include a slew of other ideas that worry universities.

The administration could wield control over the arcane but crucial accreditation process, which Mr. Trump has described as his "secret weapon" to force ideological changes. The president-elect has spoken of expanding the taxation of university endowments. And the new administration could scrap President Biden's expansive student-debt forgiveness efforts and loosen regulation of for-profit colleges.[17]

After he was elected, Trump delivered, waging a massive war to defund universities such as Columbia, Harvard and UCLA, the elite Ivies. He attacked "woke" research and departments, and ban both books and foreign students, a war discussed in more depth in the last two chapters. Trump ginned up the fervor and adoration of his base by creating a populist rhetoric against both the Corporate and Cultural Establishments. His greatest rage was directed at the Cultural Establishment, symbolized by Ivy universities, but it had a double-whammy appeal to his MAGA base. He was speaking simultaneously to their feelings of being economically ripped off by their corporate bosses and culturally degraded by coastal cultural elites. It was hardly surprising that this double blow would bind Trump's base even more tightly to him.

The Democratic Party's liberalism and DEI played into this dynamic. Trump could credibly argue that the Democrats were the "party of woke," catering to the coastal literati who saw non-college workers as ignorant and stupid. Moreover, he could show that as the Democrats focused less on class and more on identity politics, he was the only political leader speaking both to the economic needs of non-college workers and their cultural needs for respect and affirmation of their traditional values. He was standing up for them against the Corporate Establishment and the Cultural Establishment. This would help weaken the growing class economic alignment of college and non-college workers, helping the corporate elite maintain control of their entire workforce. At the same time, it was intensifying the loyalty of non-college workers to his Far-Right populist party, as the Democratic Party was seen as dominated by the coastal cultural elites and their DEI ideology.

White Christian Nationalism Is Potent in America

As the system of credentialism and the culture of higher education drew more workers to Trump, his cultural appeal was strongly reinforced by the embrace of white Christian nationalism. The power of a white Christian nationalist appeal to Americans who gain social esteem and cultural status when defined as the "real Americans" cannot be overstated. Trump's base was Evangelical, and his constant open embrace of Christian nationalism telegraphed his view that white Christian workers with traditional values were American heroes, standing up to the assault of secular culture and making America Great Again.

Trump might be a twice-divorced felon, convicted of sexual assault, who seemed to be the exact opposite of a devout Christian. He didn't go to church, and he didn't read the Bible. But he knew how to sell Bibles with his name embossed on them, and he knew how to sell an image of himself as a champion of Christian values. As a quintessential salesman, Trump success-fully branded himself as a man of God. This went way beyond calling for Americans to once again say "Merry Christmas" on the holidays. He was selling not just Bibles but the traditional worldview of a Christian nation, in which his Evangelical followers and culturally conservative white workers could feel they were the most valued members of Trump's America.

At the heart of both Far-Right populism and white Christian nationalism is the definition of "true" members of the nation and dividing them from those who are imposters and aliens. Trump's central message was that the nation was being overrun by immigrants and people who represent cultural and religious traditions at odds with the American way. He argued that the Democratic Party was built around rejecting the spiritual greatness of Amer-ica's historic white Christian identity by putting immigrants from "shithole countries" in Africa as equal to the true Americans.

In bluntly vulgar language, President Donald Trump questioned... Thursday why the U.S. would accept more immigrants from Haiti and "shithole countries" in Africa rather than places like Norway, as he rejected a bipartisan immigration deal, according to people briefed on the extraordinary Oval Office conversation.

Trump's contemptuous description of an entire continent startled lawmakers in the meeting and immediately revived charges that the president is racist. The White House did not deny his remark but issued a statement saying Trump supports immigration policies that welcome "those who can contribute to our society."[18]

The media made clear that Trump's central message was to restore Amer-ica to real Americans – and the true Americans could be divined by white Christian nationalism. Time Magazine reported on one of Trump's speeches to the Faith and Freedom Conference on June 22, 2024, captured perfectly his identity as a candidate:

The beating heart of the speech was the projection of a white Chris-tian nationalist vision. Trump told the enthusiastic crowd—many of whom sported red hats emblazoned with the words "Make America Pray Again"—that he knew they were "under siege." He declared that one of his first acts of his second term would be to set up a task force to root out "anti-Christian bias" and pledged to protect "pro-God con-text and content." He received spontaneous applause for vows to pro-mote school vouchers for private Christian schools and seal the United States' southern border against "an illegal alien invasion by the world's most sadistic criminals and savage gangs."[19]

This helps explain why Trump made his war on immigrants the head-line of his reelection campaign and a centerpiece of his second term, which rapidly built a new police state in America. Immigrants became the visceral symbol of Trump's presidency as a movement to purge the country of the millions of people who were taking the jobs of American workers and were not "true Americans;" Trump promised he would forcibly remove them, a promise he began to deliver in his 2025 "big beautiful" budget. It would also empower Trump's first executive order ending birthright citizenship; Trump was making clear you could be born here, but that wouldn't cleanse your blood and make you a lawful and "true American." Indeed, dividing the "blood" of the "true" people of the nation from the aliens is at the heart of Far-Right populism. It always pits the real patriots against those who don't belong. It makes clear that its purpose is to get rid of the elites who are favoring the aliens and to restore to the real people of the nation their rightful status as the most valued members of society.

This cultural war is at the heart of Trumpism and its religious and cult-like appeal to his base. It gives those working-class and Evangelical Americans, especially whites, who feel abandoned and worthless, a serotonin-like boost of social worth. For Evangelicals and non-college workers, this is essential to their ability to get through a day feeling assaulted minute-to-minute by all the cultural forces that attack their traditional religious and cultural values. Trump's ascendancy means that as long as he is in power, they can feel a new and strong sense of social esteem and cultural worth.

The politics of Far-Right populism is the politics of relative social worth. It delivers to the voting base of Far-Right populist political leaders and parties what they most need: the clarion message that they are valued and deserve far more social esteem than those who don't belong in the nation. The craving for social worth, by being ranked above others, is among the most primal human needs.

Trump delivers in spades to his base by fulminating daily about the horror of immigrants and coastal arrogant Communist elites – and the incredible cultural value of those in his base. Trump's 2024 campaign became a parody of horror stories and astonishing lies about immigrants that Trump repeated in his presidential debate with Kamala Harris:

> *They're eating the dogs, the people that came in, they're eating the cats, Trump said during an answer to a question about immigration. They're eating the pets of the people that live there, and this is what's happening in our country, and it's a shame.*[20]

Harris laughed. Many of the Haitians Trump was referring to in Springfield, Ohio, were not even immigrants. The comments were blatant lies. But the lies spread like wildfire:

> *And yet, tales of migrants eating pets spread throughout social media like wildfire. So did the memes and AI images of former President*

Donald Trump saving kittens and dogs in the hours leading up to the debate.... By the time the debate was over, THEY'RE EATING THE DOGS was trending on the platform X.[21]

This distracts white workers and Evangelicals who might be angry at corporate elites by focusing on the cultural elites who are responsible for their cultural victimization. It makes crystal clear that the Great Leader – with Trump himself often comparing himself to Jesus and saying that God saved him from assassination – recognizes that they are part of the chosen people. They are uniquely entitled to the respect and esteem that the nation owes them. It makes clear that they are morally and spiritually superior to immigrants and other imposters, those who are not true Americans. As an instrument of God's will, Trump's protection and approval convey a touch of God on his base. Relative social worth is everything!

The Power of Racism

The long and powerful history of racism in the US reinforces Trump's white Christian nationalism and cements his political and emotional bond to his base. The history of racism goes back to the beginning of the nation. Born in a slave society, American capitalism and culture have always been built on racial divisions. These divisions strongly reinforce the power of Far-Right populism and are a critical historical foundation of Trump's populist appeal to his base.

Trump is not usually explicitly racist; he typically does not explicitly call Black or Brown people inferior – and tends to avoid the most vulgar and blatant racial slurs. But because of the central history of race in America, he does not have to be explicit, although his 2025 edict about South Africa was clearly racist: white South Africans suffering racial discrimination could come to America, but not Indian or Black South Africans. When he goes after immigrants and others "poisoning the blood" of the US, it is not hard to decipher who he is talking about. The relative social worth he is tossing centrally into the mix is the value of white over Black and Brown. It is familiar to every American – and Trump never lets up, especially in his racially charged war on immigrants:

Vivid imagery, such as telling crowds of rally attendees that migrants will "cut your throat," are now a staple of Trump's speeches. He cites cases of U.S. women and girls allegedly murdered by immigrants in the country illegally, even as studies have shown that immigrants are less likely to commit crimesthan U.S.-born Americans.

But Trump says they are — because they are inherently worse people. He's told nearly all-white crowds in the past that they have "good genes," even before his explicit suggestion this week that non-white immigrants are genetically inferior — when he told conservative radio host Hugh Hewitt that migrants have "bad genes."

"What is so jarring to me is these are not just Nazi-like statements. These are actual Nazi sentiments," said Robert Jones, founder of the Public Religion Research Institute, the author of "The Hidden Roots of White Supremacy" and a vocal critic of Trump's rhetoric. "Hitler used the word vermin and rats multiple times in Mein Kampf to talk about Jews. These are not accidental or coincidental references. We have clear, 20th century historical precedent with this kind of political language, and we see where it leads."[22]

Far-Right populism can succeed by exploiting other social and cultural divisions than race. As just discussed, religion as well as ethnicity can serve some of the same divisive functions as race. But in developed Western capitalist nations, race has proved to be the most powerful Far-Right populist divider. In the most horrific example, Hitler built his Far-Right populism around the supremacy of the Aryan race and the "poisoning of the blood" of the German nation by the Jews. European Far-Right populism today is growing in popularity because of the mass immigration of North African, Middle Eastern and Southwest Asian peoples. Far-Right German, French and other European populists are blaming them for destroying traditional European greatness of its largely white population – and it's paying off at the polls.

In the US, race has been at the center of Far-Right populism from the founding. The Confederacy survived, as shown in Chapter 2, by giving poor "white trash" a feeling of being bonded with their white elites as chosen people over the African slaves. Feeling superior to a large slave population made the economic hardships of poor whites more than bearable. The relative social worth of whites was the foundation of the political survival of the plantation oligarchy; without racism and slavery, white trash likely would have turned on Southern white wealthy elites.

This model of racially based Far-Right populism has never faded in the US. As shown in the last chapter, it was the foundation of Jim Crow regimes and the power of the Democratic Party for a hundred years after the Civil War. It was so effective that Hitler sent his scientists to study American race theory and legal codes of Jim Crow, believing that his own regime depended on creating his own version of Far-Right American racialized populism.

Its long role in structuring how Americans think about each other and their history makes Trump's tacit racism far more powerful as a critical force seducing his voting base. Both White Christian nationalism and immigration are central to Trump's appeal. And race is the underlying not-so-hidden force behind both of them.

Because race is so embedded throughout US history, Trump's populism gains enormous force – and is easily normalized in much of the media and the public. Americans are so habituated to a culture and politics built on racial divisions that it is second nature for them to embrace a racialized populism without regarding it as racist or abnormal. This is highlighted by Trump's gaining ground among Hispanic and some Black male voters, a sign of how habituated we all are to a normalized politics based on racial division.

Trump's white working-class base is most intensely drawn in by his racialized politics. They see the Democrats blaming them for "white privilege." But Trump is not only denying any white privilege and absolving them of any racism. He has found a way to exploit their racial identity to reject Democratic identity politics and DEI and make identity politics work for him. In the ongoing contest between the identity politics central to both Far-Right populism and the mainstream Democratic Party, there's no contest about which form will appeal to white workers.

Trump's exploitation of US history as a racialized society is a game-changer, ensuring that whiteness will tie white workers in his base to MAGA and keep them tightly bonded with him against the identity politics that has replaced class politics in the Democratic Party. The Democrats will win them back only by moving back to a new form of economic populism.

The Lure of Machismo

Yet another potent form of rhetoric bonds Trump to his base. He is a master salesman of machismo. And he credibly embodies it in himself, presenting himself as the toughest politician in American history. When times are tough, ordinary people often look for "tough guys," strong enough to overcome all their enemies. Nobody played the famed Robert de Niro film role of the Godfather or Jake LaMatta-style "raging bull" boxer to ride into DC and the White House more powerfully than Trump.

The macho theme came up in the Harris campaign, when Trump made an overt and blatant appeal to young men and the attack on traditional masculinity. He made Hulk Hogan the star of his convention and made World Wide Wrestling executives like Linda McCahon part of his inner circle. Trump went on Joe Rogan – one of the biggest social media shows – to demonstrate he was Rogan's kind of "bro," a champion for all the young men who were feeling left behind and devalued. He then made stops on the other social media "manoverse" stars, including Adin Ross, Logan Paul, and the Nelk Boys, making clear how he was their guy and would change their lives for the better.

The machismo factor played naturally into a few core Far-Right populist themes. Far-Right narratives make clear that people are under siege by powerful enemies, both in the Establishment and in the alien communities posing as "true Americans." The story is clear on this: only a very tough guy – a super-machismo type – has what it takes to take on all the enemies of the people.

Machismo is also the cultural symbol of Far-Right populism's defense of traditional values. Woke cultural forces – whether of feminism, trans people or gentle pacifists or hippies – are undermining the traditional values of

American culture. And the style of Kamala Harris, who tried to appeal to everyone, only reinforced her image of a weakling trying to appease everyone around her.

Trump's defense of traditional culture boiled down to his hardcore embrace of traditional masculinity. He represented in his person the toughness that the country as a whole needed. As American appeared to be falling apart, and the world order seemed on the verge of breakdown, only a truly tough dude could hold things together.

Trump's survival of an assassination attempt – captured by his rising with a clenched fist and yelling FIGHT, FIGHT FIGHT after a bullet grazed his ear, might have clinched his nomination. Nobody could ever call Trump a sissy, even if psychologists diagnosed him as weak and deeply insecure.

Trump's machismo cemented his claim on authoritarian leadership. He had lived and acted the bully all his life. Now, he proclaimed, God and America needed the Great Leader, the authoritarian divine figure, that could save it from disaster. Trump's confident celebration of himself – as precisely the man God saved to lead – helped sell millions of voters on him.

Rationality vs. Irrationality: How Trump Used Both to Win over His Base

Among Americans who do not support Trump, the fevered adoration of "King Trump" is seen as a classic instance of the irrationality of politics. And the choice by white workers of a leader who would turn the country far more against their own interests would appear to support that judgment.

A long and growing literature has supported the idea that workers rejecting the Democratic Party and supporting Trump are voting against their own interests. Thomas Frank made this thesis famous in his 2004 best-selling work, What's the Matter with Kansas? The idea was that poor and working people in Kansas and around the country were being irrationally seduced by the cultural politics of Republicans, beginning in the Reagan revolution that aligned the GOP with Evangelicals and White Christian nationalism. Frank argued, in an early framing of the discussion above, that workers were so irrationally taken by the cultural seduction that they were abandoning their most crucial economic interests, locking them into the anxiety of the new "precariat" plagued by insecure jobs and low wages.

Frank foresaw the cultural seductions that Trump was able to exploit even more successfully than Reagan and Bush. Trump sold both cultural and economic populism while delivering the nation even more completely to Elon Musk and the billionaire class. Trump seems to have led the working class to lose their mind, insanely supporting a demagogue who would hurt them economically and ultimately even flaunt and bolster their most basic religious and cultural values by his own immoral, personal venality.

Nonetheless, there is some irrationality in the new thesis that the working class migrating to the GOP is a sign of ignorance, stupidity and irrationality.

The argument has appeal to Democrats and liberals, since it absolves them of responsibility. There is nothing wrong with them and their politics; liberals might think based on this idea. Their loss of white workers and poor people is simply a sign of irrational foolishness and bigotry in Trump's base.

The notion that what's going on here is irrational politics, driven by the lack of education and intelligence among non-college workers, is not completely wrong, but it misses the fact that liberals and Democrats are serving up the wrong platter even for a rational working class. Moreover, it also ignores the elements of rationality in working-class choices.

Let's remember that Trump was the "change agent" in both his winning campaigns, who truly appeared to rattle existing elites and seemed far more likely than the Democrats to bring big changes to a country – and its working class in decline. As we have already shown – and will document in more detail in Chapter 5 – the Democrats and Left-liberal politicians, by abandoning their own form of populism, made it appear entirely rational to bring in a wild disrupter like Trump. To support the Democrats was to get more of the same in a working-class public hungry for a massive shake-up and systemic change.

Moreover, Trump, as noted above, would carry out selective elements of a populism that would benefit the white working class in his base. True, he ran as a populist candidate for workers and governed as a loyal member of the billionaire class that he claimed to belong to. But his base voted for him based on his campaign promises – as voters often do. And both his threat and use of tariffs, as well as bullying of foreign nations and companies to create manufacturing and other jobs only in America, followed through on some of his populist rhetoric.

Moreover, it is not irrational to vote for your cultural values. Trump promised and delivered significantly on his cultural agenda to "own the libs" and attack "woke" politics on affirmative action, trans people, gays, reproductive rights and education. He assaulted public schools, subsidized private Christian colleges and universities, intimidated the liberal mass media and pushed US culture toward Evangelical and cultural symbols and ideology. For cultural conservatives of any income, voting for this agenda may be extremely rational, even if it does not speak to one's own economic interests.

What is irrational are the liberals and Democrats who are rejecting positive populism and embracing both the war system and the broader corporate regime. The political agenda itself is irrational, because it creates massive social, economic, military and environmental destruction. And it is political suicide because it opens the door to Far-Right populists who capture the rage of the public in hard times.

At the same time, there is clearly a huge dose of irrationality powering Trump's two victories, both on the part of Trump and MAGA itself, as well as his fervent base supporting him. Trump's irrationality is his policies of impoverishing his large base of working-class voters and giving the billionaires virtually all they want. His economic policies will not only reward irrationally ruling corporations and the super-wealthy but also fuel economic downturns and inequality, climate change, war and authoritarianism. This is irrationality at an existential level, since human survival is at stake.

Trump's base puts on stark display its own extreme irrationality, even though it is mixed with rational elements described above. In the short and long runs, voting unequivocally for a leader who will undermine your economic future and that of the nation is fundamentally irrational. And Trump lied to his base, seducing them with populist promises of an anti-corporate Establishment agenda while abandoning them to the predatory practices and ill will of that very Establishment.

Moreover, his culture wars, while they deliver on some of his anti-woke promises that are rational for his Evangelical and culturally conservative working-class base to support, are far from spiritually transforming the nation based on traditional or religious Christian values. For one thing, while Trump often hints at himself as being a modern Jesus, his bullying, lying, narcissistic and openly sociopathic tendencies in his speech and action subvert the cultural values he claims to support. Even his Evangelical followers recognize that Trump is a sinner of dramatic magnitude, while his culturally conservative working-class base also sees that his own personal behavior involving greed, disloyalty and extreme self-centeredness is hardly a model for their own children or for themselves.

The personal behavior of a president helps shape the culture of the nation. A president as morally flawed and corrupt as Trump will inevitably morally corrupt the nation in the name of morally saving it. As Trump was days from re-entering the White House, much of the public was mourning Jimmy Carter, an Evangelical who truly lived his Christian values in his long post-presidency. Even many of Trump's followers could see the difference between a fellow Evangelical who embodied their values in his person and life, and a president whose power they appreciated but who did not live out the values of Jesus in his life.

Moreover, it is impossible to separate culture and economics. The corporate regime – and the war system that are part of militarized capitalism – fuel powerful cultural forces that undermine the moral tenets of both Christianity and traditional conservative culture. Trump's economics accelerates and rewards profit-seeking and self-aggrandizement over all other values and codes of conduct. It becomes hard to survive in a society where the extreme power of unregulated markets and unfettered corporate oligarchy determine success. Without adopting one's own code of deregulated personal greed and self-interest, playing the game of the corporate elites, one is not likely to prosper. As I have argued in my book, The Wilding of America, the culture of militarized capitalism is one of "wilding," which affirms the value of pursuing one's own interest even when it harms other people and weakens the social fabric.

Cultural conservatism has traditionally emphasized the family and community as sacred. Of course, individualism has always been a major part of American conservative culture. But cultural conservatism in America has not traditionally supported unbridled wilding or self-interest that destroys community and leads to sociocide, the breakdown of social values and civil society itself. Even for Trump's base voting on cultural issues, choosing Trump means supporting a regime that will undermine the very values guiding your voting decision. The irrationality of Trump's base is thus both economic and cultural. It helps explain why so many think of Trump as a cult, compelling mind and body, even if it destroys you.

I Alone Can Solve It: The Cult of the Great Leader and the Attraction of Absolute Authoritarianism

Trump's machismo bled into the most seductive element of his appeal to his working-class base: his promise to solve all of the people's problems by his own personal and absolute control. Trump repeatedly said to his base and the public, "I alone can solve it." If elected, he would use his mandate to expand the power of a single American leader more than any prior president. Using new legal interpretations advanced by JD Vance and the New Right, he would subordinate all of the power of the executive branch to himself as an "imperial president." He would eliminate judicial review of his executive orders and congressional oversight of his actions to concentrate all power into himself. This authoritarian aim had been clearly shown by the January 6 coup and his long refusal to accept election results that go against him, which has been reported for years in the press:

> In Walter Isaacson's excellent biography of Steve Jobs, he quotes a colleague of Jobs as saying that he "would have made an excellent King of France." I believe the same could be said of the current occupant of the White House.
> President Donald Trump told Laura Ingraham on Fox News that filling the State Department isn't a priority because, when it comes to foreign policy, "I'm the only one that matters" (Nov. 3, 2017.) Your president brags to his base that "I am your voice" and "I alone can solve it" (Fox News, July 22, 2016). My president asked his supporters to raise their right hands and pledge allegiance to him[23]

> Duly elected presidents don't brag that they "could stand in the middle of Fifth Avenue, shoot somebody and still not lose any votes" (The Guardian, Jan. 24, 2016). Kings might. They can kill with impunity and never have to worry about voters or votes.[24]

In February 2025, Trump said that he was not subject to traditional checks and balances by courts – or by Congress. He posted on Truth Social, his social media platform, that "he who saves his country does not violate any laws," echoing a statement by Napoleon. (Richard Liscombe, "Trump under fire for likening himself to Napoleon amid attacks on judges," The Guardian, Feb. 16, 2025, theguardan.com) Trump had already been given immunity for his official acts by the Supreme Court, essentially empowering him to act without fear of being checked by judges and courts. At the same time, the MAGA Republican Party held a majority in both the Senate and House, willingly ceding all power to Trump and opening the door to his governing through executive authority without Congressional checks and balances.

Trump rapidly moved the nation from the Imperial Presidency emerging after 9/11 and the Patriot Act – allowing the President to declare emergencies suspending basic constitutional rights – toward a police state. While President George W. Bush never invoked the Patriot Act, Trump embraced the immunity given to him by the ultra-conservative Supreme Court to move toward absolutist authority. Trump exploited constitutional and legislative provisions for declaring emergencies of trade, war and invasion by immigrants. As he amped up ICE enforcement, federalized the National Guard, and sent Marines into LA and other cities in the name of purging criminal immigrants threatening the security of the nation, Trump moved rapidly in the direction of an American police state, shutting down free speech and threatening to arrest or deny habeas corpus rights not only of immigrants but also mainstream media, Democratic politicians, university leaders, faculty and students, and even lawyers and judges who ruled against him. Trump was moving to fulfill his promise that "I alone will solve it," as he placed a crown on his head.

Trump's evasion of checks and balances was not fully achieved. Courts and Congress made periodic efforts to restrain him on some executive orders, but his assertion of his rights as a "great leader" found favor in his base of voters. Already dedicated to him and thinking of him as divinely inspired after his survival of an assassination attempt, his base had already taken on elements of a cult. As he claimed total power, many in his base were already constituting a cult. Millions of MAGA voters knew that Trump might not always be polite or always be successful, but that they would unwaveringly support him to the end.

In his best-selling book, *The Cult of Trump*, Steven Hassan, an expert in cults and mind control, makes a compelling case that Trump successfully used classic strategies of cult leaders to take absolute power. The cult successfully took root because it provided two essential and overpowering benefits. First, cults offer one of the strongest forms of social bonds and community. They create and enforce a set of ties between cult members and the leader, as well as among cult members, that are virtually unbreakable. The cult community is so strong that people are prepared to die to stay part of it.

This has special resonance in an individualistic society like the US, where social bonds are relatively weak. In my book, *Bonfire*, I show how neoliberal economics championed by President Ronald Reagan have empowered corporate elites since the 1980s to weaken social solidarity in the workplace, the family and civil society. (Charles Derber, Bonfire: American Sociocide, Broken Relations and the Quest for Democracy. NY: Routledge, 2025.) The US Surgeon General, Vivek Murthy, wrote a 2024 report called "our Epidemic of Loneliness," documenting the breakdown of social ties across the nation, viewing it as a major social and public health crisis. (See Derber, Bonfire: American Sociocide, Broken Relations, and the Quest for Democracy, Chapter 4.)

Surveys show that the weakening of social connections is especially pronounced among working-class voters. Trump rallies have attracted people who are relatively socially isolated. By going from one rally to another and connecting with both Trump and fellow rally members, they find new connections. A society suffering social disconnection is distinctively resonant to Trumpism, since it cements emotionally powerful connections that give millions of people a sense of community and purpose.

Trump's cult helped lead toward something else: unchecked power. By their nature, cults offer absolute control to a single person. Cults have repeatedly shown that they are prepared to die for the leader if he orders them to do so, leading to mass suicides like the events at Jonestown and among the Heaven's Gate cult.

In his second term, Trump quickly made clear that he aimed to be an absolute ruler, not subject to the constraints of prior leaders. His vice-president, JD Vance, a Yale Law School graduate, offered the legal rationale, saying that Trump has no legal obligation to concede to judges any review or check of his "legitimate authority." Trump's MAGA party willingly ceded much of its traditional checks and balances. The courts were less submissive, but the Supreme Court had already offered him the most expansive power and immunity in US history in the Immunity and Chevron decisions. Justice Sonia Sotomayor, in her outspoken dissent on the immunity decision, said the Court had made "the President a king."

> *The Court effectively creates a law-free zone around the President, upsetting the status quo that has existed since the Founding.... "This new official-acts immunity now 'lies about like a loaded weapon' for any President that wishes to place his own interests, his own political survival, or his own financial gain, above the interests of the Nation."*
>
> *The relationship between the President and the people he serves has shifted irrevocably. In every use of official power, the President is now a king above the law.*[25]

The Chevron decision eroded the ability of government agencies to regulate corporations and exercise other traditional authority. This also helped Trump undermine the federal bureaucracy as nothing but a gigantic fraud stealing the taxpayers' hard-earned money.

His cult-like politics helped sustain the contradiction of Trump's populism by empowering the corporate oligarchy that his rhetoric assailed. Workers believed that Trump was using his absolute authority to dismantle the government and its globalist and Marxist elite Establishment working against them. The corporate class understood that Trump's absolute authority would be used to destroy a government checking their own absolute power – opening a Far-Right populist door to the greatest profits and social dominance that a corporate regime ever achieved.

Notes

1 Sonam Sheth, "Trump can't stop talking about how much he loves tariffs," Oct. 18, 2024, newsweek.com

2 Tim Reid and Gram Slatterly, "Trump pledges to take jobs and factories from allies," China, Sept. 25, 2024, reuters.

3 Maya Yang, "Trump again demands to buy Greenland in 'horrendous' call with Danish PM," *The Guardian*, Jan. 28, 2025, theguardian.com

4 Graeme Wearden and Callum Jones, "Global stock markets come under pressure amid 'Trump tariff trantrum'," *The Guardian*, Feb. 3, 2025, the guardian.com

5 Russ Douthat, "Interesting Times: Steven Bannon on 'Broligarchs vs Populism'," *New York Times*, April 7, 2025, nytimes.com

6 Russ Douthat, "Interesting Times: Steven Bannon on 'Broligarchs vs Populism'," *New York Times*, April 7, 2025, nytimes.com

7 Russ Douthat, "Interesting Times: Steven Bannon on 'Broligarchs vs Populism'," *New York Times*, April 7, 2025, nytimes.com

8 Callum Jones, "America's Brexit?" Trump's historic gamble on tariffs has been decades in the making," *The Guardian*, April 5, 2025.

9 Iza Camarillo, "Trump's Tariffs are Extremely Dumb, Just not for the Reasons You might Think," Common Dreams, April 4, 2025, commondreams.org

10 On Point, Megna Chanabarti and Gil Duran, "JD Vance and the Rise of the 'New Right'," *npr*, Aug. 1, 2024, npr.org

11 Steven Greenhouse, "He's brazenly anti-worker': US marks the first Labor Day under Trump 2," *The Guardian*, Sept. 1, 2025, theguardian.com

12 Steven Greenhouse, "He's brazenly anti-worker':US marks the first Labor Day under Trump 2," *The Guardian*, Sept. 1, 2025, theguardian.com

13 Steven Greenhouse, "He's brazenly anti-worker': US marks the first Labor Day under Trump 2," *The Guardian*, Sept. 1, 2025, theguardian.com

14 Steven Greenhouse, "He's brazenly anti-worker': US marks the first Labor Day under Trump 2," *The Guardian*, Sept. 1, 2025, theguardian.com

15 President Donald J. Trump, "Ending radical and Wasteful Government DEI Programs and Preferencing," The White House, January 20, 2025 whitehouse.gov

16 Both men attended Ivy League institutions. Vimala Patel and Sjaron Otterman, "Colleges Wonder if they will be 'the enemy' Under Trump," *NYT*, Nov. 12, 2024, nytimes.com

17 Vimel Patel and Sharon Otterman, "Colleges Wonder if They Will be 'the Enemy' under Trump," *NY Times*, Nov. 12, 2024, nytimes.com

18 Lan Frome and Jonathan Lemire, "Trump: Why allow immigrants from 'shithole countreies'?," AP, Jan. 12, 2018, apnews.com

19 Robert Jones, "Trump's Christian Natioanlist Vision," *Time*, June 22, 2024, time. com

20 Jasmine Garsd, "The stereotype of immigrants eating dogs and cats is storied – and vitriolic as ever," NPR, Sept. 11, 2024, npr.org

21 Jasmine Garsd, "The stereotype of immigrants eating dogs and cats is storied – and vitriolic as ever," NPR, Sept. 11, 2024, npr.org

22 Myah Ward, "We watched 20 Trump rallies. His racist, anti-imigrant message is getttng darker," Politico, Nov. 12, 2024, politico.com

23 *The Times of Israel*, March 7, 2016.

24 Jay Wissot, "All Hail King Donald," Vaildaily, Dec. 6, 2017, vaildaily.com

25 Sonia Sotomayor, quoted in Rebecca Beitsch and Zach Schonfeld, "Sotomayor scolds immunity decision for making presidents' king above the law," The Hill, July 1, 2024, thehill.com

4 Left-Leaning Populism
Pitchforks against Oligarchy

Yes, Left-Leaning Positive Populism Exists

As with Far-Right populism, there is a long history of Left-leaning American populism, ranging from progressive liberalism to democratic socialism. Many forms of liberalism do not challenge the corporate system and are not populist. Most forms of Leftism challenge the corporate state, but some embrace either authoritarianism or violence and represent negative populism. In the age of identity politics, Left/liberal politics tends to reject the class politics at the center of populism. But there have long been forms of Left-leaning positive populism that challenge both the corporate regime and the war system. Some of these movements ultimately succumbed to their own forms of negative populism, involving hierarchy, dogma and divisiveness. In this chapter, we look at the history of some of the major periods of positive Left-leaning populism, looking at both their successes and failures.

Politics with Class: Taking on Militarized Capitalism

Left populism is anti-establishment class politics that challenges the corporations and the war state run by the capitalist class and the military-industrial complex. It is, put simply, a populist politics seeking to end militarized capitalism and replace it with democratic socialism or some form of social democracy with universal rights and a democratic economy based on equality and social justice. Although the positive Left-leaning populist movements over the course of history take many forms, they tend to share the following characteristics:

1 They challenge the ruling establishment of militarized capitalism.
2 They attack class privilege and power.
3 They seek to unify working-class people, emphasizing the need for labor solidarity to change the corporate or capitalist system.
4 They seek to build coalitions between industrial workers and professional "post-industrial" employees to challenge growing corporate control as it spreads from the factory to the university.

DOI: 10.4324/9781003662570-5

5 They seek to build even broader coalitions between workers, students, poor people, people of color, women and activists in peace, climate and other justice movements.
6 They are anti-authoritarian and seek democracy in the economy and politics.

These are ideals of positive Left-leaning populist movements. They are rarely fully sustained in practice. Moreover, many Leftist populist movements, including those embracing Leninism or Stalinism, were never positive populist forces, always relying on authoritarianism, dogma and violence. Other positive Left-leaning populism often degrades over time into authoritarianism, dogma and violence.

In practice, Left-leaning populist movements have been historically a mix of positive and negative populism. In the US Left-leaning movements we discuss below, conflicts between the positive and negative forms often led to the destruction of the movement, as members who join for positive ideals become alienated by those who don't. As we explore which populist movements gain more support, we analyze how the maintenance of positive or negative populism shapes success.

We also tell the stories of the broader conditions that allow positive Left populist movements to succeed. These involve the intensity of hard times in the economy, the political receptivity of the two major parties to populist politics and alliances, the prevailing ideology of the public toward corporations and war, the cultural receptivity to social movements, the strength of their pro-democracy coalitions and the level of political repression wielded by ruling elites in government and throughout society.

Left-leaning populist movements began very early in the US, with roots in the movements against slavery, which became a model for future civil rights movements. After the Civil War, Left populists arose to challenge the rise of the Gilded Age Robber Barons, which set the pattern for future anti-corporate populist movements against later Gilded Ages in the 20th and 21st centuries. The anti-war movement led by socialist labor leader, Eugene Debs, against World War I foreshadowed later 20th- and 21st-century Left populist anti-war movements.

Assessing the movements and their positive or negative populism, the economic conditions they faced, their alliances with political parties, and their cultural resonance with working people helps explain the challenges and promises of populist politics. The capacity to build coalitions between industrial workers and educated New Deal liberal professionals and policymakers in the Democratic Party was a major political advancement. The New Deal coalition helped overcome the corporate Robber Barons of the 1890s and 1920s and offers lessons about how to build new anti-corporate coalitions today. But the abandonment of populist politics by the Democratic Party in the late 20th and 21st centuries turned much of the populist force and working classes over to the Right-wing, starting with Reagan and culminating in Trump.

The four most important American movements of Left positive populism in American history are:

The Abolitionist Movement: Quakers, American Blacks, Including Slaves and Ex-Slaves, Socialists, Pacifists, Workers Who Fought to Abolish Slavery

Gilded Age Populism: The Farmers and Workers Who Challenged the Robber Barons and America's First Corporate Oligarchy, But Lost Their Party

The Labor Movements and Socialists of the New Deal Era: How a Depression and Liberal Class-Based Democratic Party Helped Fuel America's Longest Populist Movements

The 1960s Generation: How civil rights and Vietnam fueled a new multiracial populist youth movement

In this chapter, we focus on the early Left populist movements of the Abolitionists and the Gilded Age Populists, as well as the New Deal and 1960s populist movements. In Chapter 6, on youth populism, we discuss in more depth the 1960s Populist Generation, and in Chapter 8, we further flesh out the story of New Deal populism, which was the most successful of the historic Left-populist movements.

The Abolitionists

Abolitionism was the first great social movement in the US. While it is not typically discussed as a form of Leftism or populism, it had many elements of Left positive populist politics. The Abolitionist movement was a radical challenge to the Establishment of the South and, in many respects, to the Constitutional Establishment of the US. It rejected the fundamental ruling institutions of the slave-holding South, including its economy, dominant form of labor and class relations, as well as its oligarchic slave-holding ruling class. Its attack on slavery was a challenge to the Constitution itself, since the Constitution treated slaves as 3/5 of a person and as devoid of any constitutional rights whatsoever.

Abolitionism was an extremely diverse movement of Quakers, educated social reformers, slaves, ex-slaves, intellectuals and writers, politicians, women, especially suffragettes, students, socialists and ordinary citizens. Most Americans were not activists in the Abolitionist movement. Liberal educated social reformers such as William Lloyd Garrison – a socialist and pacifist – led it in tandem with ex-slaves like Frederick Douglass, and they often suffered attacks from an unsympathetic public. But people from virtually every sector of the society, other than the ruling elites of the South, engaged with the movement, and a majority in the North eventually came to support ending slavery before the Civil War.

Support and activism came from the grassroots, with abolitionists including whites and blacks as well as both intellectuals and non-college workers. Activists included a minority of white Northern workers like John Murray Spear of Massachusetts, imprisoned for helping a slave. A movement of "Wide Awake" students and workers organized protests equating slavery with "wage-slavery." Intellectuals like Harriet Beecher Stowe penned Abolitionist manifestos and novels. Frederic Douglass, an ex-slave and brilliant orator and "man of the people," helped lead the movement.

Indeed, the movement can be considered a "people's movement," in the spirit of other populist movements. Stowe's *Uncle Tom's Cabin* was the most popular bestseller other than the Bible in the 19th century. Douglass was the most photographed American, hinting at the growing popular appeal of Abolitionism, despite the relatively small size of activists across the population.

The Abolitionists set the tone for all future Left populist movements by organizing their neighbors, friends and fellow workers into activist committees on their home turf that did the real work of Abolitionism:

> *The abolitionists developed their own community-level institutions that would be vital for developing consciousness and, at a face-to-face level, negotiate the diversity of the movement.... Vigilante committees emerged across the North...staffed by volunteers or stipended individuals from the African-American community or even runaways from the South. These committees documented slavery in the most personal of ways, helping catalogue the experience of individuals, while sharing their resulting knowledge broadly.... This resistance work "turned society on its hinges to let in a new dispensation on learning, religion and life."*[1]

Populist politics is always, first and foremost, about building connections and educating oneself and one's community. This is not to say, as just noted, that it was a movement embraced by the majority or actively supported by the Northern working class. A majority of white workers feared that freed slaves would take their jobs and reduce wages. Nor was it a movement against the capitalist Establishment; it was a movement against the Southern plantation ownership class and the "Slave Power" Establishment. It was populist in the sense that it opposed the Confederate Establishment with appeals to the democratic and equal rights of the people, defined in the Declaration of Independence and in the Constitution.

The opposition or fear of many white workers reflected the contradictions in many Left populist movements, which had to build very broad coalitions that included factions of different classes, races and religions. Frequently, Left populist coalitions have to win over white workers who are culturally conservative but share some economic or political interests. Moreover, most social movements, including populist ones, only succeed, even at their height, in drawing a small percentage of the public into activism itself, with the majority being supporters but not activists.

Abolitionists opposed the Southern ruling class, a plantation-owning oligarchy that used Far-Right populist appeals to rally white Southern workers to the Southern cause. In this respect, Abolitionism can be seen as the first US Leftist populism to oppose America's first Far-Right populism that was embedded in the Democratic Party of the era. The Democrats' Southern Christian nationalist form of Far-Right populism helped win the enduring loyalty of Southern whites to the Southern cause. In the 19th century, it won even Northern workers to its cause, pulling them away from Northern positive populism or Left populism.

Abraham Lincoln famously equated slavery with "wage-slavery," making clear that Abolitionism was challenging a form of labor. By doing so, Lincoln made clear that Abolitionism was partly an economic movement, challenging the South's economic system as well as sounding the clarion moral argument of the Abolitionists. Abolitionism, like most Left populist movements, was both a moral and economic movement.

Abolitionism ultimately helped defeat slavery through classic Left populist strategies. It made powerful moral arguments against a powerful ruling Establishment, insisting on its overthrow. It unified a very broad coalition of the people, including the proto-PMC of students, writers and other intellectuals coalescing with Blacks, many women, and a slowly growing number of Northern working people against a moral evil and form of political and economic repression. And it united ultimately with a powerful electoral party, the Republican Party, which would ultimately take up the cause of the movements on the ground and ensure victory. But it did not succeed in ending slavery by itself. That would require a Civil War that eliminated slavery but was driven by other interests as well.

The Gilded Age Populists

The Robber Barons of the 1890s – John D. Rockefeller, J. P. Morgan, Andrew Carnegie and Cornelius Vanderbilt – were the most powerful members of the new class of corporate elites after the Civil War who consolidated control of both the economy and the government. They became the modern corporate oligarchy, or American Establishment. They ruled ruthlessly, exploiting workers and farmers with low wages, long hours, and restrictive credit. They created vast working-class poverty as they turned themselves into America's first billionaires.

It is hardly surprising that a major populist movement of farmers and workers emerged to challenge this gang of ruling "Robbers." By the 1880s, a Famers Alliance was taking shape as the center of a new "people's movement." It created what is still called today the "populist movement" – and remains a defining moment of populism in America. Because the Populists challenged the corporate Robber Baron oligarchy, it led populism to be associated with left-wing politics, but in the 20th century, populism was increasingly viewed as any strong challenge to the Establishment, whether from the Left or the Right.

Rising in rural areas in the South and Plains, the early 1870s and 1880s Populist Movement spread across the country, with the Farmers Alliance building coalitions with urban workers and labor parties. Historian Lawrence Goodwyn, a leading chronicler of the populist movement, calls them in his book, *Democratic Promise*, one of America's greatest anti-corporate and pro-democracy movements, winning somewhere between 25 and 45 percent of the electorate in 20 states by 1894.

The farmers of the 1870s and 1880s were hit hard by the tight money regime that Morgan and other Wall Street financiers imposed. Vanderbilt, who built and owned many of the railroads on which farmers depended for supplies and marketing, was charging high prices, driving farmers into bankruptcy. As farmers fell into greater debt, financiers tightened credit terms and used their power to ensure that the "soft" or expansionary monetary policy farmers needed was prevented, driving more and more farmers into financial ruin.

In 1877, farmers in Texas first formed the Farmers Alliance as an economic movement attacking the "money trust," which was responsible for their credit crises, while also attacking mercantile elites who provided farmers' supplies and warehouses on harsh credit terms. The farmers succeeded in building alliances with major labor groups, including the Knights of Labor, who went on strike against the railroads in 1886. While supporting the Knights of Labor, the farmers issued a broad set of demands for regulating the railroads, national collective bargaining, looser monetary policy and the creation of a national banking system that would put much of Wall Street's power in the hands of government and the people.

The Alliance was famous for creating a vibrant network of lecturers who traveled and spoke to meetings of local farmers in hundreds of villages, especially across the Plains states and the Midwest. These village conversations embodied the essence of the populist spirit, relying on grassroots activism to build common awareness of how the "money trust" operated and how to fight it. These were local non-college folks getting together with their neighbors and schooling themselves in how economic power was organized against them. Some of these Populists were religious, often Protestant and some evangelical, gathering and organizing in church. It provided a model of how Left-leaning positive populism – even though the Populists of this era had some conservative Right-leaning elements – can develop as a movement of ordinary people creating community to fight for their survival and justice.

In 1892, when the Farmers Alliance had spread nationally after almost two decades, it founded the People's Party. It was an effort to create a new national political party based on a coalition of farmers and urban workers. The populists met and drafted the Omaha Declaration, a radical agenda calling for the rights of the people against the corporate Establishment. The Omaha Platform opened with this populist manifesto against the new Robber Baron Establishment destroying America and its working people:

The conditions which surround us best justify our co-operation; we meet in the midst of a nation brought to the verge of moral, political, and material ruin. Corruption dominates the ballot-box, the Legislatures, the Congress, and touches even the ermine of the bench. The people are demoralized; most of the States have been compelled to isolate the voters at the polling places to prevent universal intimidation and bribery. The newspapers are largely subsidized or muzzled, public opinion silenced, business prostrated, homes covered with mortgages, labor impoverished, and the land concentrating in the hands of capitalists. The urban workmen are denied the right to organize for self-protection, imported pauperized labor beats down their wages, a hireling standing army, unrecognized by our laws, is established to shoot them down, and they are rapidly degenerating into European conditions. The fruits of the toil of millions are boldly stolen to build up colossal fortunes for a few, unprecedented in the history of mankind; and the possessors of those, in turn, despise the republic and endanger liberty. From the same prolific womb of governmental injustice we breed the two great classes—tramps and millionaires.[2]

The People's Party demanded popular control of Wall Street, public banks, public control of the railroads, expansionary monetary policy, a graduated income tax and a range of workers' rights, including unionism, all in the service of resisting the growing anti-democratic power of corporations. While radical, it was nonviolent and grew out of the needs and views of ordinary farmers and workers. Here are its fundamental principles – pure Left populism – as declared in the Manifesto:

First—That the union of the labor forces of the United States this day consummated shall be permanent and perpetual; may its spirit enter into all hearts for the salvation of the Republic and the uplifting of mankind.

Second—Wealth belongs to him who creates it, and every dollar taken from industry without an equivalent is robbery. "If any will not work, neither shall he eat." The interests of rural and civic labor are the same; their enemies are identical.

Third—We believe that the time has come when the railroad corporations will either own the people or the people must own the railroads, and should the government enter upon the work of owning and managing all railroads, we should favor an amendment to the Constitution by which all persons engaged in the government service shall be placed under a civil-service regulation of the most rigid character, so as to

> *prevent the increase of the power of the national administration by the use of such additional government employees.*
>
> *FINANCE—We demand a national currency, safe, sound, and flexible, issued by the general government only, a full legal tender for all debts, public and private, and that without the use of banking corporations, a just, equitable, and efficient means of distribution direct to the people, at a tax not to exceed 2 per cent. per annum, to be provided as set forth in the sub-treasury plan of the Farmers' Alliance, or a better system; also by payments in discharge of its obligations for public improvements.*[3]

In their race for the 1892 presidency, with their candidate William Jennings Bryan, the People's Party succeeded in winning support not only of farmers but also of many influential labor leaders and labor parties. They won the endorsement of Terrence Powderly, the leader of the Knights of Labor, as well as Eugene Debs, a leading socialist labor organizer against the railroads. The Populists won endorsements from a large number of labor parties, including the United Labor Party, the Anti-Monopoly Party, the Union Labor Party and the Greenback Party. In the concluding speech to the Spring 1892 populist convention, Ignatius Donnelly stated:

> *We meet in the midst of a nation brought to the verge of moral, political, and material ruin. ... We seek to restore the government of the republic to the hands of the 'plain people' with whom it originated. Our doors are open to all points of the compass. ... The interests of rural and urban labor are the same; their enemies are identical.*

While the People's Party never won the mass support of urban workers that it gained among farmers, and lost the 1892 election, Goodwyn notes that the Populists influenced labor organizers and parties for several decades after the populists dissolved in 1896.

Like all US Left-leaning Populist movements, the 1890s populists, despite their pro-labor policies, had to contend with a white working class that was culturally and religiously conservative, with many raised in the South and West. They embodied many traditional Southern values. Moreover, the skilled craftsmen who helped form the AFL in the Gilded Age were appalled at the economic radicalism of the People's Party. The skilled craftsmen felt the populists challenged their superiority to factory workers and rejected many of the liberal cultural sensibilities that some of the leaders of the Populist movement embodied. The relation between class and culture has always been fraught in America and in its populist movements, as reflected both in the Abolitionist and Gilded Age Populist movements.

The People's Party, aiming to mobilize ordinary farmers and workers against the Robber Barons, faced enduring cultural hurdles. The working class itself was divided by values related to race, religion and other deep cultural issues. The majority of ordinary workers and farmers in the Gilded Age, as in the Abolitionist era and in successive eras, were cultural conservatives, with many seeing liberal, educated elites as much of an enemy Establishment against them as the corporate elites. What we now call the "culture wars" have always been a central problem facing Left populists, since Far-Right populists and their corporate allies have always found ways to present themselves as defenders of workers' traditional values and to mobilize these workers against the "cultural elites."

Ordinary workers around the country, particularly those raised in the South and West, thus saw Blacks as not only economic rivals but also part of an anti-American culture that liberal elites were helping stoke. As Right-leaning populists leaned into this Gilded Age culture war, workers and farmers often allied with their corporate bosses on cultural issues while suffering from their financial and employment ruthlessness. This led to deep splits among populist farmers; the majority were white and did not favor an integrated movement. But a significant minority created racially mixed populist agrarian groups advocating for both white and black farmers.

Perhaps the most famous populist challenging white supremacy even in the South was the Georgia populist leader, Tom Watson. Although a segregated National Famers Alliance had been formed separate from a Colored Famers Alliance, Watson openly called for unity because both black and white farmers shared the same fundamental problem.

> *Watson appealed to rural black voters by promising to respect their political and civil rights. Watson organized picnics, barbecues, and camp meetings and formed political clubs for blacks. But political cooperation did not mean socializing; blacks and whites sat separately when together. Yet that did not prevent them from cheering wildly when Watson spoke of their common plight: "You are made to hate each other because on that hatred is rested the keystone of the arch of financial despotism which enslaves you both. You are deceived and blinded because you do not see how this race antagonism perpetuates a monetary system that beggars you both. The colored tenant is in the same boat as the white tenant, the colored laborer with the white laborer and that the accident of color can make no difference in the interests of farmers, croppers and laborers."[4]*

Watson was a major leader in the People's Party, leading Populists to victory in some elections in the Jim Crow South, challenging both the "money power" and white supremacy. Black and white farmer coalitions won elections in several states in 1892 and won the state of North Carolina in 1896 under the leadership of Marion Butler (*Richard Wormser, Jim Crow Stories, "The Rise and Fall of Jim Crow," Populist Party, thirteen.org*).

But when the People's Party merged with the Democratic Party in 1896, many of these racial alliances and struggles ended with a return to the Jim

Crow of the Democratic Party. The melding with the Democrats drastically reduced the populists' economic radicalism and appeal. It also increasingly led the populists to embrace white supremacy consistent with the cultural conservatism of ordinary white workers in the South and in much of the rest of the country – as well as reflecting the Far-Right populism of the Democratic Party in that era.

The power of cultural conservatism prevented the 1880s and 1890s Gilded Age populists from ever winning over most of the white urban working class – helping explain their failure to take power. Many urban workers were fighting off immigrants as well as freed slaves as potential rivals. Like many Trumpist workers today, they were receptive to the racial and nationalist cultural appeals of corporate elites, seeking solace from their economic burdens by embracing the cultural Right populist notion that they were better off than so many other working-class groups who could not be seen as "true Americans." Other urban workers of the Gilded Age were immigrants themselves, and they embraced traditional American values and cultural conservatism as a way of proving that they were assimilating successfully as true Americans.

As we show in later chapters, the struggles of ensuing Left populist movements to build coalitions of white workers with Blacks and liberal educated PMC students, professional employees and other social reformers have always faced major cultural divisions and challenges. This reflects the enduring strength of US Far-Right populism, bred in the Southern Confederacy and taking root initially among Southern white workers and the Democratic Party in the South and across the country. It then succeeded in continuing to spread conservative racial, religious and traditional family values among white workers across America. As in the case of the Gilded Age populists, the elements of Left-leaning and Far-Right populism often mix and conflict in the movement, with both scholars and members of the populist movements themselves sometimes confused or divided about whether the movement was – or would turn – Left or Right.

Nonetheless, the Gilded Age populists were not total failures. They mobilized an entire generation of farmers against the country's first Robber Barons. They launched a populist agenda against the corporate and financial establishment that helped shape all future progressive and populist movements in America. They had a major influence on the Progressive reformers in the first two decades of the 20th century, who combated poverty, created modern social welfare and laid the groundwork for some of the New Deal that would follow. And, in many ways, their ultimate failure was a reflection of abandoning their Omaha Platform radicalism, as practical politics led them to unite with a segregationist Democratic Party seeking to tame them and highlight their core identity as white Christians rather than as workers.

New Deal Populists Are Born in the Great Depression

In the 20th and 21st centuries, new, major forms of positive and Left populism emerged. They are so important that I devote much of two later chapters to discussing them. They offer the most important insights into how a positive populism is emerging and can become a major force for defeating Trump and Far-Right populism now and in the future.

Here, I briefly preview and summarize the labor populism of the New Deal, beginning in the 1930s, and the youth populism of the 1960s. The New Deal created a new positive populist movement – differing in important ways from Abolitionism and the Gilded Age populists. It had some affinity with the Gilded Age populists by seeking to mobilize much of the nation's hard-pressed non-college working class to challenge the larger corporate system of the Robber Baron oligarchy.

While the Gilded Age populists had also challenged the Robber Barons, they mainly succeeded in mobilizing farmers rather than urban workers. The nation had not yet developed the mass base of workers that could be organized, nor did it have a Democratic Party prepared to fight for them. These two new conditions led to an earthquake in American politics, creating a positive populist Democratic Party challenging the Robber Baron Establishment to protect ordinary American workers experiencing extreme hard times.

The Democratic Party had long been rooted in the Confederacy and Jim Crow South – and had led Far-Right populism before the Civil War. That legacy continued well into the 20th century, with Woodrow Wilson being an heir and supporter of that racist and negative Southern Democratic Party populism of the Jim Crow era. The 1890s People's Party of the Gilded Age populists was taken over by and surrendered to a conservative Democratic Party with no interest in challenging Wall Street. Two decades later, the Democratic President, Woodrow Wilson, enjoyed showing the film, Birth of a Nation, in his White House. It was the most famous 20th-century film celebrating the Southern "lost cause" and the nobility of the Southern gentry. Wilson was still perpetuating the early Southern Democratic Party tradition of Far-Right populism.

The coming of the New Deal was thus an unexpected and profound transformation. It created a profound challenge to the US corporate Establishment, opening a political window for workers, the Democratic Party and the rise of positive populism in America. President Franklin D. Roosevelt and his New Deal Democrats united for the first time with a massive movement of workers fighting the ruling power of Gilded Age corporations and banks. The uniting of a populist worker movement with a mainstream governing party created the essential conditions for a victorious Left-leaning positive populism. Democratic Party populism ruled the nation from FDR's election in 1932 through the Depression and World War II. The New Deal regime lasted several decades and only came to an end with the stagflation of the 1970s and the rise of the 1980s Reagan revolution.

It was only the Depression that made the New Deal positive populism possible. Millions of workers were thrown out of their jobs and were left without homes and incomes, living in "Hoovervilles." The corporate Republican presidents of the 1920s did nothing to help them, claiming that the markets would correct themselves and that the Smoot-Hawley tariffs of the 1930s, the predecessor to Trump's massive tariffs of the 2020s, would save the workers and the country. In reality, the Smoot-Hawley tariffs deepened and sustained the Depression, doing nothing to create jobs or stimulate the economy. The failure of the Robber Barron presidents and oligarchy to help workers paved the way for the Democrats to reinvent themselves. Under FDR's leadership, they turned themselves into a party of the workers, creating a new class politics in the US that became the foundation of America's first ruling positive populism.

The New Deal integrated and modeled the crucial features of a positive populist movement that could take root and gain power in the US. First, it took seriously the pain of the hard times for workers that the Gilded Age oligarchy and political elites ignored. FDR did not know exactly how to create a new economic order when he ran for president, but he knew that the people desperately needed help and could not survive without a government coming to their rescue and actively taking steps to challenge the Gilded Age corporate Establishment. He knew he had to create a new worker-centered order based on public needs and a government serving the people rather than the oligarchy, the essence of positive populism.

When FDR won the election in 1932, he began two additional major steps to remake politics and the existing Gilded Age order. First, he reassured workers he was on their side, offering his weekly radio broadcasts that put him in direct contact with them. He spoke to workers and the poor as the real people he would serve, rather than the corporate elites. He made clear also that he looked to them to give him support. In his famous radio broadcasts, he told them he needed them to take action themselves to rewire the country for economic recovery and make the workers themselves the agents and beneficiaries of political change.

FDR was not being entirely unselfish in this approach. He knew that the Democrats could not take power and make new laws serving workers and the people without massive public support. Moreover, workers were already beginning to go out in the streets, catalyzing on their own the rallies and "people's revolt" on the streets that were spreading like wildfire across the nation.

Positive populism is always ultimately rooted in the spontaneous activism of workers and ordinary people, whether in the streets or in the factories. It requires citizens moving to assert their own desperation and needs – demanding that they be heard and served by government leaders. The Depression created the very hard times that created the most widespread worker rallies, protests and organizations for their own interests in US history. They remained largely nonviolent, but there were hundreds of thousands of activists, with many militants demanding worker rights and democratic power in the factories and in Washington.

The protests created America's most transformative positive populism movement. Workers and the poor poured into the streets of New York City, refusing to pay their unaffordable rents and stopping the police from evict-ing their neighbors. They formed breadlines around the country, including in their shanty-towns or "Hoovervilles," demanding food and public welfare from the government. And, most famously, tens of thousands of workers or-ganized spontaneous rallies at their workplaces and on the streets demanding fair wages and a new economic order that would keep them from starving. Thousands of "wildcat strikes" and occupations of factories became symbols of the new positive populism. These positive populists were nonviolent but transformative, demanding unions that would permanently be their voice for their rights and a new economic order – with many calling for some form of worker-control or socialism. They represented a genuine populist challenge to the corporate Establishment.

The movement could not have sustained itself and won decisive politi-cal victories without the support of the New Deal Democratic Party. FDR told workers that he could not make the changes they needed without their pushing him and his party as hard as they could for major change. This cre-ated a positive-spiral of class-conscious workers putting more pressure on the Democratic Party claiming to represent them. The Party responded with major empowering acts like the 1935 Wagner Act, which legalized unions for the first time in the US. This, in turn, spurred working people into more rallies and strikes in the streets and in their factories to demand their full rights. FDR was also able to pass the 1935 Social Security Act, the first na-tional social welfare system offering unemployment insurance, old-age pay-ments and insurance against workplace accidents and disabilities. This, in turn, led to strong labor organizing and the rise of fiery new labor leaders like John Lewis, who founded the new CIO, the most militant national labor organization in US history. This continued the positive-populist spiral, with FDR and New Deal Democrats responding by passing other transformative laws, including the 1938 Fair Labor Standards Act, which created a federal minimum wage, a forty-hour maximum workweek, and a minimum working age of 16, as well as a proposal for a council governing national wage and working standards.

The positive populism of the New Deal offers important lessons for the rise of a new positive populist movement today. The New Deal example created the coalition of social and labor movements with a worker-based Democratic Party oriented toward class politics and major reform of the rul-ing corporate Establishment. It promoted democracy in the workplace and democracy in government, shifting power from corporate elites and their Re-publican Party allies toward workers, the poor and other class-based allies. The demands were militant and led to a "regime change at home," but the New Deal and the masses of workers who rallied on the streets and in their factories remained nonviolent.

This New Deal labor populism was a story about workers, ordinary peo-ple and the power of an alliance that the Democratic Party can make to gain power and change the country. It is a story that leaders like Bernie Sanders know well. Sanders' anti-oligarchic mass rallies in the first months of Trump's second term may help that story resurface against Trumpist autocracy and what Sanders calls "the billionaire class."

Will American workers and unions join the fight against Trump's corporate oligarchs, as they did in the 1930s? Trump is, as Liz Shuler, the president of the AFL-CIO, the national federation of American workers, has said, the most anti-worker, anti-union president in American history. The AFL-CIO, along with the AFSCME, the nation's largest service sector union, as well as the Teachers' Union and Nurses' Union, joined the AFL-CIO to begin mounting major resistance to Trump after his re-election. They organized more than a thousand "workers against billionaires" rallies across the country on Labor Day, 2025. This came after another mass national labor protest led by major unions on May Day, 2025 and was the kick-off, according to Shuler of a year of labor mobilization against Trump leading up to the 2026 elections (Steven Greenhouse, "'He's brazenly anti-worker': US marks the first Labor Day under Trump 2.0." the Guardian, Sept 1, 2025 theguardian.com).

The 1960s Civil Rights and Anti-War Populists Fight for Justice, Peace and America's First Multiracial Democracy

In the 1960s, before the extended New Deal era came to a close under Nixon and Reagan, a second positive populist movement erupted. Once again, hundreds of thousands of ordinary Americans rallied and marched daily on the streets. They challenged the Establishment to its core, rallying for many years with mass protests and populist campaigns around the country. This positive populist movement has a somewhat different demographic on the streets than the New Deal; in some ways, more resembling Abolition. They were primarily Black people fighting for the right to vote in the South and students fighting the horrific war in Vietnam.

In some ways, this was a more radical challenge to the Establishment than the New Deal. Sparked first by courageous young Black Southerners fighting for their elementary right to speak and vote, the new civil rights movement was a challenge to a Southern Establishment that used white sheets, nooses and guns to kill challengers to their neofascist regime. In the North, students were challenging the US national security state and the military-industrial complex, a major part of the national American Establishment. It was as brutal and repressive as the Southern regime, maintaining ruthless oligarchic and militarist control of not just the US but much of the world.

The civil rights struggle was as old as the country, a nation founded partly on racism and the neofascist Confederate slave system. Abolitionism had been the first positive populist movement, rising to challenge the Confederate Establishment run as a Far-Right populist regime. The civil rights movements of the sixties had to challenge the reincarnation of the Confederate model in the 1960s South. The South continued to be ruled by racist Democratic Party elites, who used their Far-Right populism to unite "white trash" with new Southern oligarchs in defense of Jim Crow against Southern black activists.

We have seen that Abolitionism was a long and difficult struggle bred from the horrific hard times suffered by slaves. All such hard times tend to breed populist movements. Abolitionism sustained itself and ultimately gained public support by uniting a very broad coalition of Blacks and educated white liberals and Leftists. The coalition used the terrible evils of the slave system as a moral weapon against the Southern Establishment, with freed slaves like Frederick Douglass joining together in the same broad Abolitionist movement as white educated liberals like Harriet Beecher Stowe and socialist Abolitionist leaders like William Lloyd Garrison.

The Sixties movement grew out of similar horrific hard times suffered by modern Blacks disenfranchised and impoverished by Jim Crow. The new civil rights movement, like all positive populist movements, arose out of the spontaneous protests of Southern civil rights activists. They were local people who, in the 1950s, were organizing throughout the South to desegregate schools and other public facilities. In 1957, in Montgomery, Alabama, when Rosa Parks sat in a white-only front seat of a segregated bus and refused to sit in the back, she helped unleash a national populist resistance. Supported by her local NAACP civil rights organization and other courageous neighbors and fellow activists, local activists like Parks laid the groundwork for the 1960s civil rights protesters who created a nationwide positive populist revolt against the Far-Right populist regime that had ruled the South since the end of Reconstruction.

The young Black civil rights activists created fiery and effective organizations like SNCC (the Student Non-Violent Coordinating Committee), led by inspiring figures like Julian Bond, John Lewis and Marion Barry. They mobilized a massive movement seeking to finally dismantle the Southern Far-Right populist regime. Through their Freedom Rides and sit-ins in segregated diners, they created a profile of a modern nonviolent positive populism that won support, as Abolitionism did, not only from the mass of disenfranchised Blacks but much of the Northern white population. Supporters included educated young people, many of whose parents were part of FDR's New Deal. As in Abolitionism and in the New Deal, the youthful Black activists created a profile of nonviolent courage while suffering brutally violent repression.

The moral strength of nonviolence played a huge role in the building of the movement and the ultimate support of the national Democratic Party, when President Lyndon B. Johnson signed the landmark 1964 Civil Rights Act and 1965 Voting Rights Act, an iconic triumph of the movement.

The role of LBJ signals some of the differences and parallels with the New Deal. LBJ was the last great New Dealer, and he had initiated his Great Society as the latest phase of the long struggle of New Deal economic policies supporting workers against the corporate oligarchy. LBJ has the courage to back positive populism, knowing that his Democrats would lose the political support of the South and many white workers. Republicans like Goldwater, Nixon and Reagan took over the mantle of Southern Democratic Far-Right populism, leading ultimately to the Far-Right populism of Trump and MAGA Republicanism.

The positive populism of the civil rights movement was the most powerful force capable of challenging Far-Right populism. Its success, while far from a total defeat of Jim Crow and racism, came through a mass multiracial base of young, courageous activists tied with a federal Democratic Party embracing its own populist civil rights agenda against the Southern Establishment and its own Southern Democratic segregationists. Like FDR, LBJ led the Democratic Party into positive populism both on economic and social issues like race. It enabled the kind of broad coalition between a mass movement and the Democratic Party essential to positive populist triumphs.

The final element enabling that victory was the leadership of the entire movement by Martin Luther King. King emerged as the iconic symbol of nonviolence, central to any positive populism. Moreover, King moved to embrace a positive populist agenda that tied civil rights and anti-racist movements to anti-war movement and pro-labor union organizing. This moved the 1960s civil rights movement from a siloed identity movement to a positive populist movement against the corporate oligarchy and the national security Establishment.

King's positive populism also had a major effect on the student movement rising to protest the Vietnam War in the mid-1960s. King asked how he could support violence against people abroad while he was fighting to stop such violence at home. This created the conditions under which students began to develop one of the country's most important movements against war and US militarism. They would largely maintain their own nonviolence and develop a positive populist agenda not only against Vietnam but also against the war state Establishment, tied to the economic interests of oligarchic corporate elites.

The anti-war student movement was part of a "New Left" generation seeking to mobilize the nation to support a society based on "participatory democracy." We flesh this movement out in Chapter 6, since it was one of the most important positive populist movements in the US. Its manifesto of "participatory democracy" has special relevance in current struggles to challenge Trump's authoritarianism.

Despite mobilizing millions of students and older Americans, the sixties anti-Vietnam movements had important limits and failures. Elements of violence emerged, and the student activists did not reach out successfully to the masses of workers who could have helped them stop the war. Moreover, LBJ and the Democratic Party became committed to the war and did not sustain their positive populist agenda in foreign policy that they did in economic policy and that made possible the New Deal and Great Society programs at home.

Nonetheless, the anti-war, participatory democracy movements of the Vietnam era carry important lessons for pro-democratic movements in the Trump era and beyond. They demonstrate the key importance of young people in positive populist movements, while also highlighting the importance of a broad agenda uniting race and civil rights with labor struggles in an anti-corporate Establishment movement. They make clear that Left-leaning populist movements can create serious backlash among culturally conservative white workers unless they reach out to those workers and stand up for their rights and wages as part of a broader struggle against the corporate oligarchy. Positive populism has to universalize and address all the people subjected to the ruling regime.

Moreover, the anti-war lessons of the 1960s populist activism against Vietnam should make clear to the Democratic Party the cost of remaining tied to US militarism and unjust wars. LBJ did not show the courage that he displayed in civil rights and his Great Society programs when it came to Vietnam. He knew the US was likely to lose the war, but he feared that he would be impeached if he opposed it. He and other leading top Democrats of the era, much like Biden and Harris today, aligned the Democratic Party fully with the war machine, violently attacking the anti-war students and older activists in Chicago at the 1968 Democratic Convention. The Democrats' pro-war policy allowed the Republicans to take power for most of the next 30 years.

Likewise, Biden and Harris' unquestioning embrace of US militarism around the world allowed Trump to run in 2024 as the candidate who promised to shake up the US Establishment, not only at home but also abroad, with Trump promising to cut the military budget and end the Ukraine war. The lesson was that the Democratic Party's failure to embrace positive populism hurt not only the positive populist activists on the streets but also the prospect of the Democratic Party to win elections. In 2026 and beyond, the Democrats should study this outcome and change course if they want to defeat Trump and the Republican Party's Far-Right populism. How to do so is the subject of the remaining chapters of this book.

Notes

1 Charles Derber and Suren Moodliar, Dying for Capitalism. NY: Routledge, 2023, pp. 178–179.
2 ameericanyawp.com
3 The Omaha Platform.
4 Richard Wormser, Jim Crow Stories, "The Rise and Fall of Jim Crow," Populist Party, thirteen.org

5 Liberalism without Class

How the Democratic Party Handed America to Trump

Key Populist Allies: The Democratic Party as the "Bush-Lite" Establishment

The success of populist movements is based to a large degree, as suggested in the last chapter, on their capacity to find a mainstream party that embraces parts of their message and draws voters to parts of their agenda. The Southern Democratic Party played a key role in advancing the agenda of post-Civil War Far-Right populists in the Jim Crow era and beyond. On the Left, the New Deal Democratic Party of FDR was crucial in helping populist labor movements and socialists to organize and gain public support, as well as to pass laws embodying parts of their platforms.

Similarly, the Republican Party's embrace of Christian nationalism helped fuel Far-Right religious populists aligned with the Reagan Administration. Most importantly, Trump's takeover of the Republican Party with MAGA is the most powerful force building Far-Right populist movements today. Indeed, the Trump era is the first one in the post-World War II era in which the most powerful force is a Far-Right governing authoritarian party, which is directing and empowering the entire Far-Right populist authoritarian movement.

The success of Trump in transforming the GOP into a populist party is the obvious explanation of the current ascendancy of Far-Right populism. But the second fundamental reason is the Democratic Party's decisive abandonment of Left-leaning populist sympathies and alliances. In the post-World War II era, this abandonment of Democratic Party populism began with Bill Clinton and continued under Barack Obama. Both Clinton and Obama led a new Democratic Party that abandoned the New Deal and class politics, embracing identity politics and corporate trade and broader economic policy that benefited global companies at the expense of US blue-collar workers. They opened the door to Republicans, specifically Donald Trump, as the new voice of anti-global populism.

After Reagan helped destroy the New Deal regime, Bill Clinton began the Democratic Party shift away from class politics toward a "third way" centrist liberalism. In his 1996 State of the Union Address, Clinton said, famously and momentously, "The era of big government is over."

DOI: 10.4324/9781003662570-6

This was his way of telling America that the Democratic Party was no longer the party of the New Deal. Effectively, he was "re-inventing government" and the Democratic Party itself. He was celebrating the end of big government and his own revolution for a smaller government. He didn't say so explicitly, but it was a more centrist version of Reagan's revolution to end the New Deal era and let big companies and ordinary people live better and enjoy more freedom:

We know big government does not have all the answers. We know there's not a program for every problem. We have worked to give the American people a smaller, less bureaucratic government in Washington. And we have to give the American people one that lives within its means. Bll Clinton, State of the Union Message Jan. 23, 1996.

Clinton's goal of smaller government and ending deficit spending meant cutting into core parts of the New Deal:

So the first thing I would say is, we have to maintain fiscal discipline. We shouldn't spend the surplus before it materializes, and we shouldn't spend a penny of it until we have secured Social Security for the 21st century, and we ought to craft the reform in early 1999.

Secondly, we also have a Medicare Commission chaired by another DLC leader, Senator Breaux, and we have to recognize that we have to deal with that. And we ought to deal with that also in 1999. And the Democrats should not run away from making the necessary reforms in Social Security and Medicare.[1]

Cutting social security and Medicare was a death blow to Democratic Party populism. Clinton was embracing the ideals of "fiscal discipline" that have always been a corporate party's way of rejecting major public investment in the basic needs and social welfare of working people. It had the unsurprising effect of increasing the acceleration of non-college working-class voters out of the Democratic Party.

Clinton simultaneously endorsed corporate globalization and US militarism, essentially creating a double-whammy domestic and foreign policy shift. Most importantly, Clinton passed NAFTA in 1994, the iconic free trade agreement that ended trade restrictions between the US, Canada and Mexico. It was a bonanza for US companies. They finally found a way to escape remaining New Deal regulations and union wages by shifting factories to Mexico, where they could employ sweatshop workers and escape both regulatory authority and taxation.

Clinton would link NAFTA to a broader embrace of the emerging corporate global order, with trade rules fashioned by corporate lawyers and lobbyists in the World Trade Organization (the WTO) and the International Monetary Fund (the IMF). The Democrats under Clinton opened the door to outsourcing to China and to a new global regime of unrivalled corporate power and profits. The WTO and IMF allowed corporations to treat wage and environmental legislation, desperately needed by the global labor force of largely young and female sweatshop workers, as barriers to free trade. US consumers gained some cheaper prices from cars and clothing made in Mexico or China, but US workers paid the price, with millions of manufacturing jobs disappearing in the US as corporations used their new exit power to profit from cheap labor. Likewise, the WTO, IMF and World Bank all created a bonanza for Wall Street and US finance, which could invest in foreign jobs and reap the new high profits of global sweatshops and polluting factories without fear of regulation or taxation.

In effect, the 1980s Reagan Revolution was strengthened by a "Clinton Revolution" transforming the Democratic Party from the New Deal, a party of the working class and PMC liberals, into a corporate Democratic Party of corporate elites linked with minorities and PMC professional and social service employees. The new Democratic Establishment Party was commanded by sectors of Wall Street, global corporations and elite centrist policy wonks, most of them rich Democratic Party donors who framed the new corporate globalization order and benefited from it.

There were resistors in the Clinton Administration, such as Labor Secretary Robert Reich, who warned that NAFTA and broader corporate globalization were a massive assault on the US working class, turning it into an "anxious class." Reich had allies, but corporate elites won the intra-PMC liberal-party struggle. Top Clinton advisors like Rahm Emmanuel and Robert Rubin, a Wall Street tycoon who was Clinton's Secretary of the Treasury, gained a decisive victory over Democrats still wedded to the New Deal and Left-leaning populism.

Clinton's anti-populist shift helped fuel the mass movement of workers away from the Democratic Party, which they increasingly and correctly saw as another voice of the corporate Establishment, essentially the "Bush-lite" Establishment rather than the Bush Establishment of George W. Bush, who succeeded Clinton. The mass migration of the working class toward the Republicans accelerated, since both parties had abandoned a working-class populism. But Republicans offered the racial, religious and other "culture war" alternatives that gave workers who were economically diminished a cultural and social status connected to white Christian nationalism that had begun to show up in Nixon's "silent majority" politics and much more strongly in the Reagan revolution. The GOP, thanks to Democratic Party capitulation to global corporate wealth and donors, now became the new party of the working class, based not on class or economic interests but on identity and culture wars.

Obama sustained the Democratic Party's shift toward an Establishment party. He massively bailed out the big corporations and finance capitalists for the 2008 crisis they created by unfettered speculation in the housing market, leading to a housing and broader economic collapse. The year 2008 was the greatest economic crisis since the Great Depression. While it happened under Bush, Obama followed in Clinton's footsteps, saving and enriching the financial class that had caused the crisis.

> *PBS' Frontline program on Tuesday night broadcast a new one-hour report on one of the greatest and most shameful failings of the Obama administration: the lack of even a single arrest or prosecution of any senior Wall Street banker for the systemic fraud that precipitated the 2008 financial crisis: a crisis from which millions of people around the world are still suffering. What this program particularly demonstrated was that the Obama justice department, in particular the Chief of its Criminal Division, Lanny Breuer, never even tried to hold the high-level criminals accountable.*
>
> *What Obama justice officials did instead is exactly what they did in the face of high-level Bush era crimes of torture and warrantless eavesdropping: namely, acted to protect the most powerful factions in the society in the face of overwhelming evidence of serious criminality. Indeed, financial elites were not only vested with immunity for their fraud, but thrived as a result of it, even as ordinary Americans continue to suffer the effects of that crisis.[2]*

The story gets worse:

> *Worst of all, Obama justice officials both shielded and feted these Wall Street oligarchs (who, just by the way, overwhelmingly supported Obama's 2008 presidential campaign) as they simultaneously prosecuted and imprisoned powerless Americans for far more trivial transgressions. As Harvard law professor Larry Lessig put it two weeks ago when expressing anger over the DOJ's persecution of Aaron Swartz: "we live in a world where the architects of the financial crisis regularly dine at the White House." (Indeed, as "The Untouchables" put it: while no senior Wall Street executives have been prosecuted, "many small mortgage brokers, loan appraisers and even home buyers" have been).[3]*

The problem was not just Obama's bailing out the banks; it was his embrace of the larger corporate order. In Obama's two terms as president, Big Tech was consolidating corporate monopolies in a small number of trillion-dollar firms, the biggest corporations in history. But Obama never prosecuted a vigorous anti-trust policy that would have limited the enormous power of monopolies, including the "magnificent seven"-the biggest of the big Tech firms. Such a policy was essential to break down the huge political power that the biggest companies and banks were consolidating over both political parties and over America itself.

While Obama did create "Obamacare," his only major policy embodying positive populist, labor-friendly Democratic policy, Obamacare actually was a national version of the Republican Mitt Romney Massachusetts health plan and torpedoed the public option or universal health care that would have represented a true break from neoliberalism. The Democratic Party joined the Bush-lite corporate Establishment created by Clinton. By embracing the "forever" wars of the age of terrorism, Obama added a stronger Democratic Party militarism, which also served US corporate interests, particularly in securing Middle Eastern oil and creating booming politics for Exxon and Chevron. Moreover, Obama helped fuel the shift from class to identity politics that has now turned the Democratic Party into a moderate liberal Establishment machine. This has led millions of hard-pressed workers to feel that liberalism, the Democrats and Left populist movements were their enemy.

The basic turn in fortunes for workers in the Obama years makes clear just whose economic camp Obama was in:

> *the Obama era was defined by one of the largest drops in workers' share of corporate income in the modern history of the United States, according to a new report from the Economic Policy Institute:*[4]

The base of the Democratic Party began to decisively shift from the white working class to minorities and anti-racist and feminist forces, concentrated among people of color and women, as well as educated PMC elites. By 2016, at the end of Obama's second term, the Democratic Party had largely abandoned economic populism, shifting decisively from class politics to identity politics. And working-class voters knew it – and showed their disgust and anger with their vote:

> *That decline was punctuated by huge Democratic electoral losses – which strongly suggests not coincidence but causation. It suggests that the Obama-led Democratic Party kicking the working class in the face while enriching finance billionaires prompted a political backlash that ended up (misguidedly) benefiting the GOP.*
>
> *But, of course, facts like that are now supposed to just disappear – they can't be discussed, they can't be mentioned, and they absolutely cannot be thrown back in his face in an interview. It's an omerta of sorts – inconvenient facts that challenge and humiliate the Democratic Party corporatism that led to the Trump backlash cannot be mentioned.*[5]

Democratic Party populism seemed dead. The Democrats had become a second Establishment party of militarized capitalism.

Hillary Clinton and Kamala Harris continued this anti-populist, pro-Establishment trend in the Democratic Party. Joe Biden won in 2020 by running as "Joe from Scranton," a reference to his working-class roots in the most important Blue Wall industrial state of Pennsylvania. Biden did begin to challenge corporate neoliberalism with his major public investment in infrastructure and climate and his walking the picket line with striking auto workers. But he was not successful in defining himself as a break with the Clinton-Obama Establishment and was not able to overcome the Covid-linked spike in inflation, which hit the working class especially hard. Moreover, since Biden did not forcefully and openly reject the Clinton-Obama capitulation to Democratic corporate donors and elites, he did not fundamentally change the way that working people saw the Democratic Party, as became obvious when Harris succeeded him as the 2024 candidate. She ran her campaign, as I spell out shortly, as a champion of the anti-populist Democratic Party Establishment, a rhetorical friend of unions but a pillar of militarized capitalism.

The end result is that Trump, who was aggressively embracing Far-Right GOP populism, attacking both globalization and militarism, was the self-proclaimed working class's new friend. The working class accelerated its multi-decade migration from the Democratic Party into Trump's awaiting Far-Right populist welcome and embrace. Contrary to popular wisdom, this flight of the working class, not only by white workers but also many brown and some mainly male Black workers, was not entirely against their own self-interest. It was against their economic interests, but the Democratic Party had already largely abandoned working-class economic interests as central to their agenda. So there was a form of rationality among white workers to pay attention to the main issues now in play, the cultural issues surrounding race, gender and nationality that had become central to both parties.

How the Democrats Opened the Door to Trump's Far-Right Populism

In 2016 and 2024 elections, the Democrats' agendas reflected the turn of the Democratic Party into the party of the Establishment, allowing Trump and the MAGA GOP to assume the mantle of the People's Party of change. We start briefly with Hillary Clinton in 2016 and then turn to 2020, where Joe Biden embraced a touch of working-class populism and just barely beat Trump in 2020. But we focus mostly on the Harris campaign of 2024 and how it represented a Democratic Party embrace of the corporate regime and war establishment. It opened all the populist space available to Donald Trump, who finally won a Far-Right populist majority.

In 2024, the Democrats embraced the militarized corporate state, abandoned class politics and embraced a siloed identity politics, alienating and splintering the working class while cozying up to Far-Right anti-Trumpists like the Cheneys. Kamala Harris set out to prove that the Democrats were now the real defenders of the anti-Trumpist Establishment of the old corporate Republican guard. In the name of saving the nation from Trump and fascism, the Democrats turned it over to him and played a disastrous role in helping Trump take authoritarian control of the country, empowering the very corporate oligarchic Establishment that the Democrats claimed to be defending against authoritarianism.

Hillary Debuts and Joe Takes a Detour

In this brief section, I show that Hillary Clinton lost to Trump by turning over key Blue Wall states of blue-collar workers, such as Michigan and Pennsylvania, to Trump. Bernie Sanders ran in the Democratic Party as a Left-leaning positive populist. He defeated Hillary in states like Michigan, winning the working-class vote. Hillary became infamous in her 2016 race against Trump when she called workers part of a "basket of deplorables," a clear sign of her rejection of class politics and embrace of corporate rule. The comment became a meme that Trump exploited mercilessly:

> *His campaign turned that insult into an asset; supporters wore hats and shirts proudly declaring themselves deplorable. Pundits seized on the phrase, debating who does and doesn't deserve to be called that. Five years later, many believe "deplorables" – figuratively and literally – are here to stay.*[6]

Trump was able to win a surprise victory over Hillary precisely because he could take enough working-class voters, including those who had voted for Obama, to the MAGA cause. He was promising to stop the movement of auto plants to Mexico and protect workers from global corporations, rewarding only companies keeping jobs at home. Workers in the intensifying hard times of neoliberal globalization only saw Democrats as offering more protection to immigrants and minorities while anointing the first female president. This would not win over workers of either gender focused on how to keep their jobs and pay their bills.

In 2020, Joe Biden was the first Democratic candidate since Reagan to reject Reagan's "free market" neoliberal embrace of the global corporations. As Scranton Joe, he offered a pro-labor stance and delivered the most progressive economic policies since LBJ and FDR. This embrace of a new reformist class politics allowed Biden to draw back just enough workers to win his narrow majority over Trump in 2020.

But despite his genuine shift toward a pro-labor politics with elements that could be supported by Left populists like Bernie Sanders, Biden remained a largely Establishment candidate, never increasing the minimum wage, intensely supporting US militarism and wars, and failing to build an alliance with Left populist social movements like the Green New Deal and the youthful anti-war movement against the war in Gaza. Trump again stepped into the populist fertile space bred by the multiple economic, environmental and public health crises and began to recapture a working class increasingly beset by economic hard times, including persistent job insecurity and unaffordable high prices on everything from groceries to homes. Moreover, Biden never challenged the divisive and siloed identity politics that had become the dominant agenda of the Democratic Party since Reagan. This allowed Trump's Far-Right populism – expressed in policies from tariffs to Evangelicalism and white Christian Nationalism – to bring the working class more fully back into the MAGA fold.

Harris Embraces the Establishment and Helps Trump Win – The Bitter Fruit of Abandoning Left Populism

The 2024 campaign reelecting Trump brought together the many ways in which the Democratic Party abandoned Left-leaning populism and helped Trump win reelection. In a period of hard times, Kamala Harris became the Establishment candidate, not only allowing Trump to run as the "change" leader who would shake up the system but also attacking him for doing so.

In the name of saving democracy and preventing fascism, Harris ran as the candidate who would save US capitalism and its global "Pax Americana." To do so, she would build an Establishment coalition ranging from corporate hawkish Republicans like Liz Cheney and Dick Cheney to the leaders of mainstream corporate and liberal Democrats like the Clintons and Barack Obama. In the name of preventing Trumpist fascism, she aligned with authoritarian elements of the old Republican Guard and embraced the hierarchy of the US corporate regime, repeatedly calling herself a "proud capitalist." In the process, she rejected class politics for identity politics. She failed to champion a new Left populist coalition with poor people, anti-war students and climate activists who stayed home or voted for a third party or even for Trump himself.

Three factors stand out in this betrayal of Left-leaning populist movements and coalitions that could have sparked a Democratic victory. One was her view that defeating Trumpist fascism meant embracing the most authoritarian and militarized elements of the Establishment that New Deal Democrats in much of the 20th century had fought with Left-leaning social movements to democratize. As Trump was sounding notes of non-intervention and anti-war, and fiercely attacking "wasteful" US wars and the US national security Establishment, Harris was relentless in supporting US militarism in the Middle East and Ukraine and spurning the campus anti-war movement among young people. As one outraged anti-war critic put it during the campaign, Harris refused to let protesters speak and offered no change from Biden's endless arming of Israel, even as Gaza was being flattened with bombs dropped on refugee camps, hospitals, schools and UN aid centers. As one anti-war activist charged:

> *It's the continued and unprecedented support through consistent weapons supplies to the Israeli military as it carries out a horrific genocide against the Palestinian people in Gaza, where somewhere*

between 40,000 and perhaps up to 200,000 people, according to some estimates, have already been killed, 80% of the structures in Gaza have been damaged or destroyed, and nearly 2 million people are homeless, displaced and living under dire humanitarian conditions due to a tightening siege. That's the policy that Vice President Harris is committing to continue. And I think that that's, of course, outrageous.[7]

Her refusal to critique US war aid and militarism was exacerbated by her unequivocal defense of the national security establishment. She attacked Trump repeatedly for his assault on the CIA, the FBI and the Pentagon, becoming the arch-defender of the military-industrial complex and global corporate interests, which were the classic prime targets of the Left-leaning populist coalition for decades. Her touted alliance with the Cheneys, which became the leading symbol of her new bipartisan Establishment politics, symbolized the betrayal of the Left-leaning positive populist movements of Gen Z peace and climate activists who joined the disillusioned "uncommitted" and stayed home or voted third party. Her essential message to them was "how dare you challenge the CIA or the Pentagon, let alone challenge US wars and military dominance around the world?" Harris would have done well to listen to Tom Frank, author of *What's the Matter with Kansas*:

"The status quo defends itself in conservative terms, but hits the jackpot when liberals come to its aid.[8]

Harris needed to listen to this Thomas Frank reminder as well:

The problem for liberalism is not that it has been too radical; it is that it has not been radical enough.[9]

Harris' candidacy reversed Biden's shift away from Reagan's neoliberalism toward a Democratic claim to be part of the very Establishment that Trump was challenging – whether the US military or Wall Street. In the process, she was betraying the many progressive labor unions and the AFL-CIO federation that supported her. She did not call for a major attack on the billionaire class and corporate America; she left that to Trump, who was denouncing global companies for outsourcing American jobs. She never called for higher minimum wages, major taxes that would reduce skyrocketing inequality or massive anti-poverty programs. Her call for an "opportunity economy" that would help small businesses and entrepreneurs fell flat among workers angry at working hard for less, who needed a higher minimum wage and whose hard times not only included more insecure, low-paying jobs but also unaffordable groceries, rents and housing.

This all culminated as her campaign was wrapping up. Her final message was "I am a capitalist." Her campaign seized on it to secure the support of corporate leaders:

> *Kamala Harris has a message for the business world and traditional Republicans.....: that she is a 'capitalist.'"*
>
> *It's a case Harris has been building since September.... She underlined the point Tuesday...when she said in remarks her campaign immediately blasted out to reporters "I am a capitalist. I am a pragmatic capitalist."*[10]

Harris was courting the capitalist class and Republican anti-Trump allies, relying on her billionaire surrogate, Mark Cuban, to close the deal:

> *It's a message aimed at countering Donald Trump, who often portrays Harris as a socialist or communist. And Harris is tapping figures like Mark Cuban to represent her in recent days instead of others like Elizabeth Warren (who is focused on her reelection bid in Massachusetts).*
>
> *Cuban himself offered an even more colorful version of the message* in a Tuesday afternoon Yahoo Finance appearance, *saying "Kamala Harris is a hardcore capitalist" as part of his overall case that she's the better candidate for business.*[11]

All of this implicitly left Harris and the Democratic Party as the party of identity politics, both entirely compatible with the corporate Establishment and divisive of the unity across race, gender and ethnicity in the working class essential to "change the system." Harris did not constantly call explicit attention to her identity as a Black Asian-American woman. But in the absence of any class politics, it was, in fact, her identity that largely defined her campaign, fitting squarely into the "DEI" (diversity, equality, inclusion) motto that had come to define the Democratic Party since the end of the New Deal era.

The racial and gender politics of the Democratic Party could have become part of a more universalized politics had it clearly advanced a Left-populist challenge to the militarized capitalist Establishment. Instead, its silo identity politics of DEI aligned with that Establishment, pitting different elements of the working class against each other and competing for the largest sectors of the corporate pie that each minority could grab. Harris would symbolize that the real aim now was to crash the glass ceiling, not destroy the edifice or the rush of everyone to try to get into the executive suite.

DEI, the new Democratic Party credo, was embraced by "woke" corporations, who became a fitting target of Trump's Far-Right populist rhetoric. A Democratic Party based on the mainstream liberal DEI was not only aligning with corporations broadly but also assaulting white workers as "privileged," essentially enemies of the people. DEI and its language of "white privilege" was a daily assault on white workers under great economic stress and feeling anything but privileged. They may still have a diminishing form of racial privilege, but for the Democrats to accuse them constantly of privilege while offering very little populist change to defend against their subjugation to corporate elites was political suicide. Workers struggling every day to make ends meet are hardly a privileged class.

DEI not only antagonized white workers but also began to alienate Hispanics and some Black working people. As a siloed identity politics, DEI actually weakens the political power of working-class people of color. It pits identity groups against each other rather than uniting them across racial lines to challenge the corporate Establishment. In 2024, Trump picked up significant numbers of Hispanic voters and a smaller number of Black male voters, who were recognizing that DEI was dividing and weakening them rather than empowering them. This began to lead more people who cared deeply about racism to question and reject DEI as either an ideology or strategy that would help to overcome racism.

Nothing could more completely empower Trump and his populism. He could persuasively argue that the Democrats had effectively turned themselves against the majority of the working class by not only writing them off as bearers of white privilege but also abandoning the entire working class as Harris embraced her position as a "proud capitalist" and abandoned class politics.

This not only drove white workers in droves to continue their long flight from the Democratic Party of DEI to Republican populism but also, as noted above, alienated many working-class non-white voters. Harris not only lost white workers but also Black and Hispanic voters, many in traditional urban Democratic base areas. The Democratic base – spanning workers of all races – needed a full-scale attack on the corporate Establishment more than any other group. They were not fooled by the fact that many in the base shared Harris' racial identity. They knew that corporate DEI – and Democratic Party DEI – were not going to win them secure jobs or affordable groceries and homes in a neoliberal capitalism driving all the wealth created by American workers toward the executives in the corporate suite.

The Capitulation of the Left to Its Own Negative Populism

Left-leaning movements in the early 2020s revived some of their finest positive populist moments in decades. These include the revival of an activist and progressive labor movement that carried out more strikes and organizing than in any period since the New Deal era. These included the rise of militant movements in the biggest auto, steel and other manufacturing centers, Left-leaning unions rising in teaching and health care, and fierce organizing among millions of career civil servants and low-wage service workers in government.

There was major new organizing in Amazon warehouses, Starbucks cafes, opulent hotels, and other 21st-century service center entertainment and leisure industries. All of this was carried out by innovative, fiery labor leaders like Sean Fain, who went beyond collective bargaining to challenge corporate power and US wars, a true breakthrough from the labor movement of the Cold War that always fell in line in the end with corporate America and the Pax Americana.

Fain led the UAW into mass organizing not only in auto plants but also in universities, organizing not only groundskeepers and mechanics but also graduate students and adjunct faculty who could be fired as easily as Amazon workers or auto workers on the line. This connected the new labor movement with a new generation of student activists, rising most strongly against US militarism, especially the war in Gaza, but also engaged with climate action and broader human rights and social justice. The rise of labor aligned with a new Gen Z activist generation sparked hopes for a new Left positive populism to take on Trump's Far-Right populism, a hope we discuss further in the last chapter.

Harris failed to align herself with this new Left populist movement, rebuffing particularly the anti-war movements that desperately sought Democratic Party support. Her explicit rejection of demands to withhold arms from humanitarian catastrophe in Gaza was a drastic symbol of the Democratic Party's embrace of the Establishment – and it was aptly seen as such by the mass of uncommitted Democratic voters that stayed home or voted for Jill Stein in 2024.

But the movements themselves contributed to their own defeat in 2024 by following an oft-repeated capitulation to elements of negative populism in their own ranks. These include embrace of dogma and cancel culture while promoting their own kind of identity politics. This involved subtle discrediting by educated or professional progressives of working-class non-college voters and establishing their own status on the basis of higher degrees, the hierarchy of educational credentialism, and repudiation of comrades or those outside the movement who were not as radical or "woke" as they were.

Trumpism Far-Right politics was able to capitalize so successfully on its "anti-woke" populist crusade because, in fact, many Left activists, as in earlier history, saw themselves as "politically correct" and zealously attacked ordinary Americans for their language and "privilege." The language issue became symbolically important, as many Left zealots made people fear using the wrong pronoun. Some Americans began to feel terrorized that they would be punished or humiliated for selecting incorrect words or phrases to refer to racial minorities, women or other marginalized communities. The unrelenting attack on how to speak "properly" – or be subjected to cancel culture – was a suicidal form of negative Left activism and populism. It made every-day Americans feel they were being watched and persecuted not by the Right but by the PC Left, who were surveilling how they talked and the pronouns they used.

While cancel culture and PC were most intense in the identity movements organized around race and gender, they spread into class movements, which targeted hard-pressed white workers as "white privileged." They thereby blamed the very working class they were seeking to organize. This kind of PC dogma is a form of verbal violence that is experienced as real violence and can lead to physical assaults on all sides. It not only led to more flight of white workers to Trump's far-right populism but also the scary migration of significant number of Hispanic voters and a smaller percentage of Black male voters toward Trumpism.

None of this had to happen. I show in the last chapter that hope remains for a universalizing resistance of class politics and rise of Left positive populism from new labor, climate, youth and peace movements.

But this will require self-reflection among the movements of their own potential to repeatedly slide into negative populism. It will require sustained resistance in Left populist movements to siloed identity politics, politically correct dogma, cancel culture and "woke" zealotry that only empowers Far-Right white identity politics and Trumpist Far-Right populism. It will require recognition that real gains against racism and sexism will come less from DEI than from a universalizing, intersectional resistance in which workers across race, gender and religion unite for economic well-being and social justice for the entire working class and all Americans.

Notes

1 Bill Clinton, "Remarks to the Democratic Leadership National Conversation," June 4, 1998, presidency.ucsb.edu
2 Glenn Greenwald, "The Untouchables: How the Obama administration protected Wall Street from prosecutions," *The Guardian*, Jan. 23, 2013, thegarudian.com
3 Glenn Greenwald, "The Untouchables: How the Obama administration protected Wall Street from prosecutions," *The Guardian*, Jan. 23, 2013, thegarudian.com
4 David Sirota, "Obama was always in Wall Street's Corner," Jacobin, June 2, 2021, jacobin.com
5 David Sirota, "Obama was always in Wall Street's Corner," Jacobin, June 2, 2021, jacobin.com
6 Roxanne Roberts, "Hillary Clinton's 'deplorables' speech shocked voters five years ago, but some feel it was prescient," *Washington Post*, April 31, 2021, washingtonpos.com
7 "No policy change: In CNN Interview Harris refuses to condemn US military support for Israel," Aug. 30, 2024, democraynow.org
8 "30 best Thomas Frank Quotes with image," bookey.app
9 "30 best Thomas Frank Quotes with image," bookey.app
10 Ben Werschkul, "A key piece of Kamala Harris's closing message: I am a capitalist," Yahoofinane, Oct. 23, 2024, finance.yahoo.com
11 Ben Werschkul, "A key piece of Kamala Harris's closing message: I am a capitalist," Yahoofinane, Oct. 23, 2024, finance.yahoo.com

6 Lessons from Europe and the Global South
From Fascism to Social Democracy

Europe Offers Crucial Lessons about Collapse into Far-Right Populism – and Building Democracy

Europe has too many lessons about Far-Right populism to ignore. Despite important differences, today's parallels with 1930s European Far-Right populism – when Mussolini, Hitler and Franco all took major European nations into nightmarish fascist regimes – are striking. Their reconstruction after World War II into prosperous and social democracies also carries crucially important lessons.

The current shift toward a new era of Far-Right populism throughout Europe sends alarm bells and new lessons we must learn. The rise of Far-Right parties across Europe is a major development. Its scale and scope are vast and deep, as they take power in some nations and are rapidly gaining public support across almost all of the EU:

The longstanding effort to keep extremist forces out of government in Europe is officially over.

For decades, political parties of all kinds joined forces to keep the hard-right far from the levers of power. Today, this strategy – known in France as a cordon sanitaire (or firewall) – is falling apart, as populist and nationalist parties grow in strength across the Continent.

Six EU countries – Italy, Finland, Slovakia, Hungary, Croatia and the Czech Republic – have hard-right parties in government. In Sweden, the survival of the executive relies on a confidence and supply agreement with the nationalist Sweden Democrats, the second-largest force in parliament. In the Netherlands, the anti-Islamic firebrand Geert Wilders is on the verge of power, having sealed a historic deal to form the most right-wing government in recent Dutch history.

Meanwhile, hard-right parties are dominating the polls across much of Europe. In France, far-right leader Marine Le Pen's National Rally is cruising at over 30 percent, far ahead of President Emmanuel Macron's Renaissance party, according to POLITICO's Poll of Polls. Across

DOI: 10.4324/9781003662570-7

the Rhine, Alternative for Germany, a party under police surveillance for its extremist views, is polling second, head-to-head with the Social Democrats.[1]

The rising Far-Right populist parties in Europe are similar to MAGA Trumpism in rhetoric and style, and appeal to similar sectors of a rural, white, working-class base. Far-Right European parties and populists are increasingly aligned with Trump and US Far-Right populism in a global movement. The conditions fueling US populism arise out of an integrated, globalized capitalism, with interdependence driving nations into similar forms of economic, environmental, cultural and political peril.

This hints at the folly of focusing only on the US. Its relative decline is destabilizing the world, helping create major economic and political stresses leading to populist global reactions both on the Far Right and on the besieged Left around the world. Indeed, Far-Right populism has surged not only in the US and Europe but also in developing nations around the world. At the end of this chapter, I briefly consider lessons from Far-Right populism in the Global South, including examples in Latin America such as Brazil, as well as the Arab Spring populist rebellions in Egypt and Morocco.

I begin by reviewing the deep economic and political crises that gave rise to Far-Right European populism and fascism. I then show how Europe reconstructed itself after World War II by rejecting the old European corporate war parties with strong social democratic labor and Leftist populist movements. They built new social democracies and welfare states, rejecting the old Establishments of imperial European capitalism and 1930s fascism. They rejected militarized capitalism through Left populist alliances of parties and movements. But central bank neoliberalism, war in Ukraine and millions of immigrants coming to Europe have today helped refuel European Far-Right populism. Europeans need to unite new coalitions of labor and Left-leaning positive populist parties to rebuild their economies and save social democracy.

How Far-Right Populist Fascism Took over 1930s Europe

1930s European fascism, most importantly in Hitler's Germany, was caused by the punitive conditions placed on the Germans by the allies after World War I. The German economic collapse was created both by sanctions placed on the defeated Germany and the global economic depression. The global crash was created most importantly by unfettered US corporations and Wall Street speculation, debt and the market crash in 1929. This is only one of several ways in which the US contributed to the rise of European fascism.

Before World War I, Europe built relatively stable imperial corporate regimes that the US helped finance after the war to continue policing the world. But the victorious British and French Allies' sanctions on Germany, imposed partly to allow Britain to pay back huge loans from Morgan financial companies to the UK, drove Germany into an economic crisis marked by hyperinflation, followed by higher unemployment. The Great Depression in the US after the 1929 market collapse intensified the German depression and spread economic crisis throughout much of the world. The German economic crisis was far deeper than current economic problems in the US, creating catastrophic hard times that were extremely fertile grounds for Far-Right populism.

Ruling socialist and Communist parties, notably in Germany, failed to champion any progressive or populist Left positive response. They bitterly fought each other and failed to form a coalition between socialists, Communists, and social democratic parties to stop Hitler and fascism. Their exhaustion and failure opened the door to Hitler's rise and his finally winning a plurality in the 1932 parliamentary elections.

Before he joined and helped build the Nazi Party, Hitler tried to seize power in a 1923 coup in Bavaria and was jailed. He wrote the Far-Right populist manifesto, *Mein Kampf*, in prison. When he was released, he took a new tack, seeking a fascist revolution by building a parliamentary party in German electoral politics. His Far-Right rise reflected the power of aligning Far-Right populist militias and movements with a conservative political party, something that Trump successfully reproduced in his own rise to power. Trump took over the Republican Party and aligned it with Christian nationalist and armed militias while coming into power with the constitutional aura of legitimate elections.

When selected as Chancellor, Hitler used emergency powers, including the infamous 1933 Enabling Act. This allowed him to enact laws without the Reichstag's involvement, moving to destroy free media, rival parties and other democratic institutions in a few months.

Many educated Germans had dismissed Hitler as a charismatic showman who could be easily controlled by traditional conservative aristocratic and military elites as well as big companies. But as the German public and traditional conservative elites normalized Hitler's extreme rhetoric, they became more vulnerable to deeper authoritarian measures by Hitler. Hitler moved within a few months to shift parliamentary legislative power to himself as an all-powerful leader combining executive and legislative and judicial functions. He shut down Parliament when it was set on fire weeks after he became Chancellor. He began to deport thousands of Jews, gypsies, gays, handicapped people and urban "Marxists." He issued hundreds of executive orders dismantling the democratic institutions of the Weimar Republic, using frequent radio propaganda broadcasts (the "Truth Social" tweets of his day) as a way of reaching into German families and offering reassuring lies and deceptions. As one scholar wrote of Hitler:

> He lied until he got what he wanted. Unable to figure out what to do with him....(elites and the public) pretended this was acceptable. They not only underestimated him, but critically, they normalized him.[2]

We couldn't have a clearer lesson about the implications of normalizing Trump's rhetoric and accepting rule by a mainstream party tightly aligned with Far-Right populism and governing in the name of racial and religious nationalism. In the first few weeks of his second term, Trump issued hundreds of executive orders attacking voting rights, destroying separation of powers, pausing and defunding thousands of Congressionally passed spending laws, attacking and deporting immigrants, militarizing the police and domestic order, assaulting the media and journalists and comedians like Jimmy Kimmel, abolishing multiple federal agencies, firing, prosecuting, detaining and killing racial and Marxist "enemies within," and flooding the public with threats and lies. It all evokes Hitler's terrifyingly rapid destruction of German democracy.

How Europeans Built Social Democracy with Left Positive Populist Parties and Movements after World War II

Reconstructing Europe was essential after the total devastation of two European wars. Instead of going back to earlier imperial and corporate systems, European nations remade themselves in the spirit of Left positive populism. This was partly driven by limits placed on the old imperial, militarized order by the US and new anti-colonial global movements. They helped construct new democratic constitutional guidelines, which imposed strict limits on new Geman and Italian military forces and budgets. The new order spread through most of Europe, with the US taking dominion over European military affairs with the development of NATO.

The nations of Europe bonded together in the EU to build a new European order, a democratic federation seeking bonds that would eliminate wars among them. This required the leadership of a new German and broader European post-war generation, with the visceral memories of horror of the wars and genocidal violence that came from fascist and other Far-Right parties and regimes. Because memories of horror were so fresh, German youth had to take a deep dive into the dangers of authoritarianism and imperial or colonial capitalism. The power of their memories of economic hard times and fascism created by their parents and grandparents helped make possible new social labor and social democratic populist parties and movements that would take root, stabilize and flourish for more than 50 years.

The two central populist forces in reconstruction were labor unions and labor parties. They built coalitions with each other, with social democratic parties, and with Christian Democratic and more centrist Establishment parties and movements.

Germany was forced to place limits on post-war military spending of 1% of its budget, which helped transform its foreign policy toward a disarmed global human rights order. Imperial Europe increasingly rejected militarism, colonialism and war. It sought security from US-led NATO but was deeply critical of much of the US Cold War and the American war on terror.

The 1948 German codetermination law after World War II, which required all German companies with over 500 employees to elect 50% of their governing boards from workers in the company, helped create a more labor-friendly stakeholder economic order. Germany also required elected works councils mandating worker participation and joint management in corporate departments, a form of worker populism within the company.

All these labor and social democratic measures gained more power in concert with the growth and power of large unions and governing labor parties in national parliaments. They translated not only into more democratic companies but also into the embrace of universal human rights and a universal welfare system in most European countries. They enacted universal health care, affordable child care, elder care and housing, free higher education and many other social safety benefits. In Denmark, Sweden and other Nordic countries, this moved the system far toward a democratic socialism, often seen as an ideal by American self-identified labor populists like Bernie Sanders. In Germany and France, the populist forces also embraced universal welfare and rights, along with labor-friendly stakeholder capitalism.

The Second Coming of European Far-Right Populism

The social democracy of Europe created a stable and internally peaceful order within Europe itself from the mid-20th century to the first decade of the 21st century. But a series of new developments, many reflecting forces still embedded in European nations before the World Wars, created new destabilization.

These were intensified by new military tensions related to the war on terror and the expansion of Russia, as well as to decline of US global hegemony and the rise of Trumpism and Far-Right populism in the US. And mass immigration of different racial and ethnic groups into the European countries themselves, reflecting economic and social crises in the Middle East, North Africa and former colonies across the Global South, massively fueled new crises and populist anger. All these created an explosive new era of hybrid and intense economic and social hard times, breeding a potent new wave of Far-Right populist parties in France, Germany, Italy, Poland, Hungary and Sweden. It threatens a new era of European fascism, aligned with Trumpist Far-Right populism in the US.

As in America, the roots of new European Far-Right populism are deeply embedded in European history and culture. These include the power of a pre-World War I authoritarian culture and early state European capitalism that left working people without a strong economic or political voice. In most of Europe, corporate power was regulated but never disappeared in the postwar social democracies. Since the Reagan era, neoliberal austerity and "free market" policies, especially in German financial firms at the center of the EU, have taken command again. They have brought a new wave of economic crises to the European continent, hitting especially hard Southern and Eastern

European countries that do not have their own currencies to inflate their money supply. But the economic decline in Europe is serious across most of Europe, with Northern and Central European countries like Germany and the UK suffering their own very serious economic problems:

> *In both countries, voters are upset about years of stagnant growth, declining public services, rising immigration and a generalized sense that their children will be worse off than they are.*
>
> *Germany, Europe's largest economy and one-time economic engine, has not grown in five years. Its flagship carmakers, long the pride of the country's manufacturing base, are struggling to compete with Chinese rivals (and Tesla). In Britain, a decade of austerity has left the national health service, the closest thing to a national religion, reeling, and schools literally crumbling.*[3]

These divisive economic forces are feeding grounds for populism and nationalism, as countries struggle with their own economic problems and currency constraints. Most importantly, the mainstream European parties are not offering solutions.

> *Europe's political story has become one of decline: public services under pressure, crumbling infrastructure and industries struggling to compete with more dynamic foreign companies. Governments that claim to work for ordinary people often fail to deliver.*
>
> *Mainstream parties have struggled to offer big ideas in response to these big problems. Instead, voters often feel like transformative changes are off the table, and elected governments are not responsive to their needs and frustrations.*[4]

The failure of Establishment parties to respond to a deepening crisis eerily evokes the memories of the failures of major parties in the early 1930s to offer solutions that might have prevented the rise of Hitler and other fascists. As in the 1930s, economic crises are increasingly intertwined today with broader military, political and demographic crises that are feeding the new wave of neo-fascist and Far-Right parties now rising in Europe. The crises include the military tensions with Russia, which supercharges militaristic rebuilding in Europe, not only to defend against Russia but also against the rising militarization of other European countries in NATO. Meanwhile, central bank austerity is contributing strongly to the decline of European public investment, along with rising stagnation, poverty and crime. All of this is fertile ground for nationalist movements and parties linked to Far-Right populists.

European Central Bank neoliberal policies – pushing Europe toward credit crunches, high interest rates and severe declines in investment, job creation and growth – are a major factor. Starting in the late 1970s, they intensified during and after the 2008 financial crisis:

> *Macroeconomic policy within the so-called advanced economies has, for more than four decades, been dominated by "central bankism" and its ideological cousins, monetarism, ordo-liberalism and supply-si-dism. These strands of economic thinking became popular under the umbrella of neo-liberalism in the late 1970s. While they differ in both epistemological terms and in practical policy-making, these strands share a common hostility to Keynesian and other statist theories of political economy, along with a common belief in the greater efficiency of private markets for the allocation of resources within society and economy. Policy-makers within OECD-states have, in varying degrees, remained in thrall to the prejudices of neoliberal thinking, most notably to central bankism. This thraldom is characterised by the primacy of monetary policy-making as the core function of a supposedly slimmed-down state, and the corresponding subordination of fiscal policy to the disciplinary controls placed on public sector borrowing and overall state debt. This subordination has been increasingly codified in legal statutes and, in the current century, in constitutional limitations on the fiscal latitude available to states. Fiscal "consolidation", fiscal "auster-ity" are the watchwords of this incoherent and destructive fashion in political economy.*[5]

European mainstream political parties, including Social Democrats, have capitulated to the autonomy and neoliberal austerity of Central Banks up to this day, helping set the stage for the current political crisis:

> *Debates on these issues since the Great Financial Crash of 2008 and, more recently, in the wake of failed austerity programmes and the Covid-19 pandemic, have not changed the fundamental parameters governing the legitimacy of central bank autonomy. These remain largely unchallenged. What policy communities have been focssing on – adding a fiscal dimension to Eurozone macroeconomic man-agement, allowing the partial mutualisation of state debt, adding a green dimension to the ECB's mandate, analysing the relevance of (Germany's) legal rulings on Eurozone reforms – is arguably mere displacement activity, akin to re-arranging the deck chairs on the Titanic. It is, in contrast, the very case for central bank inde-pendence that requires radical re-examination. The precipitate ca-pitulation of European political elites to the "Bundesbank myth" demands the close scrutiny of contemporary and future analysts, as does the parallel capitulation of those same elites to the delusions of "neoliberalism".*[6]

European Central Bank austerity, embraced by the governing Establishment parties in Germany, France and the UK, has played a major role in the resurrection of Far-Right populist European parties. As in the early 1930s, the inability of mainstream European conservative and liberal parties to address the economic crisis has opened the door wide to Far-Right populist parties, as in the US today.

The rise of the Far-Right populist threat in Europe has been supercharged by the influx of millions of Middle Eastern, North African and Southwest Asian immigrants. Both because of the breakdown of racial homogeneity and the deepening of crises of jobs and infrastructure that mass immigration creates, immigration has become the political bombshell threatening to explode the whole system of European social democracy and replace the Established social democratic parties with Far-Right populist parties. The amount of social welfare needed – and the need for more housing, schools and the creation of an entire new infrastructure to serve desperate needs of immigrants in crisis – has become an existential threat to all working Europeans as European financial elites push European economies themselves back from social democracy toward neoliberal austerity.

Immigration in Europe, as in the US, sets up a new politics of identity and class, pitting European white workers against the immigrant workers. Had European social democrats remained strong – and built strong labor and Left-leaning populist party and movement coalitions – they might have been able to prevent the neoliberal takeover and provide their workers with rising wages and better working conditions, as well as even stronger universal welfare benefits. But the shift toward financial neoliberal policies and adverse economic and energy conditions, driving up European as well as American prices, made the European working class increasingly vulnerable to job insecurity and poverty. They became attracted to Far-Right populist appeals.

The strength of anti-immigrant Far-Right populist movements hints at the long racial homogeneity helping enable European Left positive populism and helping explain the difficulties that Left populist politics faces in racially heterogeneous nations such as the US. Even with strong working-class politics, massive immigration poses a constant threat of fascism. It reflects the visceral power of racial division and the centuries-long division of races by slavery, colonialism and segregation, which make racial unity and universal civil rights an eternal struggle. In Europe, these forces coincided with an elite turn toward neoliberalism, especially in the financial centers of Germany and France, creating more desperate economic conditions for ordinary European workers despite their social safety net protections.

The role of neoliberalism and immigration in fueling Far-Right populism in Europe will ring a bell to Americans. The same forces of neoliberal economic policies and mass immigration laid the groundwork for the rise of Trumpist Far-Right populism in the US. Indeed, the rise of Far-Right populism in Europe is linked in several important ways to the rise of Trump in the US, whose reelection in 2024 coincided with and spurred growth of Far-Right power in Europe.

The connections between US and European Far-Right populist parties were in plain view. Trump cultivated strong ties with European Far-Right leaders such as Viktor Orban, the prime minister of Hungary and head of Fidesz, its authoritarian ruling party. Trump invited Orban to Mar-A-Lago in March 2024, calling him "a great leader, a fantastic leader" in "Europe and around the world". Trump lavished repeated praise on Orban because he modeled and praised Trump's own ability to create fear and obedience in other nations:

> *Let me just tell you about world leaders. Viktor Orbán, one of the most respected men—they call him a strongman. He's a tough person. Smart. Prime minister of Hungary. They said why is the whole world blowing up? Three years ago it wasn't. Why is it blowing up? He said because you need Trump back as president. They were afraid of him. China was afraid … North Korea was afraid of him … Look, Viktor Orbán said it. He said the most respected, most feared person is Donald Trump. We had no problems when Trump was president.*[7]

Orban, known for his racist discourse, was also invited repeatedly to be a featured speaker at national US conventions of Far-Right Trumpist conservative groups such as the Conservative Political Action Committee (CPAC). Orban was cheered for the "culture war" they were waging together across the pond.

Trump wooed other Far-Right European leaders. Trump invited Far-Right leader and Italian populist Prime Minister Giorgia Meloni to Mar-a-Lago on a symbolic day, January 6, 2025. He gushed that she is "a fantastic woman… she's really taken Europe by storm." It was a mutual admiration society, with Meloni, leading the authoritarian "Brothers of Italy" party modeled on Mussolini's fascist party, saying enthusiastically she was "ready to work together" with Trump. She was the one major European leader who came to Trump's inauguration in 2025. She was touted by Politico, Reuters and other media as positioning herself as a key bridge between the European Far Right and Trump. Indeed, Meloni was working at the same time to strengthen her ties to Le Pen's National Rally party in France, hoping to consolidate a Far-Right European dominant power bloc by 2026, when French national elections might propel Le Pen to power.

Meanwhile, after Trump's reelection, his early "shadow president," Elon Musk, plunged deeply into European politics. He called in early 2025 for the triumph of the Far-Right neo-Nazi Party in Germany, the AFD, saying it alone could save Germany.

> *Elon Musk has caused outrage in Berlin after appearing to endorse the far-right, anti-immigrant Alternative für Deutschland.*

Musk, who has been named by Donald Trump to co-lead a commission aimed at reducing the size of the US federal government, wrote on his social media platform X: "Only the AfD can save Germany."

He reposted a video by a German rightwing influencer, Naomi Seibt, who criticised Friedrich Merz, the leader of the conservative Christian Democrats who has the best chance of becoming the next German chancellor, and praised Javier Milei, the libertarian president of Argentina.[8]

JD Vance also endorsed the AFD during his trip to the Munich Security Council in February 2025, just weeks before the German election. Meanwhile, Musk has used his platform, X, to telegraph support not only for the AFD in Germany but also for the Far-Right leader, Georgia Meloni, in Italy and the Far Right in the US. But the influence of Trump and corporate allies on the rise of Far-Right populism in Europe goes beyond personal connections and visits to Mar-a-Lago, though there is no doubt that building friendships with Trump will help empower and shape European Far-Right parties. Trump's economic policies are also threatening, both consciously and inadvertently, to move Europe toward economic hard times and its own nationalistic militarism, helping fuel and shape European Far-Right parties.

Trump's promise in January of 2025 to put a 25% tariff on Canada and Mexico and a 10% tariff on all goods imported to the US from China and soon, 25% on European allies, could reduce demand for European goods. Depending on the uncertain future of US tariffs, Trump's policies could lead toward a severely damaging trade war between the US and Europe, as well as with the rest of the world.

US tariffs hurt European workers and consumers. They could plunge Europe into recession, helping Far-Right parties gain more power. At the same time, US Tech and other corporate leaders, will assail European regulation of tech and other US corporations as illegal and unfair, putting more pressure on German, French and EU leaders to move Europe further back toward an American-style market capitalism. US attacks on European regulation, public spending, and expansive social welfare could gain enough traction with frightened European leaders to create new and more severe neoliberal European trends and crises that will breed more Far-Right populism, as they have in the US.

In addition, Trump's demand that Europeans radically up their contributions to their own defense could foster a new European war system that the Europeans tried to demolish after two suicidal world wars. True, European nations might be able to get a short-term economic bounce from major new military spending. But the longer-term effect, both militarily and economically, is likely to erode funds for European public investment, new civilian infrastructure, and social welfare. Meanwhile, more military funding and a new European Cold War against Russia will feed a culture of violence in Europe as it did in the US during our own Cold War. A nationalist culture of violence is like a dagger in the post-World War II social democratic Europe, and opens the door to more populist violence against its own immigrants. Crime and stabbings are already on the rise in much of Europe and the UK, partly in response to more poverty, which will only help Far-Right populist parties rise to power across Europe.

History shows that Far-Right populism tends to rise as a global wave, reflecting global economic crises and political alliances across different nations. In the early 1930s, Far-Right populism and fascism spread together across Germany, France and Spain, as well as triggering "America First" Far-Right populist forces in 1930s America. Trumpism is now linked with and fueling European Far-Right politics across Europe and the world. On February 8, 2025, leaders of major Far-Right parties in European nations such as France, the Netherlands, Italy, Hungary and Spain gathered together in Madrid, Spain, in a conference called "Make Europe Great Again." They celebrated Trump's reelection and said that his policies were their policies; they said his victory had now made them "mainstream" in Europe and that they would be building movements in their countries closely tied to Trumpism in the US. As one report noted:

> *Leaders of far-right parties in Europe came to Madrid for what, on the surface at least, amounted to a boldface names booster rally for a new Trump era.*
>
> *There was Marine Le Pen of France's far-right National Rally; the Netherland's populist, Geert Wilders; the leader of Italy's League party, Matteo Salvini. All made clear that they shared Mr. Trump's charge against what they see as "wokeism," "gender theory," and overweening environmentalism.*
>
> *For them, the American president had blown through the last barriers that had confined their parties to the political margins. The taboos had been toppled.*[9]

Meanwhile, the rise in European Far-Right populist parties will help Trump build more authoritarian populist power at home. Many are wondering whether we are now living in another horrific moment, like the early 1930s, where Far-Right populism and fascism rose together in a new globalized authoritarian movement reminiscent of the heyday of European fascism. A group of historians at the University of California, Berkeley, begins by reflecting on perceived parallels between the fascist 1930s and the rise of fascist global forces today:

> *It was a time of historic change, and society was buckling under the stress. There had been a war, then a deadly pandemic. Economic crisis was constant: Racing inflation, unemployment and changes in technology provoked extreme economic insecurity.*
>
> *But a leader emerged who understood the fear and humiliation felt by his public. He validated their rage and focused blame on a scapegoat.*

He pledged to make the nation whole again, to return it to its rightful glory. Much of the population, suffering so profoundly from the shock of loss and change and insecurity, embraced the leader as a sort of messiah. They accepted political violence, even welcomed it, and they turned away from democracy.[10]

The historians note six major parallels today with the 1930s conditions breeding fascism world-wide. These include economic and social decline, a leader attacking the "enemy within" and threatening prosecution of political rivals, and collaboration of other elites. Elite collaboration includes, today, leading politicians deferring to the new strongman and the Supreme Court issuing immunity to the new leader for his official action. (*Edward Lempinen, op.cit.*)

Issues of memory also play a key role, especially in Europe. After World War II, the visceral horror of Far-Right populism was seared into the brains of young Europeans. They could not forget or ignore. But several generations later, the memories have faded. Youth, and even their parents, see the 1930s fascist era as a distant past, increasingly remote from memory. Fading memories that make youth more quiescent, as we show in the next chapter, are always a blow to successful positive populist movements, especially since young people are crucial forces in Left populist politics.

As in the US, European Left-leaning parties and movements have become relatively weaker than in the golden era of European social democracy. Left, labor and green parties and movements in Europe remain significantly stronger than in the US. In 2024, when Le Pen's nationalist Far-Right Party looked like it might win a majority in the French parliament, four Left parties came together in a coalition to defend social democracy and resist fascism. They did not succeed in creating a stable new social democratic government, but they beat back Far-Right populism in the short term. Moreover, such anti-fascist coalitions of Left, labor and green parties - and Left-leaning populist anti-war movements - are gaining members and political representation in some European nations, and reflect the best hope for defeating European Far-Right populism today. As we show in the last chapters, these are the same forces that offer the best hope for defeating Trumpism and building solidarity and deeper democracy in the US.

Far-Right Populism in the Global South: Rise and Resistance

As noted earlier, Trump and MAGA have aligned themselves with Far-Right populists not only in Europe but also in developing nations around the world. Far-Right populism is now emerging, as it did in the 1930s, as a global tide, creating authoritarian movements and forces not only in the US and Europe but also in poor countries around the world. To conclude this chapter, I briefly consider lessons about challenging Far-Right populist regimes from the Global South.

From Latin America to the Middle East, Africa, and East Asia, Far-Right populist leaders and regimes have seen a revival in recent decades, along with resistance movements against them. Noteworthy examples in the Americas include the governments of Jair Bolsonaro in Brazil, Nayib Bukele in El Salvador and Javier Milei in Argentina, whom Trump has lavishly praised. (Felix Salmon, "Our Latin American Friends," Axios, April 15, 2025, axiox.com) The Middle East has witnessed Arab Spring resistance movements to Right-Wing authoritarian regimes in major states such as Egypt, while parallel popular resistance has occurred in North African states like Tunisia. In North Korea, a Far-Right regime has remained in power for decades, while Right-Wing populist leaders in the Philippines have ruled for over a decade.

As Trump was building connections with Far-Right populist leaders in Europe, he was doing the same in the Global South. Trump has cultivated close relations with the Bukele dictatorship in El Salvador and Milei's authoritarian regime in Argentina. (Felix Salmon, "Our Latin American Friends," Axios, April 15, 2025, axiox.com) These have been part of his effort to sustain US leadership throughout the Americas, rewarding nations there that have embraced his MAGA populist model and seeking to move the entire continent toward a politics friendly toward his oligarchy and traditional US dominance in the region. More broadly, Trump and his oligarchic allies, such as Musk, have viewed the entire world and global oligarchs as central to US interests. Trump is famous for his admiration of and cultivation of authoritarian leaders like Kim Jong Un in North Korea, Vladimir Putin in Russia and Bongbong Marcos and his predecessor, Rodrigo Duterte, in the Philippines.

While these nations have their own distinctive history and forms of Far-Right control, each shares some elements of Trumpism. All are hyper-nationalistic and have taken power in the name of enhancing the glory of the nation. Like Trump, they have seized autocratic power by defending the "true patriots" of their nations against the violent onslaught of both domestic and foreign enemies. All have ruled with an iron fist, enshrining the leader with dictatorial power. The leader has ruled with increasing cruelty and violence, turning each nation into a police state, using propaganda, armed militias and the military – under the guise of nationalism and religious authority as well as "law and order" – to defeat enemies both at home and abroad to institutionalize their own autocratic power.

Sociologist Ali Kadivar's book, *Popular Politics and the Path to Durable Democracy*, analyzes more than 80 autocratic regimes, mainly in the Global South, focusing on the resistance struggles seeking to overthrow authoritarian rulers and create sustainable democracies. (Ali Kadivar, Popular Politics and the Path to Durable Democracy. Princeton, NJ, Princeton University Press, 2022.) These autocracies have often arisen and tightened control in eras of sustained poverty involving ethnic or racial division and growing problems of crime, gangs and fear of violence. The Far-Right populist regime sometimes comes to power and holds it, as in Europe and the US authoritarian eras, when the autocrat promises to crack down with an iron fist and stop violence, purge aliens and criminals, and rebuild the economy and social order.

This was demonstrated most recently by Nayib Bukele, El Salvador's dictator, who came to power in 2019 as a Far-Right populist promising to save ordinary Salvadorans from the horrific violence of Salvadoran criminal gangs while rebuilding order and prosperity in the country. Bukele built a strategic relationship with the US, agreeing to warehouse US immigrants that Trump decided to deport into Salvadoran custody. Kilmar Abrego Garcia, a US immigrant who was legally in the US and never convicted of a crime, was sent to CECOT, a notorious prison for terrorists in El Salvador. Garcia's deportation demonstrated the horrific dangers of Trump's war on immigrants. It was turning into a potential war on anybody who was legally in the US and could now be snatched off the streets and sent to foreign jails without cause or due process.

Maryland Senator Chris Van Hollen took the unprecedented step of flying to El Salvador to talk to Garcia and try to ensure he survived and returned to the US as demanded by US judges and even the Supreme Court. But Trump defied the courts with some initial success, playing into agendas of himself and Bukele. The alliance with Trump gave Bukele new resources and legitimacy, while helping Trump carry out his new Far-Right authoritarian populism raging against immigrants. (Ashleigh Fields, "Salvadoran president mocks Van Hollen, Abrego Garcia Meeting," The Hill, April 18, 2025, thehill.com) The same mutual benefits helped Trump build alliances with dictators across the Global South.

The new authoritarian leaders in the Global South face resistance movements in many nations which offer important lessons for the anti-Trumpist resistance in the US. Case studies, including those of Kadivar and others by Erica Chenoweth and Maria F. Stephan in their important book, *Why Civil Resistance Works* (2012, Columbia University Press), show that the power of authoritarian regimes has been challenged most successfully by populist-style social movements rising among ordinary people. A long-standing dominant view is that elites opposing the autocrat will be the most successful in building forces to overturn Far-Right authoritarianism. Popular politics and resistance researchers like Kadivar and Chenowitz show that it is labor organizations and people in the streets who actually are the prime anti-authoritarian movers. The longer such genuinely populist movements build their organization and parties while sustaining protests of people on the streets, the better the chance of building the organizational power, political legitimacy and support of the public essential to overthrowing autocracy and creating an enduring democracy.

Studies of successful pro-democracy resistance in the Global South by Kadivar and by Chenowitz and Stephan show that it is typically not mainstream parties allied with the economic Establishment but movements of workers, unions and populist pro-democracy ordinary people who are most likely to defeat authoritarianism. One example is the Arab Spring of 2010 and 2011 breaking out in multiple Arab nations, including Egypt, Tunisia, Yemen, Bahrain, Libya and Syria. Tunisia's Jasmine Revolution was among the most successful, bringing down a dictator and establishing a representative democracy, but its democracy is now fragile. Egypt's Arab Spring overthrew President Hosni Mubarak but had shorter success. Nonetheless, one researcher noted the Arab Spring's early stages involved a populist explosion on the streets, familiar in American youth culture during the 1960s. Hicham Alaoui, a former Moroccan prince who left the nation and became an American researcher, observes that the initial:

"Arab Spring was like 'one giant Woodstock...Joyful anarchy empowered by internet connectivity.'"[11]

Despite failures in many Arab countries, Algeria, like Tunisia, had its own populist Arab Spring with some success, involving protests over fracking and rights to water that led to the fall of the country's authoritarian leader and new water rights. (Simon, "10 years later: Was the Arab Spring a failure?," Harvard Gazette, Feb. 8, 2021, news.harvard.edu) In other Arab nations, bloody repression and violence, including intervention from other nations, defeated anti-authoritarian revolts, sometimes led by other tribal elites, and led to either Civil War or a renewal of repressive autocratic rule. (Kadivar, ibid.; see also The Editors of Encyclopedia Britannica, "Arab Spring: pro-democracy protests," March 17, 2025, britannica.com)

Morocco's populist-style Arab Spring was led by a powerful labor movement, with a long history of building organizational legitimacy and the skills to challenge elites. When the rebellious forces of the Arab Spring swept across the Arab world, ordinary Moroccans who rallied on the streets were partly guided and buttressed by the strength and organizational capacities of the nation's national unions. (Matt Buehler, "Labor Protest in Morocco: Strikes, Concessions and the Arab Spring," Social Currents in North Africa, Oxford University Press, June 2018, academic.oup.com) The unions helped organize and sustain protestors, giving them skills, resources and legitimacy that they did not have in other Arab nations. This preserved the ruling constitutional monarch. King Mohammed VI, but led to the election of a new parliamentary leaders; and a commission was set up to write a new constitution limiting the King's power and creating more democratic rule and the democratic election of a new president and prime minister; a commission was set up to write a new constitution ensuring peaceful transition of power and democratic rule. (The Editors of Encyclopedia Britannica, "Arab Spring: pro-democracy protests," March 17, 2025, britannica.com)

In Egypt's Arab Spring, thousands of young people spilled out into the streets in another populist-style uprising. When the military failed to support Mubarak, who had ruled for 30 years, the popular rallies on the streets led to his withdrawal and ouster. While this was another instance of a successful populist revolt against an authoritarian regime, its success, as noted earlier, was short-lived. The military council that took over after Mubarak's departure was another elite group, seen by ordinary Egyptians as interested more in stability than popular rule and democracy. Due to the lack of organizational capacity of unions or other populist forces to support the skills and legitimacy of a new democratic leadership, the spirit of the people's revolt for a new democracy in Egypt was not sustained as it was in Morocco.

The Arab Spring rebellions in other Arab nations, despite initial successes, often failed in creating transitions to democracy. (Kadivar, Popular Politics and the Path to Durable Democracy. Princeton, NJ, Princeton University Press, 2022.) This was because either they were led by opposition elites of other tribes or were sabotaged by intervention of hostile forces from other countries. Other Arab Spring revolts quickly collapsed into Civil War or bloody repression from the military or foreign governments. They never had the time to allow ordinary people and unions or other popular organizations to gain legitimacy and resources that would help organize and empower spontaneous popular rallies on the streets. While populist resistance is central to defeating Far-Right authoritarianism, it fails unless it sustains itself for long-term struggle in alliance with labor or other popular-front organizations and parties that can enhance popular street protest with long-term organizational skills, resources and political legitimacy.

One final Global South example, with special relevance for the US, comes from Latin America and Brazil. Since the 1990s, Latin America has embraced social democratic and positive populist politics, as seen in Ecuador, Bolivia, and Columbia, which have fought off Far-Right populism as it was growing in the US.

> *Spasms of ethnonationalist rage gripped much of the world the 1990s – Indonesia's 1998 anti-Chinese rampage, for example. In contrast, Indigenous peoples in countries including Bolivia, Ecuador, Chile and Guatemala burst into politics as the best bearers of the social democratic tradition, adding environmentalism and cultural rights to the standard menu of economic demands. Today, many countries have retreated behind an aggrieved nationalism. For the most part, Latin Americans have not. Their reaction to the depredations of corporate globalization is rarely expressed in xenophobic, antisemitic or conspiratorial tropes, as a struggle against "globalists". Nationalism in Latin America has long been understood as a gateway to universalism.*[12]

Brazil may be the most important example. In a crucial election for democracy, former Brazilian president Luis Lula de Silva (Lula) defeated the ruling Far-Right populist and close Trump ally, President Jair Bolsonaro, in 2022. The Washington Post called the election "a race between two populists." (Zoila de Leon and Gabriele Magni, "Brazil's presidential runoff is between two populists," The Washington Post, Oct. 24, 2022, washingtonpost.com)

Lula, who had served as Brazilian president before Bolsonaro was elected Brazil's leader in 2018, won a narrow reelection match over Bolsonaro in 2022, in a race defined by concerns about democracy, Bolsonaro, a Trump look-alike in Brazil, had deeply eroded Brazil's democracy and Lula ran to save democracy and turn the government to serve the people.

Bolsonaro, a conservative nationalist military officer and one of the most influential Far-Right populist leaders in Latin America, had spent his presidency attacking democratic institutions and the integrity of free elections, governing as a close ally and admirer of Trump. Known as "the Trump of the Tropics," he campaigned on prosecuting crime, gang violence, immigrants, and communist Leftists; he promised to protect the true Brazilian people against all their enemies. He aligned with classic Far-Right populist "free market" policies to abolish many government agencies, erode public regulation, promote fossil fuel energies, and save the struggling capitalist economy. He also condemned abortion and supported Right-Wing Evangelical religious groups.

He was strongly supported by the corporate elites, who embraced his neoliberal economics, and some poor and working-class people who feared growing violence and crime and wanted a strong leader. Bolsonaro ran a Brazilian culture war against Lula and labor, modeling himself again on Trump. (BBC, "Who is Bolsonaro beyond the sound bites?," Oct. 28, 2018, bbc.com)

President Lula, the head of Brazil's Left-Wing Labor Party, has been the most famous modern positive populist in Latin America. He ran as a defender of democracy, campaigning to protect Brazilian freedom from Bolsonaro's increasingly autocratic regime. As a longtime leader of the Brazilian Labor Party, he had credibility as a representative of poor and working-class Brazilians who desperately needed a government to support their voice and needs.

Lula ran and governed on a labor platform to protect ordinary Brazilians against the Brazilian corporate oligarchy and its alliance with Bolsonaro. He promoted raising the minimum wage, taxing the rich, expansionary fiscal policies to rebuild the Brazilian economy and create new jobs and major expansion of Brazilian social welfare programs. In the years following his reelection, Lula's policies faced global economic pressures but were able to create some new economic growth and more jobs, higher minimum wages and broader social welfare, including a progressive tax system overhaul forcing corporate elites to pay far more than under Bolsonaro.

To deal with crime and violence, he supported anti-crime measures and increased public safety, believing that his Left populist agenda could only survive and win continuing support of Brazilian workers with increasing public safety. Though tough on crime, Lula was a positive populist, recognizing that his class politics to support the Brazilian worker against the oligarchy could only take root both by attacking violence from criminal gangs as well as the economic and political violence of Bolsonaro's oligarchic authoritarianism. (de Leon and Magni, Wash. Post. Op cit. See also Mauricio Savarese,

"Brazil's economy improves during Lula's first year back, but a political divide remains," AP Jan. 2, 2024, ap.com)

After Bolsonaro's loss in 2022, he emulated Trump again, trying to orchestrate a coup against Lula's reelection campaign. In a polarized Brazil, he mobilized conservative militants and wealthy corporate supporters in mass protests against the election, modeled on Trump's January 6 coup. Because of the country's intense class divisions and culture war, his coup could have succeeded.

Why he failed helps illuminate the most important lessons for Americans seeking to oppose and defeat Trump after his reelection. On the one hand, lawyers and the Brazilian Supreme Court have held firm, resisting the assault on the law by Bolsonaro and his wealthy allies. The Supreme Court resolutely defended both the rule of law and fair elections, rejecting Bolsonaro's autocratic maneuvers and, in 2024, banning him from running for elections until 2030 for abuse of power and false electoral claims. (AP, "Brazil's Bolsonaro barred from running for office," NBC News, July 1, 2023, nbcnews.com)

The crucial role of lawyers and Brazil's Supreme Court is one major lesson for American pro-democracy movements. Trump, in his second term, was empowered not only by an ultra-conservative Supreme Court that he helped appoint but also by the capitulation of major legal firms to his demands, despite his repeated attacks on lawyers, judges and the rule of law, including the right of the judiciary to review his executive orders. The Brazilian case shows that defeating authoritarianism is partly in the hands of courageous lawyers and judges prepared to rule against autocratic powerful figures and movements that break the law.

A second lesson involves Lula's form of positive populist politics. Unlike the Democratic Party's abandonment of class politics in 2024, documented in the last chapter, Lula made good on his populist promises to bring prosperity and justice to the poor and Brazil's hard-pressed working class. His strong stance against the oligarchy and the corporate politics of Brazilian capitalism stands in vivid contrast to Kamala Harris's losing campaign against Trump, running as a "proud capitalist" and offering no clear anti-corporate agenda to help save the hard-pressed US working classes. Had Harris taken up more of Lula's class politics, she might have won over more US workers who voted for Trump because they did not see her as shaking up the US oligarchy and ensuring a new pro-worker economy at home and abroad.

A third lesson is the power of the coalition Lula made with the MST, known as the Landless Workers Movement, a remarkable positive populist movement that has over two million members. The MST played a vital role in mobilizing public support against Bolsonaro and helping Lula get out of prison and win reelection on a transformative agenda. The success of the Landless Workers Movement in opposing Brazilian corporate oligarchy and the authoritarian power of Bolsonaro is another clear measure of the centrality of coalition between a mass popular movement and a leading political party in defeating autocracy and overcoming corporate rule. (Vincent Bevins, "This Land is our Land," The Nation, May, 2025, thenation.com)

While Lula supported law and order policies against Brazilian gangs and violent crime, he never departed from a non-violent positive populism. He realized that many Brazilians, including many conservative workers, wanted a strong leader and did not shrink from an aggressive state role, either in fighting crime or corporate power. But his support for a strong leadership remained consistent with democratic rule and free elections as well as the creation of a democratic pro-worker economy.

Lula realized that democracy depended on a major change in Brazilian oligarchic power that would give ordinary workers a reason to believe that he was not part of "the Establishment" and would genuinely offer ordinary people a new economic path along with a democratic voice. This is precisely the message that the Democrats need to hear as they struggle to find a way to win back America's workers and save democracy with positive populism.

Notes

1 Giovanna Coi, "Mapped: Europe's Rapidly Rising Right," Politico, May 24, 2024, politico.eu
2 "The Rise of the Nazis: Establishing Dictatorship: The Plot to Destroy Democracy From Within," Keene State College, keene.edu
3 Katrin Bennhold and Amanda Taub, "Haking Democracy," *NY Times*, Jan. 28, 2025, nytimes.com
4 Katrin Bennhold and Amanda Taub, "Haking Democracy," *NY Times*, Jan. 28, 2025, nytimes.com
5 Jeremy Leaman, "Central Bankism: Fashionable but Destructive. Monetary Policy in the EU Just Money," Feb. 26, 2021, justmoney.org
6 Jeremy Leaman, "Central Bankism: Fashionable but Destructive. Monetary Policy in the EU Just Money," Feb. 26, 2021, justmoney.org
7 Ryan Cooper, "Donald Trump loves dictators," The American Prospect, Sept. 12, 2024, prospect.org
8 Kate Connolly, "Outrage as Elon Musk claims only AfD can save Germany," *The Guardian*, Dec. 20, 2024, theguardian.com
9 Emma Bubala, Far-Right Leaders Really in Spain to "Make Europe Great Again," *NY Times*, Feb. 8, 2025, nytimes.com
10 Edward Lempinen, "Fascism shattered. Europe a century ago - and historians hear echoes today in the US," UC, Berkeley, Sept. 9, 2024, news.berkely.edu
11 Clea Simon, "10 years later: Was the Arab Spring a failure?," Harvard Gazette, Feb. 8, 2021, news.harvard.edu
12 Greg Grandin, "Want to beat authoritarianism?" Look at Latin America. *The Guardian*, April 25, 2025, theguardian.com

7 Young People as Populists: Education, Universities, and Democracy

Youth as Sparkplugs of Populism

In the 1960s, American young people sparked a formidable wave of populist activism on the Left. This included thousands of Southern Black students and other young people who participated in sit-ins at segregated diners and risked beatings while taking segregated buses to integrate transportation and public facilities across the South. Thousands of Northern civil rights students came south to support them and risked their own lives as they tried to register Black voters and help create multiracial democracy. Soon, hundreds of thousands of new student activists helped build another mass movement against the war in Vietnam. The peace movement was part of a broader youth movement that tried to organize a multiracial participatory democracy in the workplace and economy, as well as in politics.

Young people have long played leading roles in populist movements and politics. Following many historical precedents, US young people by the early 2020s had started up major campus anti-war movements against the war in Gaza, founded and led movements against gun violence and mass shootings, became important climate activists, organized with anti-racist movements against police violence, joined Me Too and other feminist movements for reproductive rights, and allied with labor movements in organizing workers and students on campuses that are becoming more corporate. Some students become labor organizers in other work settings when they graduate. Gen Z is the first generation with social media and Internet skills that help them reach out to large audiences and organize protests in a hurry – and often with remarkable efficiency.

The level of activism among Gen Z is surprisingly high. Fifty-one percent of Gen Zers have attended a rally or protest on a specific social issue. 61% of Gen Z volunteers for a cause they see as meaningful. Thirty-two percent of Gen Z are regularly involved in activism or social justice work. As summarized by a United Way survey of Gen Z activism in March, 2024:

> *Nearly one-third of Gen Zers (32%) are regularly engaged in activism or social justice work (compared to 24% of millennials), demonstrating*

DOI: 10.4324/9781003662570-8

*a significant Gen Z commitment to societal change. This engagement
deepens among college students, where the percentage escalates to
nearly 40%. In the realm of public demonstrations, over half of Gen
Zers (51%) have participated in rallies or protests to support specific
causes or social issues, with a slight increase to 56% observed among
those in higher ed.*[1]

The causes that Gen Z are most focused on include inflation and cost
of living, healthcare, affordable housing and income inequality, along with
climate change and gun control. Forty percent or more of Gen-Zers rated
each of these as issues they are passionate about. (United Way NCNA,
"The Gen Z Activism Survey," March 5, 2024, unitedwaynca.org) All of
these issues relate to the economy and social justice – and they all breed
economic populism.

It is hardly surprising that young people are sparkplugs of positive populism. They are not as wedded to the existing order and prevailing ideologies, and they are eager to learn about the world from a fresh perspective.
They have not been subjected to the decades of institutionalized hierarchy
and indoctrination of older people. Many enter education settings where the
idealized norm is to develop critical thinking and create new knowledge.
Campuses are becoming more corporatized and repressive but remain among
the most liberal and progressive institutions in the US. Young people are less
activist today than they were in the 1960s, for reasons we explore in this
chapter, but remain a major source of hope for Left positive populism and
opposition to Trumpism and Far-Right populism.

For Peace and Participatory Democracy: The 1960s
Populist Generation

In 1964, thousands of students from the North joined Freedom Summer to
go South and to register Black voters in Alabama, Mississippi, and other
segregated states. In the summer of 1965, I joined another large migration of
students south to organize voter registration and fight for multiracial democracy. Inspired by Martin Luther King, these young people formed legend-
ary organizations, such as the Student Non-Violent Coordinated Committee
(SNCC) and Students for Democratic Society (SDS). They became an important part of the social infrastructure of a Left populist movement led by
young people. In the 1962 Port Huron Statement, a manifesto written by one
of the SDS founders, Tom Hayden, they became committed to "participatory
democracy" as their main objective.

*we seek the establishment of a participatory democracy, governed by
two central aims: that the individual share in those social decisions de-
termining the quality and direction of his life; that society be organized*

to encourage independence in men and provide the media for their common participation.[2]

"Participatory Democracy" defined the entire sixties movement. It was a populist agenda because the youthful activists defined participation as democratic voice and power in every area of their lives. They wanted participatory democracy in the school and classroom, the family, the workplace, the larger economy and all levels of government.

They would see our current crisis of democracy as the latest version of the authoritarianism they were fighting – both for civil rights in the authoritarian South and in the government against the Vietnam War. What helped them make history was their belief that young people themselves could wield great power. This faith in the power of youth helped them become prime movers for massive social change toward participatory democracy. The Port Huron Statement said that their movement must

> *"consist of younger people...and be directed to the recruitment of young people. The university is the obvious beginning point."*[3]

This belief in youth – as one of the centers of Left populism – was intertwined with their analysis of the rising importance of the university. They saw it as an increasingly crucial institution in America. This reflected their own status as students in an economy moving toward post-industrialism and a need for a more highly educated workforce. They were becoming early members of a potent PMC – a credentialed new class. But they also understood that the university – and their own future work-lives – were increasingly subject to corporate control and militarism. This led them to a profound critique of the university itself, which remains as powerful and true today as it was in their own era:

> *First, the university is located in a permanent position of social influence. Its educational function makes it indispensable and automatically makes it a crucial institution in the formation of social attitudes. Second, in an unbelievably complicated world, it is the central institution for organizing, evaluating, and transmitting knowledge. Third, the extent to which academic resources presently is used to buttress immoral social practice is revealed first, by the extent to which defense contracts make the universities engineers of the arms race. Too, the use of modern social science as a manipulative tool reveals itself in the "human relations" consultants to the modern corporation, who introduce trivial sops to give laborers feelings of "participation" or "belonging," while actually deluding them in order to further exploit their labor. And, of course, the use of motivational research is already infamous as a manipulative aspect of American politics. But these social uses of the*

universities' resources also demonstrate the unchangeable reliance by men of power on the men and storehouses of knowledge: this makes the university functionally tied to society in new ways, revealing new potentialities, new levers for change. Fourth, the university is the only mainstream institution that is open to participation by individuals of nearly any viewpoint.

These, at least, are facts, no matter how dull the teaching, how paternalistic the rules, how irrelevant the research that goes on. Social relevance, the accessibility to knowledge, and internal openness – these together make the university a potential base and agency for a movement of social change.[4]

These insights about the connection between the increasingly corporatized and militarized university and the larger crises of US society helped shape the sixties movements into a kind of Left populism. Their direct experience – on and off campus with civil rights issues and the Vietnam War – helped turn an entire generation into a populist movement to overthrow militarized capitalism. The focus was building a deep multiracial democracy in the South as well as the rest of the country and seeking to end US wars like Vietnam, all part of a populist "New Left" seeking to transform the US into a "participatory democracy."

Martin Luther King himself evolved from an exclusive focus on civil rights to a vision of a "promised land" which would institutionalize peace and justice in a new labor-friendly economy and multiracial democracy. King died marching with garbage workers on strike in Memphis in 1968; King had a premonition he might die, but he viewed his mission as social and economic justice for workers of all races as well as a civil right to overcome racism. This was his own spiritually driven populism, expressed to a crowd in Memphis the night before he was assassinated:

And so the first question that the Levite asked was, "If I stop to help this man, what will happen to me?" But then the Good Samaritan came by. And he reversed the question: "If I do not stop to help this man, what will happen to him?."

That's the question before you tonight. Not, "If I stop to help the sanitation workers, what will happen to all of the hours that I usually spend in my office every day and every week as a pastor?" The question is not, "If I stop to help this man in need, what will happen to me?" "If I do no stop to help the sanitation workers, what will happen to them?" That's the question.[5]

King's magnanimity of spirit translated into a politics that inevitably required looking well beyond civil rights to the entire structure of the economic and political system. King played an important role in helping inspire the

1960s youthful New Left populism – committed to overthrowing the Establishment and "changing the system."

Following King's example, the sixties students were heavily focused on fighting racism but did not lapse into siloed identity politics. They kept their eye on the ball of universalized resistance, uniting different races and ethnicities against the larger corporate oligarchy and war system that is always the central target of a Left populism in a capitalist society. They made substantial progress on racial change and justice by integrating anti-racist struggles with a broader populist challenge to the hierarchies and command systems of militarized capitalism. King, who symbolized this evolution, asked how he could end violence in the racist South if he supported an American system that was waging war and broader violence against people of all races across the world.

Movements like 1964's Freedom Summer carry some lessons for young people today confronting the authoritarianism of Trumpist Far-Right populism. Until 1965, the South was a system of white supremacy that melded racism and White Christian values with corporate power. It was brutally violent, and both Black and white young activists in Freedom Summer were harassed by police, arrested, beaten, shot and murdered. But the largely non-violent tactics of the civil rights activists, modeled by Martin Luther King, ultimately proved successful in winning significant support in the public and Washington, DC, leading to civil rights legislation that was a major step away from authoritarianism toward multiracial democracy. We need to learn the lesson today of the struggle for democracy in Freedom Summer, which I summarize here from my own experience:

Freedom Summer helped unleash a major effort to bring democracy to Mississippi. Voting rights were seen as part of an educational, economic and political transformation. Voting rights activists helped establish 41 freedom schools for more than 3,000 young Black people, helping provide literacy, history and organizing skills that would allow the struggle to continue.

It would take my Freedom Summer in 1965 to move closer to the first new phase of multiracial democracy. In that summer, I lived with a Black family for several months and continued the voting rights and education work begun in 1964. Like the 1964 workers, we faced constant violence, arrested by the police the first day and followed by armed men who once managed to get into our car and tried to strangle us. Despite this violence, we succeeded in registering thousands of new Black voters, and in 1965 we had won enough national support that President Lyndon B. Johnson signed the Civil Rights Act before summer's end. It was the most comprehensive voting rights act passed since Reconstruction, outlawing "abridgement" or "denial" of voting rights to any racial or minority group in every state.

I never imagined then that 60 years later, we would desperately need another Freedom Summer, this time to create multiracial democracy across not just the South but the entire nation. Once again, we face election denialism, white Christian nationalism and a revived American fascism. We need Freedom Summer more urgently than 60 years ago, because now we face an election that could be our last – and will take years of new Freedom Summers to win and get real democracy.[6]

The student movement gained strength by aligning with the Democratic Party that it was challenging. The Southern Democrats were still wedded in the early 1960s to Jim Crow, but the student movements were smart enough to realize that to win, they needed to ally with a national liberal or Left-leaning political party. The Democratic Party under LBJ embodied the last generation of New Deal Democrats, who were sympathetic to important elements of the economic and racial demands of the movements. The coalition between a liberal National Democratic Party and the Left-leaning populist youth movements proved difficult but it was a recipe for fighting American fascism in the South. The sixties students denounced the corporate and racist policies of the Democratic Party but recognized that their New Left social movements needed to align with the Democrats and push them toward a New Left populism. They lamenteda:

Democratic Party which tolerates the perverse unity of liberalism and racism, prevents the social change wanted by Negroes, peace protesters, labor unions, students, reform Democrats, and other liberals. Worse, the party...prevents...sweeping urban reform, disarmament and inspection, public regulation of major industries; these and other issues are never heard in the body that is supposed to represent the best thoughts and interests of all Americans.

An imperative task is to demand a Democratic Party responsible to their interests.[7]

It demonstrated the insight that Left populist movements can win major victories and help steer the nation away from fascism and authoritarianism by aligning with a major political party and uniting struggles on the ground with national electoral politics. The 1960s movement intensified their fight against the bipartisan war in Vietnam and militaristic Democrats, even as they aligned with elements of the Democratic Party where they could find common ground. But they didn't abandon their populist "change the system" politics or their fight against militarized capitalism. They recognized that you can only defeat Far-Right populism with Left populism, even if you need to compromise in building broad successful coalitions.

A final lesson is that young activists had to continuously struggle to keep their left populist movements positive rather than negative. Despite landmark successes, the Sixties movements began to decline and disappear by the early 1970s. Part of this reflected the rise in dogma, political correctness, competition for movement leadership, and activist groups that began to embrace violence. All of these negative forces weakened the movements, which began to look more like negative populism of the Far Right and the destructive elements of the militarized capitalism they were fighting.

The rise of dogma in the late 1960s SDS, led by orthodox Marxist groups like Progressive Labor (PL), perpetuated a long history of political correctness and dogmatism in Leftist class movements against capitalism, both in Europe and the US. Students were not able to avoid their own internal strife about who was "more radical" or "more ideologically pure." This created angry divisions within the student organizations and alienated the larger public from the movements themselves. Moreover, the privileged economic background of some student activists alienated many of the working-class people they hope to win over to oppose the Vietnam War and corporate power. Building bridges across class and culture proved difficult. The majority of the white student movement, in contrast to Left-leaning students, academics and social service professionals during the Great Depression and the New Deal, could not build strong personal and ideological ties to the working-class majority they were hoping to empower.

In the South, the civil rights struggles experienced their own forms of class and racial division, turning some Left organizations and movements from positive to negative populism. Many SNCC Black members believed that affluent white activists, protected by skin color and money, were taking attention and leadership in the movement away from them. As both black and white activists were violently assaulted by Southerners hating their presence, some decided it was time to "grab the gun" and fight back. Some young white activists decided to flee to safety in the North or burned out and joined the corporate rat race or the communes of the countercultural hippies, who retreated from politics into a new personal lifestyle.

The rise of negative populism did not destroy all the positive ideals and populist action of the 1960s movements. They helped raise a new fundamental critique of US wars and global dominance, with a new generation keenly aware of the violence of the military-industrial complex. They ingrained a new consciousness of civil rights that ended Jim Crow as a ruling Southern system and helped foster a fight for multi-radical democracy that is critically important in confronting the latest era of Trumpism. They helped begin a new conversation about poverty that would eventually lead to struggles against the Reagan revolution's enshrinement of corporate oligarchy and globalization.

This led to new struggles, such as the "Turtles and Teamsters" 1999 Battle of Seattle, that helped inaugurate a new Left-leaning populist struggle against globalization. The legacy of the Sixties also included the Left populist Occupy Wall Street movement of the 21st century, which brought thousands of mostly young people into encampments on the streets in scores of US cities across the country. They were protesting the big banks getting bailed out for as reward for their financial speculation, which was destroying the economic prospects of the younger generation. And as we see in the rest of this chapter and the next one, the sixties populists helped create a history of struggle against militarized capitalism and for democracy. While Trumpist rhetoric tried to appropriate that populist history for Far-Right movements critiquing global corporations and war, a new wave of labor and youth movements today is also building on that legacy.

Gen Z and Populist Movements Today: The Glimmers of New Positive Populist Student Movements

In the Spring of 2023, after the October 7 Hamas attacks, the Israeli government launched a prolonged, unrelenting attack, killing more than 60 thousand Palestinians in Gaza at this writing, mostly women and children who were non-combatants. It was one of the first mass anti-war movements on US campuses since the 1960s. Mass encampments by student protesters on campuses like Columbia, Harvard and USC brought back memories of 1960s student anti-war protests on the same campuses. At the same time, as discussed more in the next chapter, young people were already building mass movements against climate change, gun violence at home, racism, sexism and corporate power.

The reelection of Trump also brought fear into all these movements. They began to realize that new and severe repression by Trump's Far-Right populism was a grave existential generational threat. It was targeting "woke" education and creating new repression of protest and speech by increasingly corporatized universities. It terrified many students into submission but also laid the groundwork for new youth movements seeking to bring moral and social justice ideals into some form of resistance to build a deeper and more sustainable democracy.

Gen Z would bear the burden of building a pro-democracy movement or capitulating to a new authoritarianism. Even beyond that, Gen Z climate activists faced human extinction from either environmental death or nuclear war. They had also been trained in grammar schools about how to save themselves from mass shooters. They began to understand that this was a life-and-death generational crisis, both for themselves personally and for the human species. Studies show this has had big implications:

climate anxiety is greatest for Gen Z – those born between 1997 and 2012 – who have been bombarded with news of climate disasters on social media. They feel betrayed, she says, by government inaction and dismayed when told they are overreacting to what they see as an existential threat. More than half of the 16- to 25-year-olds in the Lancet survey said they believe humanity is doomed. And close to 40 percent said that fears about the future have made them reluctant to have children of their own.

*While Wray views such findings as "incredibly sad," she believes
that distress about climate change can be transformed into a "super-
fuel" to generate positive change. "Anger can be hugely motivating,"
she says. "When it is based in a real sense of injustice, it shows that
your conscience is alive, that your sense of being morally transgressed
is intact."*[8]

In the rest of this chapter, as well as the next chapter, we look at the prospects, both positive and negative, of a new generation of positive populist
activists. They need to take some relevant lessons from the sixties despite the
enormous generational differences in the conditions and challenges they face.
They also face the current weakened state of American Left-leaning politics
in the face of Far-Right populist ascendancy. Much depends on whether they
meet the challenge.

Hard Times: Then and Now

Much has been made of the differences in the hard times, especially in terms
of good jobs and economic security as well as the cost of education and
housing, that are more intense today than in the 1960s. The deeper economic
challenges confronting Gen Z has turned many of them to the corporate
world and locked them into Wall Street rat race more intensely than their
1960s Boomer predecessors. The idea that today's students face a more uncertain job market, greater inflation and potential long-term severe recession
threatening their lifestyles is true, but it is not the full story about the hard
times challenging both generations. Moreover, the hard times story cuts both
ways in terms of political responses it elicits.

When I went into the job market in the 1970s, I also faced competitive
challenges, not entirely different than the ones today. Jobs appeared to be
contracting as the Vietnam War and foreign competition from a resurgent
Europe also made Boomer students want to keep their noses to the grind-
stone. But until the late 1970s, it is true that some Boomers felt they could
"drop out" and "drop in" later when they wanted to get a job.

Until the stagflation crisis of the late 1970s, the economic hard times faced
by Boomer generation students were less frightening and constraining than
those students feel today. The intense competitive pressures faced by contemporary students, students tell me in my classes, give them no time to be social
activists. Many say they want to solve the climate crisis and make the world
more peaceful and just but can't imagine "fighting the system," which they
are studying so hard to succeed in.

But hard times, as I have emphasized frequently in this book, are historically a catalyst of activism. Gen Z faces existential poly-crises involving
the global economy, climate and other environmental crises, gun violence,
wars that could escalate into nuclear conflict, and loss of face-to-face community bred by social media. The end of important rights and the crisis of

authoritarianism also help make Gen Z a particularly belabored generation, having to fight to ensure the very survival of life and the planet. Moreover, their economic anxieties have historically produced inclinations to distrust corporations and oligarchs, who are undermining their future jobs and incomes to protect their own well-being.

Hard times, then, both paralyze and spur activism in today's youth. Many don't relate to politics at all, focusing on getting ahead in grades and winning the race toward lucrative corporate jobs. Many see themselves as forced to be "returns on their parents' investment," given the super-high college tuitions their parents have spent to educated them. Others keep running the corporate rat race but believe they will make a difference by bringing environmental awareness and sustainability into the business world, along with more embrace of racial and gender justice. Many tell me that they have a commitment to end poverty and low wages through charity, nonprofit organizations or fighting for universal human rights such as health care and higher education.

The contradiction between feeling paralyzed and being motivated to make a difference in the world is partly balanced through Gen Z's immersion in social media. Many students tell us that social media enables a kind of activism that saves time but allows them to build online communities and reach large number of fellow activists and public audiences through TikTok, Instagram and a large variety of other social media platforms that permit or enable online activist groups. Students are skeptical about social media as enabling a kind of "click activism," which makes you feel good because you signed an online petition. On the other hand, whether in anti-war work or climate justice or economic justice activism, many other students feel that social media has enabled them to build activist communities and solidarity not only online but also on the ground on campus and in the streets. Social media plays a huge role in catalyzing activism in Gen Z:

> *34% of 8-to-17-year-olds say the internet has inspired them to take action about a cause whilst 43% of Gen Z say the internet makes them feel their voices matter. These are stats which are echoed by our own research as 75% of our community said that social media has caused them to take action whilst an additional 75% of our community said that social media is an effective way to spread info and take action on a social cause or political issue.*[9]

Social media is deeply contradictory from an activist and populist perspective. It can lead to passive "click activism" and create a generation pretending to care and make a difference. But it also gives everyone access to online communities and movements that make many activist options possible: petition, lobby lawmakers, work to influence large audiences to support national and global democratic causes both online and offline.

Repression on Campus and in the Streets: Then and Now

The Trumpist targeting of "woke" universities is just one facet of a broader assault on protest and free speech, both on campus and in the streets. Trump put education and the university in his Far-Right populist bulls-eye. He blamed "woke" education as the engine driving Marxism, DEI and other liberal-to-Left ideologies that he claimed were destroying traditional American greatness and the very survival of Western Christian culture and civilization. He has promised full-scale war on "woke" universities, as reported by the New York Times:

> Mr. Trump has said he thought that colleges and universities need to be reclaimed from "Marxist maniacs," and his running mate, JD Vance, has described universities as "the enemy."
>
> Republicans have often trained their focus mainly on highly selective campuses, but their proposed policies could have a wider impact. The Heritage Foundation's Project 2025 – an outline for Mr. Trump's second term that he has tried to distance himself from – calls for sweeping changes, like privatizing all student loans, rolling back protections for transgender students, and paring back diversity efforts on campus.
>
> "This is a moment of enormity for American higher education," said Lynn Pasquerella, president of the American Association of Colleges and Universities. "Many of President Trump's top advisers are the architects of Project 2025, which seeks to dismantle higher education, not reform it, and to replace what they perceive as woke Marxist ideology with their own conservative ideology."
>
> Some items on Republicans' wish lists, like eliminating the Department of Education, will be challenging to achieve. But their plans include a slew of other ideas that worry universities.
>
> The administration could wield control over the arcane but crucial accreditation process, which Mr. Trump has described as his "secret weapon" to force ideological changes. The president-elect has spoken of expanding the taxation of university endowments. And the new administration could scrap President Biden's expansive student-debt forgiveness efforts and loosen regulation of for-profit colleges.[10]

The Trumpist economic, legal and cultural attack on universities and the idea of a "liberal education" aligned with the increasing control of big corporations and donors who now feel entitled to openly fund and reshape higher education – including reshaping curricula and protest on campus. In the 21st century, a growing analysis of the "corporatization of the university" has focused on the influence of corporate and other conservative donors in turning the university toward a bureaucratic jobs-oriented machine replacing the traditional liberal arts institution that rhetorically prized free speech and the right to protest.

After the huge protests against the Gaza war in the Spring of 2023, the MAGA Congressional hawks brutally attacked universities for not taking a strong enough stand to stop protest on campus. Pressured also by large donors who felt more entitled to intervene in academic affairs, university administrators rethought their approach to student activism and coordinated informally to enforce far more severe repression on activist students and faculty. By the Fall of 2024, they had achieved considerable success, as the level of campus encampments and protests declined significantly in the Fall semester and activist students and faculty became increasingly fearful and more passive, afraid for their jobs and careers. The move of Trump back into the White House in 2025 and his immediate unprecedented assault on the university, seeking to defund research and take over academic programs and departments, increased fears of repression in the university, media, workplace and throughout society, both making activism more personally dangerous and quieting the kind of populism on activism and the streets seen at the height of the 1960s.

When Harvard finally pushed back and refused to comply with Trump's attack after his reelection, suing him for political interference, it came only after combating the compromise and capitulation urged by top corporate elites and major donors on the Harvard Corporation, the board running the school. Billionaire donors pushed the Harvard president for months to pursue more negotiation and compliance with Trump. Even after Harvard sued Trump, corporate elites with close ties to and power at Harvard, kept up the pressure for Harvard to settle. (Rob Copeland, Maureen Farrell and Michael S. Schmidt, "As Harvard is Hailed a Hero, Some Donors Still Want to Strike a Deal," NY Times, April 22, 2025, nytimes.com)

While such corporate influence and student repression undoubtedly have cowed both universities and students, it is not new. Ronald Reagan was elected in the 1980s by making campus radicals a central political target. He began his attack on universities in the 1960s, recognizing the political power of going after student protesters. He called Berkeley activists on the University of California "trash," and aligned with white Christian conservatives who were calling activist campuses like Berkeley "un-American" and traitors to the country, painting radical students as spreading anti-American values and turning the country over to Communists.

Reagan declared that many leftist campus movements had transcended legitimate protest, with the actions of "beatniks, radicals and filthy speech advocates" having become more to do "with rioting, with anarchy" than "academic freedom." He blamed university administrators and faculty, who "press their particular value judgments" on students, for "a leadership gap and a morality and decency gap" on campus, and suggested a code of conduct be imposed on faculty to "force them to serve as examples of good behavior and decency."[11]

Reagan had taken some of his cues from President Nixon's own crusades against the Sixties anti-war activists. Nixon won his presidential campaign in 1968, and his reelection in 1972, by rallying the "silent majority" of working Americans against Marxist and violent campus radicals. While most Americans shared doubts about Vietnam, Nixon succeeded politically by making ordinary Americans hate the anti-war protesters more than they hated the war.

Nixon succeeded partly because the Left protests and campaigns increasingly succumbed, as noted earlier, to negative rather than positive populism. The "silent majority" felt attacked by the protesters, whose horror at the war often led them to denounce everything American, including ordinary citizens supporting the war or not joining the anti-war resistance.

As repression increases, Left populists should learn the lesson that they cannot reduce their anti-war activism or give up but need to remain vigilant to sustain a positive populist form of activism. They need to recognize that many of their most important aims – including their deep moral and political opposition to the billionaire class, the war system, and American authoritarianism – is shared by a large majority of the population, including millions of those who voted for Trump. Much of the public believed Trump's anti-war and pro-worker rhetoric and correctly saw the Harris Democrats, aligned with Old Guard Republican corporate elites and Cheney war hawks, as the true Establishment. Ironically, their vote for Trump was, for many, a vote against the corporate Establishment and US wars, suggesting a public potentially receptive to a populist Left challenging many parts of militarized capitalism.

In the first few months of his second term, Trump massively increased his assault on the universities, delivering fully on his campaign promises. His crackdown on Columbia University, threatening to withdraw $8 billion dollars of federal funding if it did not expel student protesters, scrutinize all international students on visas for possible deportation because of their political views, remove senior faculty specializing in Middle Eastern studies and Black studies, defund diversity, health, climate change and other taboo subjects, scrutinize students and faculty online posts and scholarship for possible "anti-American" bias, and put in receivership its Middle East program and redirect its entire research and teaching agenda in a way consistent with Trump's policies.

Trump created a list of over 60 universities that would be subject to loss of federal funding and potential lawsuits if they did not comply with similar elements of Trump's political views and priorities. Trump threatened Harvard with over $8 billion in federal cuts.

A letter to Harvard from the Trump administration ... demanded that the university reduce the power of students and faculty members over the university's affairs; report foreign students who commit conduct violations immediately to federal authorities; and bring in an outside

*party to ensure that each academic department is "viewpoint diverse,"
among other steps.*[12]

Harvard finally summoned the courage to resist, with Alan Garber, Harvard's President, saying that:

> *"No government – regardless of which party is in power – should dictate what private universities can teach, whom they can admit and hire, and which areas of study and inquiry they can pursue."*[13]

This was an important step in the growth of resistance, supporting international and other students who were top targets of Tramp's Far-Right populism against immigrants, progressives and students. In the 1960s, the universities did not do enough to protect their students and encourage their critical thought and activism. The need to do so now is critical for the development of a new youth-inspired positive populist movement that can help defeat Trumpist authoritarianism.

In the last chapter, I look in greater detail at Trump's massive assault on American universities, showing how it is paralyzing students with fear while also catalyzing students to side with deported international students and join protests in support of their free speech rights and defense of both their universities and American democracy. Trump's assumption that students and young people would be too afraid and focused on their own job prospects to engage or lead new populist struggles was not entirely wrong. But it failed to recognize how deeply his attack on the universities and his tariffs blowing up the economy might create a new era of populist student activism.

Gen Z at the Crossroads: Contradictory Prospects

The forces I have described – including the nature of current hard times, the corporatization of the university and targeting of liberal arts and student protest by wealthy donors, the increased campus repression tied to broader political repression and threats central to the Trumpist regime, and the decline of the activist student and broader Left relative both to the Sixties and to the ascendancy of the Far Right – all contribute to a view that Gen Z is fated to become a silent or politically complicit generation. Many believe that they are lacking social and political solidarity, as they compete to win the race to Wall Street and celebrate the "America First" of Trumpism. As the society elected Trump, it appeared that Gen Z might get on the bandwagon. And all these forces contribute to making the erosion of any Gen Z positive populism – or any form of activist politics – a reality.

At the same time, there is substantial evidence to the contrary. Media pundits, researchers, pollsters and much of Gen Z itself see young people – and especially students – as tending toward activism and social justice. They also have documented that Gen Z, both offline and online, has been one of the most progressive generations since the 1960s. Their commitment to activist causes like ending climate change, ending gun violence, ending racism and sexism, avoiding unnecessary wars and reducing the influence of the military-industrial complex, and challenging the big money billionaires and global corporations dominating the US economy and government is surprisingly well documented. As one analyst summarizes it:

> *Political protests around the world are being shaped by Gen Z, a co-hort of digital natives who are coming of age and using social media to share progressive views and organize resistance to corporate elites and authoritarianism on and off of campus.*
>
> *Generation Z, commonly meaning those born between 1997 and 2012, has become the face of global political activism. This cohort is deeply engaged in social and political causes, and uses the power of social media to mobilise support and drive change. Their political activism is characterised by a blend of online and offline efforts underpinned by strong moral convictions and the value of personal experiences. Gen Z's approach to activism is highly inclusive and intersectional, which enables them to build coalitions across different movements. This amplifies their impact and fosters a holistic approach to social change. They have redefined what it means to be an activist in the modern world.*[14]

This is evident both in their activist movements online and on the ground, with public opinion polls showing young people far more to the Left than to the Right. Their concern about economic inequality is high, with many young people fearing that the billionaire class is a predator on their own futures. Perhaps that is why major industrial unions like the United Auto Workers are now finding graduate students and faculty as one of their largest new receptive audiences, open to joining unions. The popularity among many young people of Luigi Mangioni, who killed the CEO of UnitedHealthcare because of "Ill will toward corporate America" found largest support among young people. When Mangioni printed "deny and dispose" on his bullets, he was speaking to the feeling of a whole generation that it was facing denial and deposition, not only from health insurance companies but also from corporate and government leaders who were not listening to them.

Moreover, the ideology of the general public has also been misread because of the Trump victory. Polls have consistently shown that large American majorities disapprove of big money in politics and the dominant power of big global corporations and billionaires like Elon Musk in outsourcing their jobs and cutting public spending they desperately need for health care, higher education, affordable housing, and environmental protection. Even some of the conservative voters who voted for Trump began to wake up after the election and realize that Trump was going to enrich and empower the corporate oligarchy that they thought he was going to curb.

None of this proves that populist activism on the Left is destined to grow much stronger and replace Trumpist Far-Right populism. But it does point to facts and possibilities for the rise of a new Left positive populism both among the young and across all ages that can challenge the existential perils inherent in Trump's oligarchic capitalism.

Notes

1 United Way NCNA, "The Gen Z Activism Survey," March 5, 2024, united-waynca.org
2 Port Huron Statement, sds-1960s.org
3 Port Huron Statement, sds-1960s.org
4 Port Huron Statement, sds-1960s.org
5 Martin Luther King Jr., "I see the promised land," April 3, 1968, edchange.org
6 Derber, "1964's Freedom Summer Offers a Model of the Voting Rights Work We need to do," Truthout, April 21, 2024, Truthout.org
7 Port Huron Statement, sds-org
8 Richard Shiffman, "For Gen Z, Climae Chane is a heavy emotional burden," YaleEnvironment360, April 28, 2022, e360.yale.edu
9 "Gen Z on activism," Aug. 17, 2022, imageinsights.com
10 Vimel Patel and Sharon Otterman, "Colleges Wonder if they will be the "enemy" under Trump," *NY Times*, Nov. 12, 2024, nytimes.com
11 "Ronald Reagan on the unrest on college campuses, 1967 History Resources," The Gilder Lehrman Institute of American History, Aug. 15, 1967, gilderlehrman.org
12 Vimal Patel, "Harvard says it will not comply with Trump's Admnistration's Demands," NYT, April 14, 2025, nyt.com
13 Vimal Patel, "Harvard says it will not comply with Trump's Admnistration's Demands," NYT, April 14, 2025, nyt.com
14 Solomon Winyi, "Genn Z are not the future. They are a formidable force in the present," Aug. 14, 2024, blogs.lse.ac.uk

8   Resist and Overcome

Positive Populism against Autocracy and Regime Change at Home

Speaking to the Hidden Radical Majority: The Contradictory Power of Left Populism Today

After Trump's 2024 reelection, liberals and the Left were scared and demoralized. They saw that the US public had given a small but decisive majority to a man called a fascist by his own top generals and policy chiefs in his first term. They saw the Democratic Party defeated in all the decisive swing states. They saw Trump gearing up to follow through with new generals, judges, billionaire Cabinet officials and other oligarchic advisors who were more youthful, brutal, smart and ready to steer Trump's attack on democracy and the rights of millions of Americans to the worst possible conclusions. And they thought the majority of Americans would celebrate his most cruel and violent achievements. All this led many to burn out from politics and to give up hope – at least until Trump was out of office. And while many said they would resist Trump's worst policies in any way they could, they felt they had no clear path forward.

This is all understandable, as the Trump era is bringing serious threats not only to basic rights and civil liberties but also to the economy and survival of the planet. His winning of a popular majority of voters showed that millions of Americans appeared prepared to follow him if he followed through on his promises. But the conclusion that the American public is committed to the actual policies that Trump will carry out is wrong. The public was drawn by Trump's populist rhetoric and rage at the system. But they were not embracing the rule of America's corporate oligarchy, nor cheering the corporate billionaires that he put into greater power in his new Administration.

In fact, a first glance suggests quite the opposite: that millions of Americans who voted for him were hoping to celebrate Trump's attack on the corporate Establishment that he railed against in his campaign. After his first six months, close to 60% of Americans said they disapproved of his economic policies and the state of his economy. Moreover, polls show that the public was turning against the cruelty and violence of his ICE police state assault on immigrants, with the majority opposed to his horrific deportation policies

DOI: 10.4324/9781003662570-9

and aware that immigrants also had rights and played an important role in the US economy.

Trump's tariff and trade wars, as well as his anti-worker budgetary policies and his anti-immigration policies, have deepened the economic problems of working people, increased the gap between billionaires and everyone else, and are destabilizing the economy. Trumpism is increasing risks of recession, both in the US and globally. As Trump's continuing trade and tariff wars destabilize the US economy, severely harming workers who voted for him, the support for a class politics and positive populist agenda will grow. Trump's own brand of populism will have far less credibility, as he has become the Establishment, controlling the executive branch, Congress and the backing of the Supreme Court. This will open up major new space for the resistance to Trump – and expand the positive populist majority of voters, including many voters who voted for him and whose populist views I document further in this chapter.

Moreover, even if the economy were to stabilize and it becomes more difficult for a Left-leaning populist majority to win support or shape policies nationally during Trump's second term, there are at least 20 "blue" states and thousands of localities where this "hidden populist majority" has a chance of exercising real power. It can engage and, in some instances, take over state and local Democratic parties, as well as social movements on the ground, that could be both a foundation of resistance to Trumpist rule nationally and laboratories for enacting Left-leaning populist governance and policies.

In this chapter, I show how the "hidden populist majority" already began to build foundations of massive national resistance against Trumpism in the first six months of Trump's second term. In the final section of the chapter, I look at prospects for regional, state and local Left-leaning populism, as well as growing national resistance, keeping in mind that populism typically starts and grows at home – and expands as the economy destabilizes and moves toward new downturns, job losses, affordability crises and recession.

Positive populism is the expression of new communities and activism of ordinary people. They are congregating in their own neighborhoods, workplaces and local civic organizations and town halls as economic and social crises intensify. They are expanding rapidly toward mass national positive populist movements – to transform the country to help save working and middle classes in ever-more serious economic, environmental and socio-political crises. The resistance to defeat Trumpism must not only begin dismantling his ruling corporate oligarchy but also build a new sustainable democracy, far different from the pre-Trump era.

National Strategy and Prospects: Building a Left-Leaning US Populist Majority to Challenge Trump

We need a new assessment of the prospects of a populist Left in the Trump era and beyond, based on a central contradiction. On the one hand, a populist

Left, like any form of populism, must be radical, that is, seek to shake up the ruling Establishment and create a new order that more fully represents the interests of ordinary people. But to gain power, it also has to win over a majority of voters, and thus requires a big-tent coalition with millions of Americans who don't see themselves as Leftist or even liberal. Coalition "big tent" politics that might work for the Left would seem to contradict maintaining a radical Left-leaning agenda.

But the contradiction is itself a partial illusion. It assumes that the US majority supports the actual corporate oligarchic policies Trump is putting in place. There are many forms of evidence showing that this is not true. The evidence goes well beyond the point that Trump came back into office with a 41% favorability rating, the lowest in 50 years for an incoming president as he started to shape his new Administration; in its first six months, it dropped even lower, especially on key issues of the economy, as the jobs and affordability crises intensified due to Trump's tariff, trade and budget policies. The working classes recognized the growing threat of serious new economic downturns and recession, linked to his war on immigrants as well as his tariffs and budget.

Even more significant is a form of hidden populism in the working classes and the public itself, one commanding a majority in years of polling that we documented in Chapter 1. We go deeper into the polls here and show how they help to explain not only Trump's own victory but also his new vulnerability as he turns the government over to corporate elites and creates serious economic crises imperiling America's workers.

These hidden sensibilities and attitudes reflect the anti-Establishment radicalism of populism itself, whether coming from the Right or the Left. As discussed throughout this book, populism is rejection of the ruling Establishment and the creation of a new system accountable to ordinary and working people rather than elites. The majority of voters who elected Trump were radicals in this sense: they were supporting Trump's full-throated rhetorical attack and rage at the ruling Establishment. They rejected Harris and the Democrats, as documented earlier, because they saw her and the Democratic Party as the candidate of the Establishment, not offering any change. They voted for Trump because they saw him as the "change agent" who would shake up the corporate Establishment and help the "forgotten worker."

Unless Trump were to follow through on his rhetoric to attack and take down the billionaires and corporate power –which he has already shown he will not do– some of the majority who voted for him will become even more disillusioned with Trump and stop supporting him. If Trump's tariffs, trade wars, budget, and immigration policies continue to destabilize the economy and move it toward recession, the majority of Americans who have long told pollsters that they disapprove of big corporations and corporate control of America will have to look at Trump differently. The most fevered MAGA base will support Trump to the end, with many wanting more of his white

Christian nationalism and satisfied with massive deportation of immigrants. But their own economic populism will open some of them to a new political conversation, especially as the very hard times created by his economic policies get worse.

Left-leaning positive populists need the support of a big tent coalition to win over a popular majority. But contrary to conventional wisdom, the plurality of Americans – and on many issues the majority, as shown by polling data – is actually deeply populist itself, distrusting or hating the corporate oligarchy, while a majority also approves of labor and unions. They are looking to vote for those who share their anger at the elites. That is why they voted for Trump, and explains why they may be willing to listen to a positive populist movement that follows through on the anti-corporate and pro-worker rhetoric that Trump promised, as he now delivers to the billionaire class and oligarchy almost all they want.

Millions of ordinary Americans will become increasingly open to a new positive populism as it becomes obvious how Trump's policies are enriching billionaires by harming millions of American workers and leading toward even more economic insecurity and a new potential great recession. Democrats will win them over only by offering the positive populist agenda that can save workers in increasingly desperate times, much as the New Deal won workers by seeking to save their economic and democratic future. Trump's chaos and anti-worker policies, as they create grounds for a new great economic collapse, will reinforce and intensify the anti-corporate views of the hidden populist majority, creating more fertile ground for a positive populism rejecting Trump's authoritarian populist lies and failures.

What Americans Believe: Stories from Trump World and the Bipartisan Populist Majorities in the American Public

Recognizing that a majority of Americans are angry at corporate elites and support workers and unions opens the door to solving the contradictions facing Left populists. They need to reach far beyond people who identify as Leftist in order to win a majority. But they can build a big-tent coalition if they ally not only with labor and rising Left movements but with many non-voters, conservatives and even some Trumpists who are looking for the anti-Establishment alternative to ruling corporations and billionaires. They thought Trump would deliver; he did exactly the opposite when it comes to challenging the corporate Establishment.

This is no easy new path – it is filled with pitfalls. In the Trumpist era, the Left populist plurality may be prevented by the repressive national Far-Right order – or fail because of its own weaknesses and mistakes – to achieve its goals. As noted above, it may have to retreat in certain phases from winning national campaigns in the short term, turning toward building resistance and power at the regional, state and local levels. But if Left populists can sustain their anti-corporate assault on the Establishment and fight for rule by ordinary people, they have the potential to win over voters across the country, including those who don't think of themselves as Left or liberal.

These include the culturally conservative workers in Michigan and Pennsylvania who voted for Bernie Sanders in the 2016 Democratic primaries for president. Success will require moving the conversation from the identity politics of the current Democratic Party to the class politics that many liberals sympathize with but have moved away from because of the seductions of identity politics. Success will require allying on economic and class issues with a broad range of non-college cultural centrists and conservatives in the working and middle classes who reject DEI and the broader cultural liberalism or educated elites.

This is a daunting challenge, but there have been historic successes of this approach, as in the New Deal era. It remains a possibility because the hidden radicalism of sectors of the anti-Establishment majority opens the door to the potential of a populist Left-leaning movement that already has a plurality and can actually attract and build a popular majority by becoming more populist rather than going "mainstream" and embracing the rule of the Establishment. Remember, you build a positive populist plurality or majority by winning only a fraction of Trump populists, as well as a sector of independents, not the majority of the hard-core MAGA base who will never abandon him. At the same time, you win back some of the Hispanic and Black male vote, as well as some of the white workers, the parts of the traditional Democratic base that voted for Trump in 2024.

Stories began to emerge quickly after Trump's 2024 reelection that many Trump voters were now ready for him to get serious about holding the billionaires and bankers to account and taking on the big corporations sending jobs abroad, keeping wages low or raising prices on groceries and housing. Journalist Chris McGreal, reporting for the Guardian from Saginaw, Michigan, interviewed Trump voters and MAGA leaders who had voted for Trump. They are ready for some serious Trumpist anti-corporate populism.

Saginaw is a bellwether blue-collar Michigan county that voted for Trump in 2016, for Biden in 2020 and for Trump again in 2024. Saginaw represents precisely the culturally conservative non-college workers who are critical swing voters, drawn to Trump for religious and cultural reasons but also laser-focused on economic, kitchen-table issues confronting Trump and the nation in 2025 and beyond.

McGreal talked with Lori Patterson, chair of the local Saginaw Republican Party and a big Trump supporter. She supports MAGA, voted twice for Trump, and is a fan of his immigration and border policies as well as his crime and foreign policies. He's tough enough to earn the respect of America's enemies. But she also wants him to follow through on a new phase of his populist anti-corporate policies. She told McGreal that she was "steadfast in her belief that Donald Trump will complete his oft-made promise to 'drain the swamp.'" McGreal writes that:

She believes Trump will take on the corporate giants she said wield too much control over US politics and citizens' lives even as the incoming US president assembles a cabinet stacked with billionaires.[1]

Patterson explains further to McGreal:

"The industrial complex, they're enriching themselves, and it's supposed to be about the people," said Patterson. "Trump made mistakes in his first term. He wasn't a politician. He didn't know how to really drain that swamp like he wanted to. He trusted some of the wrong people. He learned that lesson this time."

Erik Kowalewski, Saginaw's Deputy Chair of the Saginaw Republican Party, agreed. He tells McGreal that Trump "knows what his supporters want" and is not going to let the billionaires take his eye off the ball. Karen Abate, a Saginaw Trumpist voter who is a member of the Republican County executive committee, sees a need for change, as corporations, freed from government regulation, are betraying their workers. She used to feel that "the system was working" for workers and families like hers but is discovering "that it doesn't":

"These kids today cannot afford to live on their own, they can't afford their own home. It's not because they're not working hard enough. It there's just there's no money left at the end of the day," she said.

Abate continues:

"The pendulum has swung so far. Things have gotten so out of line. Companies ought to be able to police themselves and not hurt people, and it's just gotten way, way out of line. It's time that it swings back the other way," she said.

Now she sees "a dire need for reform." And Patterson, the MAGA chair, agrees, as does Kowaleski, saying Saginaw MAGA leaders are looking for what can only be described as populist change. They

want Trump to target what they regard as corporate control over their daily lives, from the food and the medicines they consume to what many regard as the fleecing of their taxes by the military-industrial complex to fund weapons shipped to Ukraine and Israel.

They have hope that RFK Jr. will target Big Food and Big Pharma, bringing big companies to heel.

"RFK is going to expose the chemicals that are in our foods. It's terrible that our foods here in the United States are so different than like of those in the UK. Why are our ingredients so different?" she said.

"The problem is when they're putting that stuff in our foods, they're making us more unhealthy which is, in turn, helping big pharma because pharma is making profit off of us being unhealthy."

The Trumpist voters don't need any further cues: they rattle off a list of populist complaints to McGreal:

> *Patterson and a group of Trump voters at the Republican offices in Saginaw tick off the links they see between between the mass production of unhealthy foods, big pharma profiting from drugs prescribed to treat the resulting medical conditions and a health industry raking in huge profits while millions of Americans are dragged down by medical debt.*
>
> *"Medical debt is really disheartening," said Patterson. "If someone has cancer or something like that, they're putting all their their savings and everything into it, and that should not happen. When it costs $100 to administer an aspirin, that's ridiculous. That's just taking money from people."*

In his farewell address, Joe Biden seemed to sum up the Trumpist voters' populist complaints:

> *"Today, an oligarchy is taking shape in America of extreme wealth, power and influence that really threatens our entire democracy, our basic rights and freedom."*

McGreal says that Trumpist voters like Patterson and her colleagues "do not disagree with Biden's attack on the concentration of power in the hands of the unelected." What they believe is that Trump will and must now truly "drain the corporate swamp." They believe that he is strong enough to do it, while Biden was way too weak.

The story unearthed by journalists like McGreal suggests that Trump's anti-corporate populist rhetoric has taken hold of at least a sector of his Republican Party base. In Chapter 1, I introduced polling data showing that a supermajority of American voters disapproved of big companies and banks while approving of labor and unions that could rein them in. The data showed that the decline in approval for big companies and banks has been going on for more than 50 years, and that approval of big business is now the lowest since the early 1960s. The corresponding populist long-term trend is rising support for US workers and unions, now higher than at any stage since the 1960s, with 55% of the public in support of the workers and unions.

We can add here that big companies and big banks, according to Pew, were the only two major institutions in America with 40% or lower ratings; all other institutions – from labor parties to universities to small businesses – had far higher ratings, as summarized in this 2022 poll chart.

Small businesses are broadly popular with the public, in contrast with large corporations and banks

% who say each of the following has a ____ effect on the way things are going in the country these days

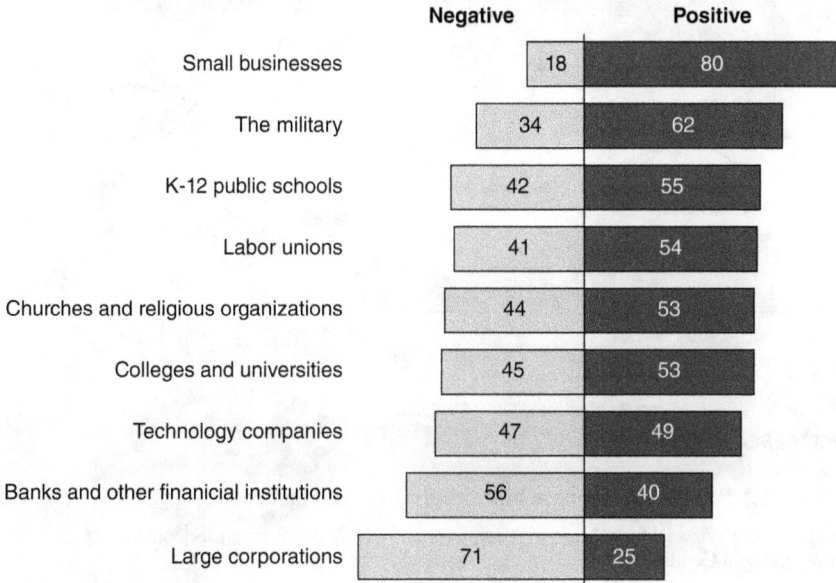

	Negative	Positive
Small businesses	18	80
The military	34	62
K-12 public schools	42	55
Labor unions	41	54
Churches and religious organizations	44	53
Colleges and universities	45	53
Technology companies	47	49
Banks and other finanicial institutions	56	40
Large corporations	71	25

Note: No answer responses not shown.
Source: Survey of U.S. adults conducted Oct. 10–16, 2022.

PEW RESEARCH CENTER

Figure 8.1 Big companies and big banks have low public approval.

This is suggestive of a hidden populist majority of Americans who distrust big corporations and banks while being far more supportive of other American institutions closer to "the people." The anti-corporate populist mind-set cannot just be explained by a generalized distrust in social institutions; unions, schools and small businesses get big public support. And the Saginaw populism is consistent with nationwide GOP polling data.

Indeed, the supermajority voter disapproval of big corporations and banks was notable among both Republicans and Democrats, but the disapproval and decline were more striking among Republicans. This helps put in context the stories coming out of key Trumpist voting centers like Saginaw. Dating from the first Trump years, the level of Republican support for big companies and big banks plummeted strikingly, more so than among Democrats. Pew found the same collapse of Republicans' support for big corporations and banks from 2019 to 2022:

Republicans' views of banks, large corporations have become much less positive since 2019

*% who say____ have a **positive effect** on the way things are going in the country these days*

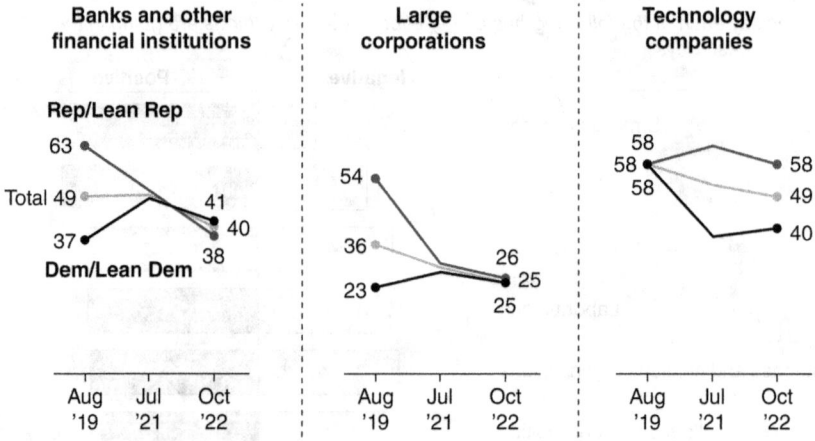

Figure 8.2 Republicans oppose big corporations and banks.

(Republicans' views of banks, large corporations have become much less positive since 2019, Pew Research Center, Nov. 17, 2022, pewresearch.org)

Republicans' positive views of large corporations fell 52% from 2019 to 2022, according to the Pew poll. A 2021 Gallup poll on the same topic corroborated the steep drop in Republican views toward big business. A 2021 *New York Times* poll indicated that 78% of Republicans think corporations have too much power.

Some of this reflects the Trumpist attack on "woke" corporations being too liberal or DEI. But much more is involved. Democratic approval of big companies has also collapsed. Only 25% of Democrats had positive views of corporations in the 2022 poll. Another Pew poll shows big banks are also disapproved of by both Republicans and Democrats, including conservative Republicans and liberal Democrats expressing disapproval of big companies and banks at almost equal levels.

Commentaries by both Pew and Gallup, analyzing the drastic public decline in support of big corporations and banks across the board, suggest the collapse was due to the dramatic increase in corporate power, beginning recently in the 2010 Citizens United Supreme Court decision giving corporations the constitutional right to put unlimited money into politics as a form

Comparable majorities of liberal Democrats, conservative Republicans say banks and financial institutions have a negative impact on the country

% who say each of the following has a ____ effect on the way things are going in the country these days

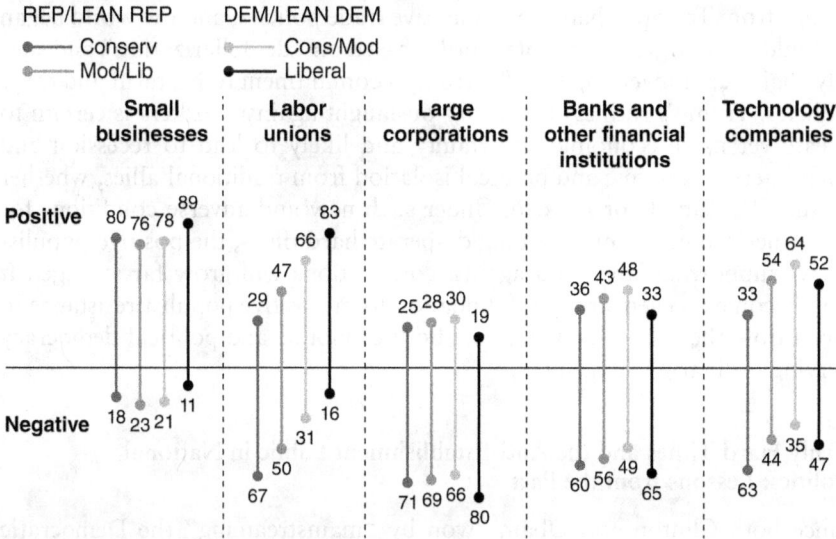

REP/LEAN REP ● —— Conserv ● —— Mod/Lib

DEM/LEAN DEM ● —— Cons/Mod ● —— Liberal

	Small businesses	Labor unions	Large corporations	Banks and other financial institutions	Technology companies
Positive	80 76 78 89	83 66 47 29	25 28 30 19	36 43 48 33	64 54 52 33
Negative	18 23 21 11	16 31 50 67	71 69 66 80	60 56 49 65	44 35 47 63

Note: No answer responses not shown.
Source: Survey of U.S. adults conducted Oct. 10–16, 2022.

PEW RESEARCH CENTER

Figure 8.3 Both democrats and republicans disapprove of big corporations.

of free speech. These political rights given to big money, tied to concentration of corporate and bank market power, led to dramatic increase in profits and the reduction in wages linked to decline in union power. Trump accelerated the problem by refusing to attack corporate monopolies and enforce any anti-trust action – thus leading to some competition that might have checked corporations – even as he was supporting his corporate oligarchy in all the other ways discussed throughout this book.

These positive populist views are bipartisan, shared by Democrats and Republicans alike, who share negative views of big corporations and positive views of unions. Young people are distinctive in their strong antagonism to big companies, while they also disapproved more than older adults of the military and are strongly supportive of unions and labor. ("Young people less likley than older adults to say the military and churchaes have positive effect on the country," pewresearch.org) Positive populism is thus growing in the new generation, even though it is spreading, as suggested by this data, across older demographics and much of the US population as well.

It is important to note that this bipartisan anti-corporate and pro-worker majority existed before Trump's tariff, trade and budgetary policies destabilized the economy further and created higher risks of a full-scale recession or even a possible depression. The dollar weakened, trading partners sought refuge from Trump's chaotic and punitive trade policies, and the world began to build an new global economic order based on "de-dollarization" and supply chains circumventing the US. Trump's commitment to his tariff and trade policies. Trump's ruthless budgetary onslaught against workers is certain to create yet more economic uncertainty and likely to lead to recession and longer-term economic and political isolation from traditional allies, whether in the EU, Canada or Mexico. Under such new and adverse conditions for the American economy, breeding desperate hard times, the positive populist views supporting labor and against corporations will grow far stronger. It will become an even stronger foundation for a positive populist resistance to overthrow the oligarchy and create both economic and political democracy serving ordinary Americans.

Truly Hard Times and the Anti-Establishment Public in National Politics: Lessons from the Past

Since both Clinton and Obama won by "mainstreaming" the Democratic Party and joining the Establishment, they have pulled liberals away from the idea that a more Leftist Democratic Party, tied to popular movements, could be a recipe for victory. But Harris' defeat showed the weakness of a Democratic Party embracing Establishment politics. In fact, as hard times become harder, the populism of the mainstream will grow stronger and will force a reckoning with the truth of an emerging anti-Establishment American public. As hard times get harder, realizing that winning the majority means challenging the corporate power elite will become more obvious. In other words, as hard times grow overwhelmingly bad, going mainstream means going populist, and not the faux populism of Trump.

We can consider again two eras of very hard times that we have briefly discussed. One was in Europe after World War II. Europe had committed suicide after two devastatingly destructive wars. Entire European economies were ruined, both in the Allied and fascist nations. Their political systems and very societies were also largely destroyed, either under occupation or desperately needing economic rescue from the US.

The depth of the hard times meant that Europe could not go back to earlier aristocratic and corporate systems and imperialistic elites that had brought on the Great Depression and wars. Europe had to reconstruct their entire societies. This is populism on a grand scale. In Europe, it meant questioning everything in their history and ruling systems. The only way forward was a transformative politics that built a new system with strong economic, cultural and political guardrails against reverting to the old Establishment and system.

Out of the ashes of the ruins of the old system, the Europeans built a new social democracy. This was a largely populist endeavor. It was designed to be ruled more than any earlier European regimes by the people and to serve the interests and welfare of working people rather than aristocrats or corporate elites. It took several decades of introspection and new generational visions to build success – but it came in spades. By the 1970s, Europe was becoming an integrated, peaceful and prosperous continent, with a universal social welfare system protecting the security of more ordinary European working people than any prior European order. It also built a new democratic order, a democracy that extended into the economy and gave workers codetermination voices on corporate boards, workers' councils and, most important, in, massive labor movements and labor parties that ruled major European nations in the late 20th century.

As often happens, success carried with it seeds of defeat. As Europeans prospered, people from their former colonies were struggling with intense hard times, forcing them to migrate to a newly wealthy Europe for survival. This upended the new European order and put major economic burdens on European social democracies, just when global neoliberal policies were migrating from Wall Street and the US over to Europe, embraced by financial firms and central banks in Germany, France and other nations in the EU. All of this helped build the new Far-Right populism that now opposes the Left-leaning populist politics and institutions that the Social Democrats built. But the European Left populism of social democracy was so successful with the public that even the rising Far-Right European populist parties are not now challenging the foundations of the expansive social welfare system or stakeholder-based economics, where workers have significant voices.

A second historical era with lessons about future very hard times and populism is the New Deal in the US. The Great Depression after 1929 threw about one-third of US workers out of work. Millions lost their homes as well as their jobs. As President Hoover did nothing, promising that the markets would self-correct, voters fled three successive 1920s corporate Republican presidents and elected FDR, an American aristocrat who promised to change the system, end the Depression, and turn America from the rule of rich corporate speculators and the wealthy to a new system that would put workers more in control than ever before, both in the economy and the government.

FDR was more reformist than revolutionary. But given the intensity of hard times, there was no way out of the Depression other than major changes in the economy and government, all of which had populist elements. One involved rejecting the Robber Barons who still ran America while mobilizing an activist government speaking and acting for the recovery and empowerment of workers. Forcing out the oligarchy of wealthy corporate titans who made up the Establishment meant building solidarity among workers and helping organize unions that would fight for worker interests in their companies and in the national government.

The spectacular outbreak of wildcat strikes and sit-downs in factories by workers demanding justice and power was one of the great populist achievements in US history. Hundreds of thousands of workers took part in the massive effort to legalize and build unions throughout America. Fiery labor leaders like John L. Lewis built the new CIO, an industrial labor federation that rejected the racism and elitism of skilled craftsmen, sought to build a new labor populism uniting all workers across sectors and skill levels to challenge corporate power. New Deal workers pressed for a greater democratic role for all workers in factories, offices and in the government. This widespread worker populism, bred by the massive crisis of the Great Depression, helped create the most successful Left-leaning populist era in America.

Part of the New Deal success was the coalition that emerged between the educated New Deal liberal elites, who ran FDR's Administration, and the non-college mass of ordinary workers. Crucial PMC advisors to FDR were Labor Secretary Frances Perkins, Secretary of Commerce Harry Hopkins, Secretary of Agriculture Henry Wallace, and top aides Cordell Hull and Harold Ickes – called the "Brain Trust." They were part of the educated elites and hardly populist in style, but they overwhelmingly supported the new labor movement on the ground. Many of the PMC New Deal architects had socialist leanings like Henry Wallace, who became FDR's Vice-President in 1940 and Eleanor Roosevelt, the President's wife.

The enormity of the Great Depression and the crisis faced by increasingly activist workers led New Deal politicians and policy advisors to embrace a strong coalition with populist non-college workers, who were the New Deal base and leading unionization drives all across America. This coalition reflects the contradictions and compromises inherent in successful populist politics. As in the New Deal, populist and radical working people on the ground, who included socialist and communist unions and activists in the 1930s, accepted coalitions with a Democratic Party that embraced them as their new base, even if they didn't share all of their populist tendencies. FDR helped consolidate that populist coalition by telling his corporate critics, who called him "a traitor to his class" that he welcomed their accusations and stood firm with the workers, proud to be a traitor to the uncaring rich.

The New Deal achieved major changes in American capitalism, creating a public goods economy that involved the government in creating millions of jobs to put Americans back to work. The New Deal began to create a form of American social democracy, with some parallels to the system growing up in Europe. In his first 100 days, FDR created his Public Works Administration (PWA) and the Civilian Conservation Corps (CCC) and created hundreds of thousands of jobs for the unemployed, planting millions of trees, building highways and huge dams, constructing public buildings and bridges, cleaning and expanding public forests, and investing in other infrastructure essential to rebuilding the economy and creating over 8.5 million jobs. The government created and took ownership of major enterprises like the Tennessee Valley Authority, which became a model of what we would now call a form of green populism, along with the massive public investment in planting trees, preserving wilderness on public lands, and investing in other clean power projects. Wall Street and finance capital survived. But the New Deal made government and "the people" partners in a new public goods economy, investing hundreds of billions in today's dollars on goods and services created by and for the people.

At the same time, the New Deal was advancing another central goal of Left populism: building the power of the working class against the corporate oligarchy. In 1935, FDR signed the Wagner Act, the first law in US history to recognize and legalize unions. In 1937, he signed the Fair Labor Standards Act, protecting the rights, security and health of US workers. These seminal laws were a crowning achievement for the hundreds of thousands of workers who had been fighting for unions and built a key coalition between the New Deal Democratic Party and the working class that helped unleash a new massive union drive in FDR's second term.

Never in US history did so many workers take over their factories, engage in wildcat strikes, organize street protests to rally the public to their cause against their corporate bosses, and succeed in building a labor movement that led to more than 40% of all workers being unionized after World War II.

The activism and solidarity of the workers in challenging the Robber Barons and the old order reflected the populism inherent in the American majority during very hard times. For ordinary people, populism meant survival. Continuation of the existing Establishment, which had done nothing to end the Depression, meant endless suffering or death.

The workers in the North often were cultural conservatives and did not like seeing poor Blacks get a lot of New Deal welfare or support. The New Deal withheld some of that support. But the New Deal also survived and endured because it understood the art of coalition between a governing national party and populist movements on the ground.

In a lesson for today, the Democrats could attract workers into their fold with class-based economic populist politics, even though many of these workers were culturally conservative. They could govern with a universalizing populist agenda, uniting working people who embodied a variety of cultural values and racial identities. This may unfold as part of a "new New Deal" or "Green New Deal" that moves the nation beyond the rule of the oligarchy, in an affirmative program not just to resist and go back to the pre-Trump era but to move to finally end oligarchic rule in America and establish a form of economic and social democracy. It must speak to the most basic needs of work people for secure and meaningful work, access to vital health and education needs, and creation of a sustainable green environment and a genuine democracy of and by the people.

Truly Hard Times: The Rise of a New Anti-Establishment and Anti-Trump National Populist Coalition

In post-war Europe and the US New Deal, hard times became so overwhelmingly hard that a populist current of ideas and feelings spread widely among ordinary people and became a new majority. The hidden radical or anti-Establishment populist majority that the polls document will become less hidden as hard times intensify and we move full steam into new economic, environmental, and political crises in the second Trump term and beyond.

The emergence of new truly overwhelming hard times is inevitable. Trump himself is inaugurating a new era of authoritarianism that will cause economic, racial, military and political chaos. As highlighted above, Trump's tariff, trade and budgetary policies are destabilizing an already fragile economy, and may well catapult America into a serious and deep recession. As Trump builds and enriches further his new corporate oligarchy, his budget and his trade and tariff wars increase risks of massive job loss and unaffordable price shocks. We can expect both supply and demand crises as tariffs drive nations trading with America to find new partners and markets. As Trump's budgets reduce consumer demand from workers struggling to keep their jobs and pay their grocery bills, many more Americans, including many more of his supporters, will join with anti-Trumpists to try to save themselves from the deluge that Trump's economic policies and authoritarianism will unleash.

But contrary to the Harris path, the way to defeat Trump and to build a more democratic and just America is not by embracing the old Establishment, the corporate oligarchy that has become Trump's greatest ally. As hard times intensify, it will become more evident how deeply the corporate state, whether in its pre-Trump or Trumpist incarnation, will plunge the US and much of the world into challenges and mass suffering, breeding populist anger and responses. With Trump now the ruling Establishment, the illusions of his populist rhetoric and disasters of Far-Right policies will continue to undermine the economic security and support of the workers who voted for them. Many working-class voters who voted for Trump will join a new and more visible populist majority, whose shared anger at the oligarchic corporate machine can help unite working people across race, gender and other cultural differences to fight together against the economic turbulence and crises engulfing all of them.

The emerging truly hard times, becoming more of a genuine emergency for working people as the economy destabilizes and weakens, will create conditions more analogous to the 1930s crises leading to the New Deal. This will boost a new positive populist majority. At this writing, the communities and activists that could create a new New Deal – one both positive-populist and Green – are already visible. It includes a coalition between ordinary Americans horrified by Trump's war against immigrants and the poor; young people organizing for jobs, housing, peace, climate action and against gun violence; the rising labor movement that is now organizing in universities as well as factories, and a class politics led by Left politicians like Bernie Sanders, AOC and the progressive caucus in the Democratic Party, seeking to expand their base both in the PMC – or educated professional-middle class – and among a majority of workers and voters across all races. In many ways, this coalition could replicate and represent dimensions of the New Deal populist coalition among non-college working-class people, often culturally conservative, and PMC-educated liberals in the Democratic Party who were committed to class politics and embraced a coalition with both culturally conservative and liberal non-college workers.

There are three fundamental elements essential to creating and building this new populist majority coalition. The first is recognizing the unfolding severity of the emerging truly hard times. Trump's authoritarianism and oligarchy will breed major economic crises, experienced as very personal by workers who cannot pay their rent or grocery bills and worry about keeping a job. These emotionally charged personal troubles will grow as the economic crises caused by Trump's tariffs, trade wars, massive budget cuts, and war against immigrants begin to fully impact the country: creating economic and emotional shock.

The rising demand and supply crises will overwhelm millions of American workers already suffering job insecurity and price shocks. These shocks will intensify as American allies in Europe, Canada and Mexico seek alternative supply chains and markets, isolating the American economy – all linked to Trump's chaotic and punitive international policies. Trump's climate policies and military and foreign policy will pour fuel on the economic crisis flame, creating environmental disaster, possible escalation of conflict into nuclear war, social division, political violence and breakdown of democracy.

Second, the rise of extreme economic hard times will be aggravated by hegemonic crises in global capitalism, produced by the relative decline of the US and the rise of China and other global competitors to the US. This again can sound abstract but is very personal for working Americans who cannot pay their rent or grocery bills. The breakdown of the existing global order of "Pax Americana" ensures economic rivalry, instability and conflict that will lead to nationalist competition as well as wars of competitive expansion by Great Powers similar to those of the World War I era. American workers will feel this in their daily lives, as they struggle to keep their jobs and afford their health care, housing and groceries.

While Biden introduced elements of Keynsian public investment and regulation that helped stabilize the economy, Trump and the revival of neoliberalism across much of the world are creating corporate oligarchies running most developed nations and global austerity policies and speculation that will create growing economic crises. As in the 1920s, the failures to invest in public goods and to curb corporate speculation in a deregulated corporate regime are almost certain to turn markets downward and begin new crashes, similar to the 2008 great financial crisis. Another Great Depression or Great Recession to come will create the extreme hard times likely to breed a yet larger populist majority that will eventually reject Trumpist populism for the real deal.

Third, the emerging very hard times must stir a new revival of American labor, with parallels to the labor organizing and union activism of the New Deal. In the first year of Trump's second term, the AFL-CIO and major national unions mounted massive labor protests against Trump's war on unions and working people. Tens of thousands of workers, led by some of America's biggest unions, joined protests against Trump on May Day and Labor Day of 2025, with vocal protests headlined as "Workers Against Billionaires." But many unions remained relatively quiet, leaving questions about whether unions could lead a new version of the mass positive populist seen in the New Deal. This issue is discussed below in the context of the increasing proletarianization and unionization of educated professionals in workplaces, government, and universities. A proletarianized PMC may play an important role helping mobilize industrial workers also facing increasing job insecurity and affordability crises.

The PMC Joins the Working Class: The Proletarianization of the Professional and the New Post-Industrial Populist Coalition

Crucial to the new majoritarian populist coalition is the corporatization of the university and other knowledge-based sites of students and professionals, the highly educated and credentialed PMC. Remember that a new populist majority requires a coalition of populist non-college workers with Left-leaning PMC students and liberal professional employees, who are a growing sector of the population, the new base of the Democratic Party, and a central player in the 21st century Left. When the PMC and working class find common ground, remarkable populist coalitions can emerge, as in the New Deal.

This new coalition is likely to grow because of the growing intrusion and control of the corporate oligarchy into the universities, hospitals employing PMC doctors and nurses, and other central economic sites of the PMC. The corporatization of the university may be one of the most important forces enabling a new labor-PMC coalition. Students and faculty increasingly find their research funding, salaries and job security dependent on corporate priorities. This has increased hard times, especially for graduate students and adjunct faculty, who are now one of the most fertile employee bases for rapid unionization. The UAW, led by auto worker leader and Left populist, Shawn Fain, is organizing heavily on US campuses, aligning himself with students and faculty who are anti-war and increasingly anti-corporate. Fain could be one of several new John L. Lewis firebrands creating a new labor movement and populist coalition not only in factories but also on campuses around the country.

The corporatization of the universities is spreading into other non-profit institutions where PMC work, including big media, hospitals, public schools, welfare agencies and government itself. Indeed, the public sector, composed of millions of PMC civil servants and targeted by Trump as the "deep state," is, along with the university, the central economic site for the PMC. Trump-ism is turning both public sector PMC civil servants as well as those in the university and other non-profits into newly vulnerable employees, desperate for funding and security; they will increasingly align with PMC employees in companies and non-college working-class employees in all these settings.

The PMC was identified by sociologist Alvin Gouldner as a rising new class with contradictory interests. It served corporate interests in manage-rial roles, but professionals like doctors and scientists also were increas-ingly employees subject to corporate control. In an earlier work, I wrote extensively both about the rise of a new professional class and, in my book, *Professionals as Workers*, its increasing subordination to corporate power, maintaining some technical autonomy but losing control over the aims and agendas of its work.

The populism of the sixties was largely a PMC Left revolt, which corpora-tions succeeded in painting as anti-working-class and anti-Americans. But before the New Deal, throughout the New Deal era, and continuing and deepening in the 21st century, the PMC is both growing and becoming the spearhead of a new Left politics. As discussed in the last chapter, students have helped create some of the most energized Left movements in the US since the 1930s and beyond. As their conditions become more proletarianized, and they see themselves identified and treated as increasingly disposable workers, they have become more identified with class politics and Left-leaning popu-list movements, whether to save the environment or prevent gun violence or deepen democracy in their own worksites and the broader economy.

The proletarianization of the PMC, as the corporate oligarchy moves to take over universities, government and other sites where professionals work and congregate, is centrally important. It intensifies the prospect of hard times for a growing and more educated and entitled sector of the labor force. They already are leading champions of movements to save the world from the poly-crises of climate change, war and poverty and extreme inequality. As their own job prospects become more perilous in the growing crisis of jobs and affordable prices, far more acute in an emerging recession linked to Trump's tariffs, trade wars and budget, they become more directly subject to the control of the oligarchy. Their class politics – and identification with other workers – will increase.

Education has always been a key component of social change and radi-cal movements. Educated groups led social movements at the very begin-ning of America, including the abolitionists who wrote best-selling books to arouse the public to end slavery. The access to education by the majority of Europeans helped fuel the rise of populist social democracy and univer-sal rights and social welfare. Progressive reformers all through the Progres-sive era and into the New Deal were part of broader coalitions seeking to end poverty, regulate corporations and create a better world for workers across race and gender.

The PMC now holds one important key to the future prospects of Left positive populism. It has its own cultural and economic interests in meritocracy and educational credentials. But it also increasingly finds that its credentials are not saving itself from the invasion and power of the corporate world. Whether it can bridge cultural and political differences with the non-college industrial working class, and reintroduce class politics with its own economic freedom and well-being at stake, is critical for the future of the Left, positive populism and the ability to defeat Trump and deepen a sustainable democracy both in the economy and politics.

The major new effort by the UAW to organize students, faculty and other university workers is part of the PMC's populist beginning. It continues with the biggest American union confederation, the AFL-CIO, uniting and working closely with the Service Employees International Union (SEIU), the American Federation of Government Employees (AFGE) and the American Federation of State, County and Municipal workers (AFSCME), as well as large and activist teachers' and nurses' unions. These are all huge and progressive unions in America's government and service sector, which now constitutes 70% of the US economy. Their members include both PMC and non-college working-class service workers, who both face job insecurity and affordability. The attacks on their unions and their government agencies is intensifying as the wrecking ball of Project 2025 and the Trump-DOGE machinery rolls into place. All these developments point to the urgency and rise of a PMC-working-class coalition. They are beginning to join together to forge a new labor movement to save American government, basic worker rights, federal government workers, and public goods and safety nets essential to all Americans in the working class and PMC.

As discussed in Chapters 3 and 4, Trump emerged as the most anti-union president in modern times, surpassing even Ronald Reagan in the intensity and scope of his war against labor and unions. While he was elected based on claims of protecting workers' jobs and bringing down the prices they paid for groceries, rent, mortgage and health care, he did exactly the opposite.

As he fired tens of thousands of workers employed by the federal government, while also joining in legal suits to de-constitutionalize unions brought by Elon Musk and Jeff Bezos, the world's two richest corporate oligarchs. Trump had already made clear whose side he was on. By Labor Day, 2025, both working people and major unions, including the AFL-CIO, the American national labor federation, were vocally denouncing Trump's betrayal of workers and unions:

In her annual State of the Unions address, AFL-CIO president Shuler said on Wednesday: "The state of working people in this country is they're under attack." She added: "We want cheaper groceries, and we get tanks on our streets. We want more affordable healthcare, and we get 16 million Americans about to be kicked off their coverage." Shuler said unions will hold close to 1,000 rallies and other events this Labor Day across the US to kick off a year of mobilization.

Jenny Smith, a home-care worker in Champaign, Illinois, said Trump's plan to end overtime and minimum-wage protections for home-care workers shows contempt for struggling, low-wage workers. "Trump doesn't know what it means to go to work day after day to earn a living," she said. "If you take away these wage protections, it will take money out of these workers' pockets. The majority of these workers are Black, brown and single mothers. You're taking from their children's mouths."

Smith voiced dismay that Trump hasn't made good on his promise to reduce prices. "I'm very disappointed that prices aren't going down," she said. "I just bought a dozen eggs for $6."

She added: "I don't think he cares about us, but he does care about the billionaires."

Trump has taken numerous steps that will weaken safety protections for workers. He is cutting staffing by 12% at the Occupational Safety and Health Administration (Osha). His administration has proposed eliminating a requirement for adequate lighting on construction sites. It is reducing the fines that small businesses pay for violating safety rules. It has proposed blocking the government's mine-safety district managers from ordering upgrades in mine ventilation and safety. It has slowed action on Biden's effort to protect workers from high temperatures.[2]

On Labor Day, 2025, more than 1000 massive union-led protests, organized by the AFL-CIO, scores of major unions, and partnering organizations, took place in all fifty states.

The AFL-CIO said on its website the protests are intended to be a "celebration of working people" and a "celebration of the power we have when we come together in a union—the power to take back our country for working people, not billionaires." Many of Monday's demonstrations are expected to be held in small towns, not just big cities, which Saqib Bhatti, executive director of Action Center on Race and the Economy, told USA TODAY is because "it's important to show that there is opposition to the Trump-billionaire agenda in every community big and small." Becky Pringle, president of the National Education Association, which partnered with the AFL-CIO, said the protests will "demonstrate our rejection of corruption and lawlessness and predatory policies," citing cuts to Medicare and tax breaks for the wealthy.[3]

The Labor Day protests by unions followed massive labor protests that had helped build the resistance on May Day, a few months earlier. While the role of unions in the resistance was not discussed widely in the media, the huge success of both the May Day and Labor Day protests suggested this should not be understood as labor acceptance or union acquiescence to Trump. Many unions had, indeed, remained relatively quiet, and a significant percentage of Trump's base remained non-college workers in unions. But the leadership of America's largest unions, with exceptions of conservative unions like the Teamsters, was increasingly involved in building mass resistance to Trump.

Moreover, as noted in the May Day and Labor Day protests, America's activist union leaders were gaining increasing buy-in among their members. This included America largest service union, the SEIU, The American Federation of Government Employees (AFGE) and the Federation of Federal Employees (NFEE), the National Education Association and many of its local educational affiliates, restaurant workers' local unions, local health care unions, hotel workers, carpenters' organizations, and many other unions. While not yet on the scale of New Deal labor mobilization, labor resistance was growing. In the May Day and Labor Day mass protests, it demonstrated labor, representing both industrial labor and the PMC, could build vital coalitions with community groups and other pro-democracy civic activists, and lead an ever-larger resistance:

> The range of issues being protested — mass deportations, cuts made by the billionaire Elon Musk's Department of Government Efficiency, efforts to undermine the power of unions — was almost as broad as the locations of the protests, with demonstrators outside the Indiana State Capitol, in a park in Savannah, Ga., and on a highway overpass in Tempe, Ariz...
>
> In Boston, a Labor Day parade appeared to double as a kind of demonstration, with labor leaders carrying signs reading "Workers Over Billionaires," the organizing slogan for many of the events on Monday. The Massachusetts governor, Maura Healey, marched alongside her fellow Democrat, Senator Elizabeth Warren.
>
> In Manhattan, a crowd of several hundred people gathered near Trump Tower as traffic sped by along Fifth Avenue. Jonathan Gartrelle, a nonprofit worker from Jamaica, Queens, said he believed that opposition to the Trump administration was not a fruitless struggle.
>
> "The ruling class, the governing class, the people that have all the money" were betting that most people "won't act because they're paralyzed by fear," Mr. Gartrelle said. "But throughout history, when you underestimate anything, that is the point at which you fail."[4]

Despite the huge scale of the May Day and Labor Day protests, which rallied in both small and huge street rallies in cities and towns in every state of the country, union leaders still had to contend with the problem of conservative members in their organizations, many of whom voted for Trump. At least three factors were helping labor leaders build resistance in the face of cultural and political differences among workers. First, many working-class Trump voters were having second doubts about Trump, feeling he had betrayed them in his tax breaks for billionaires, attacks on unions, and his budget bill that led to mass firings and loss of benefits for them. Second, the rising number of Black, Brown, and female workers in unions - well represented by leaders of the Teachers, Nurses, and the AFL-CIO itself -were more likely to be culturally liberal and stridently opposed to Trumpist values and policies.

Third, a growing number of workers and union members were college-educated and professional employees. They were experiencing their own deeper proletarianization as Trump slashed budgets in health care, education, science, environmental protection, weather forecasting and disaster management. All PMC sectors were increasingly at risk – and were increasingly unionized. The PMC was growing and building ties with non-college workers, a recipe for potentially massively expanding worker interaction across education and cultural differences. It opened up new opportunities for unions to mobilize a more educated and culturally diverse labor force into the resistance.

The new role of education and the PMC in fueling a labor-based populist resistance is a critical area. Education and intersection of PMC and industrial workers is essential to building the majority populist coalition. In the high-tech society, knowledge and post-industrial labor play an increasingly important role in the economy. This has major effects on the cultural orientation of the workforce and the potential for labor mobilization.

Education for labor and resistance is housed partly in public schools and universities but emerges throughout the society. Education takes place not only in schools and colleges but in family conversations, workplace and union organizations, the news media, parent-teacher associations and other civil society organizations. Democratization is closely related to education. In all forms of education, inside and outside of schools, people learn critical thinking and gain access to knowledge that helps offer a sense of empowerment. Today's positive populism is linked to the education and shared economic crises faced by both the non-college and PMC sectors of the labor force - and the interaction and alliance that develops between them.

In the final section, I show the rapid rise of a new mass positive populist movement with some of the features of both the New Deal and 1960s populist movements. They melded non-college industrial workers with young people, students and progressive professionals. The melding of the PMC with labor and unions has always offered new potential for positive populist movements – and this remains even more important today.

Remember that educated professionals played a leading role in the New Deal. They helped create and administer New Deal policy and helped create a labor framework that included rights for professionals employed in government and corporations. While smaller in numbers than today, they were crucial allies fighting with industrial workers against the Robber Baron oligarchy of the 1930s. In the 1960s, students in the PMC played a critical role in both civil rights and anti-war populism of the period. The number of students had risen significantly since the 1930s. They were politicized and radicalized by their education, the beginnings of contraction in their job markets, and their role as cannon-fodder for the Vietnam War.

Students today are the Gen Z standard-bearers of the PMC. Within the first few months of Trump's second term, they were subjected to their own existential economic, environmental and political pressures risks. They faced their own civil rights and war crises. As in the sixties, they have become an important force linking unions and labor activism with broader social justice and pro-democracy action. The new PMC-industrial worker labor coalition beginning to emerge in Trump 2.0 was beginning to demonstrate success in joining with allies beyond the labor movement itself: civil rights, feminist, pro-immigrant, and pro-democracy forces integral to the anti-Trump resistance, as shown in the next section.

The PMC - both students and professional employees in government and the service sector as well as the university itself - have been pummeled by Trump's chaotic and destructive economic policies as well as by his larger authoritarian attack on democracy, science and knowledge. These are a death threat to the PMC. They put the PMC in grave jeopardy just as Trump's trade policies and oligarchic war on workers was putting the industrial workforce at existential risk.

Trump's assault on the university and both student and faculty's right to free speech, academic freedom and peaceful protest has been just the most obvious element of Trump's attack on the PMC. His tariff, trade and anti-immigrant wars, and his 2025 budget, all created an economic crisis severely impacting both the PMC and industrial workers. It may help bring them together. Trump's economic policies grew on top of the economic problems of a declining American Empire emerging even before Trump, as the US faced new competition from China and other rapidly developing nations.

As this assault was beginning, it was happening in the context of the new organizing drive by the UAW and other major American unions seeking to organize students and university workers, from faculty to custodians, into unions on campus. This had the effect of linking the university – the institutional foundation of the PMC – in organizational and populist ways with workers around the country, a major feature of the New Deal. Some new form of the New Deal populist movements would become increasingly urgent as Trump's tariffs and other catastrophic socio-economic and political policies were driving the US and global economy into a ditch that will ultimately be solved only through democratic populist transformations, moving beyond the New Deal, toward a fully democratic economy and politics.

Universalizing Resistance: Rebuilding Positive Populism

Successful positive populism always requires a very broad coalition. History has shown that the coalition must include not only the worker and PMC base discussed here but also an even broader set of communities, especially those singled out and most at risk from the Far-Right Christian national-ism of Trump and MAGA. This includes Black, brown and other people of color, who, like immigrants, are in the economic and political crosshairs of Trump. It also includes women, another group whose basic rights are always under attack by Far-Right populist regimes. These communities have long been politically mobilized and organized to cope with the enduring power of Far-Right forces in the US, as well as to help lead other low-income working people seeking economic rights and justice. Civil rights and women's rights organizations had long been at the forefront of campaigns for economic jus-tice and workers' rights, as human rights, civil rights and voting rights. It was not surprising that they emerged as important players in the opposition to Trump in his first term and in the early resistance to his white Christian nationalism and corporate oligarchy after his 2024 reelection.

This points to another major element of a universalizing resistance. Work-ers and the PMC, as well as people of color, immigrants and women, have long been central to the Democratic Party since the Gilded Age, when immigrant workers poured into Robber Baron factories and worked under brutal condi-tions. We have seen that positive populist coalitions that have won success, especially in the New Deal, have built crucial connections between populist workers and activists on the streets with the Democratic Party. Moreover, when the Democratic Party has failed to challenge the Establishment and em-brace its natural populist base, it loses to Republicans, as happened after the Democratic Party embraced the war-state Establishment in the Vietnam era. Any new successful positive populism will thus require that the Democratic Party remember its history, respond to leading populist champions such as Bernie Sanders and AOC, and empower the growing Progressive Caucus of the Democratic Party emerging in the wake of Trump's reelection. They can win only by transforming the Party after Harris' disastrous defeat into a posi-tive populist party aligning with the vast movements of workers, students, women, people of color and immigrants protesting on the streets almost im-mediately after Trump's reelection.

Weakened and demoralized in the early months of Trump's second term, the Democratic Party suffered low approval ratings of 27% in April of 2025. They can only regain enduring support if they seriously listen to their natu-ral base of populist allies rallying against Trump's authoritarian and corpo-rate policies. This includes not only unionized workers and students but also other deeply vulnerable working and low-income people targeted by Trump's brutal, Far-Right populist regime. Mirroring past white Christian national-ist regimes, Trump has long been attacking immigrants, people of color and women; they all organized to regain their basic economic and political rights eroded under Trump's first term and faced far deeper attacks from Trump in his second term.

Protecting undocumented immigrants and those with asylum claims, green cards or student visas became a focus of many of the earliest positive populist mass protests in Trump's second term, reflecting horror at Trump's rising police state and growing public awareness of the economic fallout of purging immigrant workers essential to American agriculture, construction and services. Trump rounded up Venezuelan immigrants in the first few months of his second term, falsely claiming they were all part of a notorious criminal gang; he deported scores of them to a notorious prison for terrorists in El Salvador. In April 2025, the Roberts Supreme Court finally unanimously ordered Trump to "facilitate" the return of Kilmar Abrego Garcia, who held a green card, was married to a US citizen and was not part of any criminal gang. Trump refused to carry out the Supreme Court order, creating an unprecedented constitutional crisis.

Immigrant rights activists and immigrants themselves were major players in the early positive populist resistance rising after Trump's reelection. Tens of thousands of US citizens joined with them in massive rallies to defend basic human rights for both immigrants and US citizens. When Trump defied Supreme Court ruling to return Garcia from the Salvadoran prison, he also said that US citizens themselves could be deported for crimes or "domestic terrorism," referencing peaceful protests at Tesla auto dealers. Trump soon ordered US citizens, including children, to snatch and deport Americans he claimed were criminals; Trump also declared large sectors of the Southwest US border, in Arizona, New Mexico and California, as an extended part of a US military base. Authoritzing the US military to help police arrest immigrants and stop crime, is a form of martial law blatantly violating the Constitution. (Tara Copp and Lolita Baldor, US Army to control land of Mexico border as part of base, migrants to be detained, officials say, AP, April 14, 2025, ap.com) Millions of American citizens were beginning to understand that the assault on immigrant rights could easily morph into an attack on their own free speech and due process rights, with the president invoking military, trade and political emergencies to cement his authoritarian rule.

There was a natural connection between immigrants and youth in a rising anti-Trump positive populist resistance. Many of the most publicized Trumpist assaults targeted immigrants studying on green cards or student visas on US campuses. When Trump sent ICE and police to snatch them off the street, he was creating an assault on the students almost always important in positive populist movements. Moreover, he was assaulting the university, the central institution of the PMC, especially its youth. And immigrants, like young people, were subject to increasingly repressive corporate control by oligarchs who were their abusive bosses in the case of low-wage immigrants and by big corporate donors in their universities in the case of students.

In assaulting immigrants, Trump was unwittingly helping positive populist resistance coalesce around workers as well as students. Millions of immigrant workers are central to the US economy. Deporting them could create a massive labor shortage, raising prices and creating a supply-side crisis for the food and low-income services that many Americans depend on. Since many of these immigrant workers are organized by the Farm Workers or major service unions, the assault on immigrants drastically weakens the economy, and has created both an economic and moral foundation for an essential coalition of positive populist resistance between labor and immigrants, as well as youth and immigrants.

Millions of immigrants are people of color, another crucial link underlying the rise of a positive populist coalition of resistance. Black slaves were the original target of Far-Right populism in America, and Black people remained the primary target of Jim Crow. Trump's white Christian Nationalism was just the latest stage of Jim Crow, with the civil rights community mobilizing against Trump as the 21st reincarnation of a Far-Right racist regime, targeting most fiercely immigrants who were people of color, with classic nationalist and xenophobic attacks always intended to unite "white trash" and all white workers with their bosses.

Black and brown people have always been close to the heart of anti-Trump resistance, with Blacks rallying in major protests of the Black Lives Matter movement in Trump's first term after the police killed George Floyd. Trump attacked Black Lives Matter as a "domestic terrorist" movement burning down American cities, though most of its protests were peaceful, if sometimes disruptive. Trump was arguing for eliminating Martin Luther King Day as a national holiday, attacking diversity, banning Black history books and defunding Black cultural museums, seeking to end Black Studies programs in schools and universities, while calling for no limits on guns for his MAGA base that was heavily armed.

Most importantly, Trump was slashing the social safety nets, such as Medicaid and SNAP, that millions of Black, Brown and other low-income workers are most dependent on for survival. DOGE and Musk's sledgehammer was a class-wide weapon hurting most of all Black and Brown, as well as white, low-income workers; meanwhile, Trump was destroying union and worker rights also essential to their survival. Given these assaults, Blacks and other people of color were destined to play a central role in any successful anti-Trump populist resistance.

Civil rights groups have stepped up in the wake of ongoing police violence against Blacks and the intensifying Trump threat to people of color's most basic rights: to vote and speak freely on the streets. Moving in the spirit of January 6, in early months of his second term, Trump initiated a series of executive orders that sought power of his federal Administration to illegally take over from the states the power to rewrite voting rules and protections, with Blacks at particular risk. In April 2025, a leading national electoral rights center, the Brennan Center for Justice, issued this fearsome and crucial warning:

> *President Donald Trump last Tuesday issued an executive order that aims to illegally overhaul and take control of major parts of the nation's*

election systems. He claimed extraordinary unilateral authority to reg-
ulate federal elections and usurp the powers of Congress, the states,
and an independent bipartisan federal agency. This violates the Con-
stitution and various federal laws. If implemented, the order could dis-
enfranchise millions of American citizens, compromise the security of
sensitive personal data, and disrupt election administration across the
country....

The order purports to require citizens to produce a passport or simi-
lar document to register to vote. The order's limited list of acceptable
documents would mean that most Americans would have to present a
passport to register using the mail registration form. Only about half
of Americans hold a passport, putting millions of eligible voters at risk
of being blocked from voting. Research shows that younger Americans,
Americans of color, and lower-income Americans are less likely to have
ready access to documents like passports and birth certificates. And
millions of married women who have changed their names may not
have citizenship documents that match their current legal name.

It does this by giving illegal instructions to the Election Assistance
Commission (EAC), an independent bipartisan agency that supports
election administration, to change the federal voter registration form.
Not only does the president lack the power to order the commission to
do this, but adding such a requirement to the federal form would vio-
late federal law and the Constitution. States that don't comply would
face cuts to federal funding.[5]

Trump's authoritarianism is a threat to multiracial democracy, and Trump's
political allies began ratcheting up their attacks even further in Trump's second term. The populist resistance to Trump was led partly by civil rights
organizations such as the NAACP, Black Voters Matters, and the Southern
Poverty Law Center, as well as Black civil rights and constitutional attorney
activists like the Black NAACP's leading attorney, Gwen Ifill. Black political
leaders, like Senator Corey Booker, who stood and spoke for 25 hours on
the Senate floor in April 2025, with the longest filibuster ever given in the
Senate, was joined by scores of urban Black mayors and Democratic Representatives like Texan Democrat Jasmine Crockett, who all helped lead the
populist resistance to Trump as it exploded after his reelection. They were
working and rallying to defend not only Black and Brown people's most basic
constitutional rights but also their economic survival. As noted earlier, Rev.
William Barber was leading a mass movement of poor people, Black, Brown
and white, to bring people of color into alliance with white workers to attack
the corporate Establishment and end poverty in America.

Blacks and other people of color have long been the base of the Democratic Party. As the Democrats regroup to defeat Trump, they have no chance
of victory without mobilizing their Black base. As in the Sixties populist
movement, it took a Democratic President, LBJ, who allied the Democratic

Party with the civil rights movement and Martin Luther King, to create multiracial democracy and end poverty. The same alliance is essential today with Barber being today's champion of the intertwined positive populist fight for economic justice and civil rights.

After Trump's reelection, he accelerated his calls to limit voting rights – issuing numerous executive orders making it more difficult to register by demanding birth certificates or passports, eliminating voting by mail, purging voters from the rolls for minor typos and limiting the time when votes can be cast and counted. Black voting rights groups continued and intensified their long struggle for Black voting rights and multiracial democracy, essential to both Black economic survival and political rights.

Latosha Brown, one of the founders of Black Voters Matter, has been organizing for more than a decade to secure Black Voting Rights in Georgia and other areas of the Deep South. Black Voters Matter takes its inspiration from the populist civil rights movement of the 1960s, embedding itself in communities of poor people and building communities on the group, with a strong focus on anti-poverty work and voting rights, led by Black women like Brown. Brown embodies the positive populist spirit:

> *We don't come to our community members like they are just votes to be rounded up or counted like jelly beans. We're coming in as friends, with hugs and love." In the spirit of Freedom Summer and specifically quoting Martin Luther King, she says: "We always tell people 'Power at its best is love implementing the demands of justice.'"*[6]

Latosha Brown and her Black Voters Matter points to another group central to a positive populist successful Trump resistance: women. Like Blacks and immigrants, women are always a major target and victim of Far-Right populism. The modern Christian Nationalist movement rising under Reagan and triumphing under Trump grew out of a major culture war and political assault on women's role outside the home, inside the workplace and in politics more broadly. Abortion was a galvanizing issue for the Far Right as Trump came to power, a stalking horse for a broader assault on feminism and a return to the feminine mystique that claimed God had destined women to be wives and mothers.

Some of the protests after his reelection were branded the "hands-off" movement. The language symbolized the key importance of Trump's and his Supreme Court's attack on women and abortion. Hundreds of thousands of women protestors chanting "hands-off my body" became an iconic symbol of the cry for freedom among all groups, each demanding that Trump gets his hands off their own bodies, social security, health care, education, and their rights to speak and protest.

Women's issues were beginning to universalize, as Trumpism and Christian Nationalists attacked women's increasing role and ascent in the workplace. Since the rise of second-wave feminism in the 1960s, women had been organizing for equal rights in the economy and the workplace. Women are 47% of workers in America; they are over 55% of service workers, the majority sector of the US economy. By the Trump era, many of the most important and populist unions – including the biggest service sector unions like SEIU and AFSCME, teachers' unions, nurses' unions, and the AFL-CIO – America's largest workers' federation led by Liz Shuler – were headed by women. The worker-PMC coalition central to positive populism includes women as a major force; they are the majority of protesters and voters in the resistance. Black women, like Latosha Brown and Gwen Ifill, were also among the most mobilized community of American positive-populist activists, working across class lines to help poor women in the South to gain economic and voting rights even as Black women in the North helped lead urban struggles for abortion, job and family benefits.

The leading role for women reflects their greater support for collective values and solidarity over traditional American individualism. Studies show that values of caring, support, and solidarity are stronger among women. These "feminized values" are central to any positive populist movement. (Katherine Adam and Charles Derber, The New Feminized Majority, NY: Routledge, 2008)

Like Blacks, women are a crucial base of the Democratic Party. The resistance of populists on the streets had to transform the Democratic Party, moving it toward the "Fight Oligarchy" positive populist agenda modeled by AOC. A growing number of female Representatives in Congress, notably in the Progressive Caucus, were moving in that direction in the first months of Trump's second term.

Women's organizations played a major role in the resistance. In Trump's first term, organizations like Planned Parenthood, Reproductive Freedom For All and the Center for Reproductive Rights had already played a major role in mobilizing women to save abortion. While they failed, the economic justice and political freedom championed by positive populists in Trump's second term were more urgently needed by women, already suffering denial of their most basic bodily freedom. In Trump's second term, they faced assaults on their most important economic and political freedom; women were learning Far-Right populism has always been built around traditional family values dictating women's role was in the home. Women are major participants in the resistance, fighting again for equality in the workplace and economy as well as the political sphere. Because they are so centrally targeted by Far-Right populism, they are natural leaders of positive populist anti-Trumpist movements.

Positive Populism Starts at Home: Stages of the Resistance

The psychiatrist, Elisabeth Kubler-Ross, introduced a famous theory of the stages of grief people go through when someone they love dies. Millions who have lost family and friends have found it useful. It may be helpful to the millions of Americans who believe that Trump's reelection means the loss of any meaningful US democracy – and perhaps the loss of all that they hold dear, including not only their own jobs, wages, and freedom from poverty but also life on the planet because of Trump's policies on climate change. A quick look at Kubler-Ross's stages may offer initial help to the positive populists who need to resist and defeat Trump. They are confronting a deep grief that could paralyze them and destroy the massive resistance that needs to be built – and quickly. And all are entangled with not just stopping Trump but confronting the broader economic, environmental, cultural and authoritarian poly-crises that his policies will unleash and building the new populist politics that can transform the ruling corporate regime and truly build democracy.

Kubler-Ross's most widely accepted formulation was her five-stage model, involving the experience and processing of five deep responses to death and grief:

1 Denial
2 Anger
3 Bargaining
4 Depression
5 Acceptance

Undoubtedly, all these stages are common, both among individuals grieving loved ones and Americans who experience Trump's reelection as a kind of both economic and political death. Early denial and anger seem almost inevitable in the case of catastrophic personal or political losses, as does some depression. Acceptance, though, while perhaps essential in some form, may seem too passive and self-defeating in dealing with the political grief tied to Trump's victory and rule.

Trump's reelection was a staggering loss – and it drove millions out of politics or into depression and paralysis. That could become a form of tacit "acceptance," in which refusal to participate further is a subtle way of accepting new, unpalatable realities. But given the history of past political cycles, which have also brought terrible new leaders to office, there is reason to believe, based on a rising resistance against Trump and his oligarchy, that this is not a permanent loss.

Each earlier Far-Right populist success, as shown earlier, has given way eventually to some form of limited but meaningful democratic reconstruction. Far-Right populism does terrible damage – and for long periods – but it ultimately gives way to its contradictions and failures that lead a majority to abandon it, as well as to the inevitable rise of new generations looking for something better. And if these don't arise, foreign interventions, through war or other military or economic intervention, help ultimately to end Far-Right populist rule.

This has been true both in the US and in Europe. In Europe, the worst phase of Far-Right populism was the reign of fascism in major European nations such as Germany, Italy and France. It would take World War II to drive fascism out of power in Europe. Rising social democracies, driven by strong positive populist new generations, built a far more enduring new social democratic Europe.

The longest reign of Far-Right populism in the US was the Southern White Christian nationalist form, beginning in the Confederacy of the slave-system and perpetuated regionally in Far-Right Jim Crow states. This system never fully disappeared – and is partially resurrected in Trumpism on the national level and in some conservative states. But change has happened – and always does.

Trump's reelection was devastating, breeding both denial and anger, as well as great sadness. But there was also resistance right from the beginning of Trump's reelection, from the Democratic Party, judges, labor unions, and a rising tide of workers, students and the general public, whose basic economic security and political rights were threatened.

There was resistance in the first weeks of Trump's reelection by the national Democratic Party to his worst Cabinet picks and judges' rejections of some of his executive orders. The Democrats also had to organize to block Trump's unconstitutional efforts to shut down their own fundraising apparatus, ActBlue. On April 27, 2024, the media reported that Trump had ordered his Justice Department to investigate and prosecute the Democrat's long-standing main organization to raise funds for its federal and state candidates for high office. As Congressman Jamie Raskin, a constitutional lawyer, put it:

> *"Today's presidential decree targeting the campaign infrastructure of the Democratic party with precisely zero evidence of wrongdoing is the kind of edict you'd expect from a power-mad dictator in a Banana Republic," said House Judiciary Committee Ranking Member Jamie Raskin (D-Md.). "This president, with his approval ratings underwater and sinking like a stone, is desperately seeking to undermine his political opposition by cutting off their access to funding."*[7]

The Democrats also began organizing to stop Trump's most dangerous prosecutions of all his other "enemies of the people"– whether unions, the media or universities – and to halt his unconstitutional freeze on massive amounts of federal spending. Early efforts by the national Democrats involved using every legislative and legal tool at their disposal to halt unconstitutional budget slashes, stop destruction of entire federal agencies and programs, and undo unconstitutional Trumpist assaults on science, public health and the environment. Positive populist activists not only had to save working people from economic devastation but also had to fight bans of books, takeovers of research and academic programs and fight Trump's effort to shut down the Department of Education and Department of Labor.

All these Trump initiatives violate federal law and free speech, threatening American workers' most basic economic rights and job-security, as well as their constitutional rights. New executive orders kept assaulting the right to vote, making registration more difficult and purging voting rolls, especially among low-income Americans. They added major new restrictions on times and ways to vote that hit low-income workers and the unemployed especially hard.

Within several months of his reelection, Trump was amping up threats to voting that made commentators concerned whether 2026 elections could be held fairly – or even at all. Trump and his top officials were issuing threats to election officials, who might face prosecution for just clerical errors. Trump issued executive orders and other edicts to ban mail-in voting, require voter identification, ban electronic voting machines in blue states, and prosecute both voters and election officials voting centers for minor or accidental mistakes. Would enough people take the risk and volunteer to serve in election centers?

Trump also demanded that Texas lead Red States in gerrymandering state voting districts. Texas complied, denying Democrats five legitimate House seats. This set off a race across the country, with other Red states, like Missouri, also gerrymandering their electoral map to deny Democrats seats. Democrats, led by Governor Gavin Newsom in California, threated to do their own partisan redistricting as their only way to preserve chances of winning elections in 2026 and beyond.

Meanwhile, as Robert Kuttner wrote in regard to Trump's early order to prove citizenship to vote, the Supreme Court continued to rule in Trump's favor, extending the constitutional mandate of presidential power they had already provided him in their 2024 Immunity decision:

> *In March, Trump signed an executive order requiring all prospective voters to provide documentary proof of U.S. citizenship. In April, a district court judge enjoined DHS from carrying out Trump's order. Since then, however, the Supreme Court has ruled in Trump v. CASA that district court decisions do not apply nationwide. So the Trump order on proof of citizenship in voting could be revived.*
>
> *Trump is pursuing his characteristic strategy of flooding the zone, in this case demanding voter information, threatening election officials with prosecution for even technical violations, and deterring voting by demanding proof of citizenship, while targeting naturalized citizens on another front.*[8]

With the Supreme Court's complicity, many believed that Trump was mobilizing to actually make elections impossible, perhaps by declaring another of his many emergencies that would suspend basic voting rights or cripple them in a way to ensure MAGA victories. This would follow Trump's strategy of deny constitutional rights by declaring economic emergencies, trade deficit emergencies, and immigrant invasions, all suspending Americans' basic rights. Beyond his electoral schemes, Trump was imprisoning and deporting immigrants and protesters without any due process. Erwin Chemerinsky and Laurence Tribe, among America's most renowned constitutional lawyers, wrote that Trump was undoing the core checks and balances in the Constitution – and that "We should all be very, very afraid." (Erwin Chemerinsky and Laurence Tribe, "We Should All be Very, Very Afraid," NY Times, April 9, 2025, nytimes.com) Regarding Trump's deportations of Abrego Garcia to Salvador prisons without judicial review, Chemerinsky and Tribe wrote:

> *There can be no doubt what this means.*
> *There would be nothing to stop the government from jailing its critics in another country and then claiming, as it is now, that the courts have no jurisdiction to remedy the situation. Armed with this power, the government would know that Immigration and Customs Enforcement or the F.B.I. or any federal law enforcement agency could apprehend any people, ignore the requirements for due process and ship them to El Salvador or any country that would take them. These individuals would have no legal recourse whatsoever from any American court. The administration could create its own gulags with no more judicial review than existed when Stalin did the same thing in the Soviet Union.*[9]

Two weeks after Trump's reelection, pro-democracy lawyers and legal groups, such as the ACLU and labor law groups associated with the AFL-CIO, were bringing scores of lawsuits against Trump to nullify his attacks on immigrants, his executive orders on freezing federal funds across the board, shutting down agencies like USAID and the Departments of Education, his aggressive attacks on unions shutting down much the Department of Labor, the NLRB and firing tens of thousands of government employees, while eliminating the unions of tens of thousands of government employees. these were all central goals of the US corporate oligarchy and seen by corporate elites as their best and perhaps final chance to consolidate their power.

National resistance to Trump's autocracy and oligarchy exploded in the streets in cities and towns across the country in the next few months after his reelection. Thousands of people tried to block Musk and his aides from physically getting into the Labor Department, the Treasury Department, the Department of Education, the Consumer Financial Protection Bureau and the Office of Personnel Management, where he was accessing sensitive personal information on thousands of civil servants and citizens. On May Day and Labor Day, 2025, tens of thousands of union member, led by the AFL-CIO, protested Trump's all-out assault on unions.

Activists gathered in DC and around the country to protest Trump's and Musk's attacks on public schools and the Department of Education, on public health clinics, on environmental regulations and consumer protection, and on immigrants. Tens of thousands of protesters and hundreds of thousands of others phoned their Congress representatives to fight Trump's wrecking ball immediately. They targeted not only Musk but also the OMB led by Project 2025 leader Russell Vought, as he gained Senate confirmation and immediately sought to cut funding from virtually every agency of the federal government, almost all of which are central to the economic survival of working people and the target of oligarchs since the New Deal. And around the country, local citizens stood in opposition to ICE officials and police trying to find and evict immigrants in their communities.

The public protests were loud, creative, angry and massive, as headlined in media reports two or three weeks after Trump's reelection:

> *"Democracy is not a spectator sport! Do something," said a sign held aloft by one demonstrator in Philadelphia.*
>
> *The protests were a result of a movement that has organized online under the hashtags #buildtheresistance and #50501, which stands for 50 protests, 50 states, one day. Websites and accounts across social media issued calls for action, with messages such as "reject fascism" and "defend our democracy."*
>
> *"Democracy is not a spectator sport! Do something," said a sign.*
>
> *Outside the state Capitol in Lansing, Michigan, a crowd of about 1,000 people gathered in freezing temperatures.*
>
> *Catie Miglietti, from the Ann Arbor area, said Musk's access to the Treasury Department data was especially concerning to her. She painted a sign depicting Musk puppeteering Trump from his outraised arm – evoking Musk's straight-arm gesture during a January speech that some have interpreted as a Nazi salute.*
>
> *"If we don't stop it and get Congress to do something, it's an attack on democracy," Miglietti said.*
>
> *In Columbus, Ohio, protesters outside the Statehouse shouted, "Wake up USA! Stop the coup that's underway!"*[10]

Much of the protest was spontaneous, an uprising by outraged Americans who had little prior engagement with protests or activism and reflected small but crucial forms of personal and community resistance:

> *I'm appalled by democracy's changes in the last, well, specifically two weeks – but it started a long time ago," said Margaret Wilmeth, a self-described senior citizen from Columbus. "So I'm just trying to put a presence into resistance."*
>
> *Craig and Robin Schroeder drove nearly two hours from their home in Findlay for the demonstration. They described the appointment of*

Defense Secretary Pete Hegseth as a slap to Ohio's military families. The Senate narrowly confirmed Hegseth after questions from members in both parties over his qualifications to lead the military, especially amid allegations of heavy alcohol use and aggressive behavior toward women.

"This is my first protest ever, but I can't imagine a more worthwhile one," said Robin Schroeder, 47.

Demonstrations in several cities piled criticism on Musk and the Department of Government Efficiency.

"DOGE is not legit," read one poster on the state Capitol steps in Jefferson, Missouri, where dozens of protesters gathered. "Why does Elon have your Social Security info???"[11]

Popular resistance just kept growing, with the huge No Kings protest in June 2025, bringing as many as six million people onto the streets, followed by the women's and anti-Trump budget "freedom" protests on July 4, 2025. A genuine resistance was building across the entire country and among virtually all ages, ethnicities, education and occupations. This was reflecting what the populist and consumer firebrand activist, Ralph Nader, called "civic self-respect" and "civic resistance." (Ralph Nader, Civic Self-Respect, Seven Stories Press, 2025) Nader's Raiders, a national network of community-based citizen activists, had long challenged the oligarchy's corporate policies endangering American workers' cars, jobs, daily consumer product prices and quality, health, education and environmental protection. The outpouring of citizen activists – Nader's vision of a democracy empowered by citizens coming together in their community and fighting the oligarchy power every day in every stage of their life appeared to be emerging at a scale that Nader had been arguing was essential – and possible – for years.

In the Trump era, especially his second term, millions of protestors infected with Nader's citizen-activist spirit were facing the greatest threat of their lifetime. Seeing much of his own lifetime citizen activist achievements and democratic participation at risk, Nader called for a citizen activist revolution against the corporate state and the "dictatorship" that Trump was creating to create an American fascism.

Indeed, Nader, a lawyer as well as iconic citizen-activist, drafted a 17-article Impeachment of Trump. Impeachment had been tried twice in the first term. In the second term, Nader made a persuasive case that Trump had now violated American rights so profoundly – in a blooming neo-fascist revolution – that Impeachment was now an essential remedy, a call that would be taken up by many Democratic Party positive populists, such as Rep. Jamie Raskin, also a constitutional scholar and lawyer. To read Nader's impeachment is to read one of the most blunt and incisive indictment of Trump as dictatorship, with Nader enumerating all of the detailed violations of democratic principles, laws and basic rights in his brief but compelling call for Trump's Impeachment. (Ralph Nader,

"Resignation-Legions of Impeachable Offenses," letter to President Donald J. Trump," titled "Articles of Impeachment Against Donald J. Trump," from Ralph Nader, Washington, D.C.)

Alongside this populist resistance of activist-citizens and working people and students on the streets, mass consumer boycotts of media conglomerates like Disney, many states and cities began their own broad-based legal and official resistance, with state Attorney Generals suing him for trying to end birthright citizenship and helping to put reproductive rights in their constitutions. Many localities refused to cooperate with federal agents seeking to find and deport immigrants. As Trump II ruled, turning over more and more of the government and country to his oligarchy, more cities and states passed anti-corporate, labor-friendly, environmental and social justice measures reflecting positive populist values.

At minimum, this suggests that Kubler-Ross's initial model does not exhaust all the possibilities. Indeed, a second model derived from her first has also come into use in grief counseling, with seven stages:

1 **Shock:** intense and sometimes paralyzing surprise at the loss
2 **Denial:** disbelief and the need to look for evidence to confirm the loss
3 **Anger and frustration:** a mix of acknowledgment that some things have changed and anger toward this change
4 **Depression:** lack of energy and intense sadness
5 **Testing:** experimenting with the new situation to discover what it actually means in your life
6 **Decision:** a rising optimism about learning how to manage the new situation
7 **Integration:** acceptance of the new reality, reflection on what you learned, and stepping out in the world as a renewed person

This model may prove more useful in aligning our psychological reactions with the political lessons of history. It acknowledges the inevitable initial shock, denial and depression that Trump's return to the White House brought. At the same time, it looks like a series of unfolding stages, in which those opposing Trump combine anger with new positive choices to begin to rebuild their lives and political commitments and movements. There is "experimentation" to discover what this means in your life and a possible "rising optimism" about managing the huge change. Finally, there is "reflection on what you learned" and "stepping out in the world as a renewed person."

In personal life, dealing with death, Kubler-Ross's stages are documented by research on people dealing with the death of loved ones. It is valuable to think about this second set of seven stages as not just a more hopeful prognosis for people suffering political grief, though it is that. It is also an acknowledgment or type of documentation of the long historical reality of renewal and change. It recognizes that all Far-Right populist rules, at least in the US, have ultimately given way to resistance and rise of more democratic governance. If we look at the history, we can find genuine grounds for "stepping out in the world as a renewed person."

In politics, the relevant subject is not just ourselves as individuals but as members of families, friends, social networks, workplaces, political parties and social movements. In fact, we should apply the seven Kubler-Ross stages to the most relevant political collectivities and social movements. The important question is how democratic, positive populist movements collectively navigate each stage and use anger, testing, decision and ultimately integration to re-enter the political world as a "renewed movement."

Many progressive and Left-leaning groups are beginning to move through these stages as they try as they respond to the reality of Trump's reelection. After Trump's win, there has been exhaustion, anger, depression and shock. There will be strong temptations to deny what has happened or drop out, partly because of fear of opposing Trump. Many stopped watching the news and stopped thinking about or talking about politics. Many will want to leave the country. Some have, and more will.

But Trump's Far-Right radicalism – enveloped in the never-ending monologue of his lies, threats and grievances as well as his policies leading toward a police state in his war against immigrants as well as destabilizing the economy and increasing the threat of long-term recession as well as long-term environmental and military crises and inflaming of crises in relation with traditional allies such as Canada, Mexico and Europe – quickly began to wake many people up to the need to move beyond the early stages of shock, denial and depression. Trump's rapid-fire tsunami of his policy positions starting on Day 1 of his second term intensified these early stages of depression and denial but also pushed people toward the later, more "activist" or integrative Kubler-Ross's stages.

Within a few months, videos displaying Trump's authoritarian assault on immigrants and international students aroused the public; one showed an innocent Tufts graduate student and Fulbright Scholar, Rumeysa Ozturk, snatched off the streets by masked ICE police for writing an opinion piece in a Tufts newspaper a year earlier, scaring millions of Americans fearful for their own safety and freedoms. (Dalia Faheid and Gloria Pazmino, "A PhD student was snatched by masked officers in broad daylight. Then she was flown 1500 miles away," CNN, March 29, 2025, cnn.com) The fear escalated as the Trump Administration defied Federal District Court judges and the Supreme Court and, as noted above, deported another innocent immigrant with a green card, Kilmar Abrego Garcia, as well as hundreds of Venezuelan immigrants. As discussed earlier, Garcia was kidnapped and deported without any due process, helping catalyze a far larger mass resistance involving hundreds of thousands of Americans protesting on the streets, with populist activist organizations like Indivisible and the ACLU telling Garcia's story and organizing mass protests all over the country. (Indivisible, "Crisis and Cruelty: Illegal Abductions, Court Defiance and the Case of Kilmar Abrego Garcia," no date, indivisible.org)

Trump's Far-Right broader authoritarian politics have been so overwhelming that they bear a quick repetition. They include unconstitutional use of ICE and the military – and invoking one emergency or war threat after another – to go after immigrants and other of his enemies in US cities in the name of stopping a non-existent Venezuelan invasion and restoring law and order, his use of the Justice Department to prosecute his political enemies, his rejection of constitutional reproductive rights and birthright citizenship rights, his mass firing of civil servants, his mass cuts orchestrated initially by Elon Musk at DOGE to social welfare and assaults on Social Security, Medicare and Medicaid, his blatantly corrupt deals with his corporate oligarchs giving them huge government contracts for massive payments to himself and his business, his crypto, real estate, sneaker, whisky and other blatant grifting schemes, his all-out attack on unions, his war to control down critical thinking and defund universities like Harvard and the University of Pennsylvania, among hundreds of others, his nationwide campaign to ban books and "woke" curricula in elementary schools, high schools and public libraries, his campaign to defund or abolish hundreds of government programs and regulatory "deep state" agencies essential to the health and safety of ordinary workers, his assault on environmental regulation and public health, his withdrawal from the World Health Organization and the Paris Climate Accords, his imperial chaos abroad, his tariffs and trade wars drastically shaking up the markets, his brutality toward immigrants, his constant racial and gender slurs, and his violent repression of rioters and protesters, as well as his ongoing election denialism on full display January 6 and his ongoing executive orders to weaken voter rights and create the view that all elections were rigged. At this writing, these are already catalyzing positive populist movements stirring much of the public – moving them more quickly down the seven stages of grief and renewal that Kubler-Ross offers.

The final three stages – testing, decision and integration – can all be seen as processes moving individuals and movements from burnout and surrender to activist renewal. They have been observed in millions of people dealing with the death of loved ones. History of Far-Right and positive democratic populist movements suggest the same tendencies to rebuild in the face of calamity, and to find the resources to renew a vibrant democratic movement in the face of horrific Far-Right populist regimes, a movement that has already led millions of ordinary Americans out into the streets, outraged by Trump's naked authoritarianism based on the joint rule of an autocrat and his oligarchy.

Principles of Emerging Resistance

As stages of resistance and renewal emerge, positive populists leading the charge will need to keep in mind some key reflections about how to respond to political catastrophe and the way to overcome the hurdles and threats that they will face. Here, we just briefly list and reflect on them.

1   The trauma of defeat to Trump and his Far-Right populism is deep and real. It creates overwhelming shock and denial. Many will experience it as a political near-death. There is no question that most will need a period of recovery involving rest and reflection. Forcing all people and movements to respond immediately – whether with petitions or mass marches – may be counterproductive.

   At the same time, the first few months after Trump's reelection, with hundreds of thousands of people protesting all over the country against Trump's disastrous tariffs, his war on government, his deportation of immigrants and open assault on rights of free speech and protest that included threats to deport US citizens who were "criminals," and his unconstitutional defiance of judges and the Supreme Court, show that many people respond to trauma with an immediate fury and want to hit back right away. When leading positive populist politicians like Bernie Sanders and Alexandria-Ocasio-Cortez launched their April 2025 "Fight Oligarchy" tour, they attracted huge crowds of between 10,000 and 35,000 ordinary Americans in red states like Idaho, Utah, Nebraska, Kansas, Texas, and Montana, as well as in swing states like Arizona and Colorado.

   These enormous turnouts for the most positive populist politicians in America showed the potential for a positive populist resistance. That so many people reacted so quickly suggests that Trump is likely to face a long-term resistance with many affinities to the New Deal as economic turbulence and prospects of severe downturn and recession loom larger. And the mass street protests within weeks of Trump's reelection served a purpose – not only for those who spontaneously demonstrated on the streets – but for the rise of a longer-term positive populist movement that could ultimately defeat Trump and his billionaire oligarchy.

   In April 2025, as she was joining Sanders in her "Fight Oligarchy" tour, AOC was getting the highest favorability ratings of any Democrat. Indeed, on April 17, one of America's leading pollsters, Nate Silver, predicted that AOC would be the 2028 Democratic Party presidential candidate. (Pocharapon Neammanee, "Nate Silver Predicts Who Will Be the 2028 Democratic Presidential Candidate," HuffPost, April 17, 2025, huffpost.com) If true, this would be a major step forward for the Democrats, moving toward the positive populist agenda that can speak to the hidden populist bipartisan American majority and winning back many of the New Deal working-class Democrats who voted for Trump.

   As Trump's trade, tariff and budget policies spiked prices and job losses, increasing risks of stagflation and recession, the populist labor politics of the New Deal will become common sense, the only way to save most

Americans working paycheck to paycheck from falling into poverty and long-term deep economic insecurity.

Many working people might now see in Cortez a 21st-century New Deal for them to return and support. Indeed, Cortez was a cosponsor of the Green New Deal legislation introduced during Trump's first term and calling for massive investment in jobs and job training for America's working class in hard-pressed states like Michigan, Wisconsin and Pennsylvania. Sanders had also defeated Hillary Clinton in many of these states' 2016 presidential Democratic primaries, with workers seeing in Sanders and Cortez a positive populist agenda that would speak to them and highlight them as central players in the fight against big corporations and the ruling oligarchy.

Many moderate Democrats fear that such outspoken populism cannot win over a culturally conservative working class. But remember that positive populism is a recipe for economic transformative measures helping all workers, whatever their cultural values. Positive populism is class politics that speaks to every American worker's interests, whatever their position on divisive "cultural wars." The art of positive populist success is empathy and unity with working people of different religions, ethnicities and cultural values, including culturally conservative workers whom liberals and Democrats have so often "dissed."

Put differently, positive populism is founded on a transformative politics build to destroy the ruling corporate oligarchy, but it can only succeed with radical empathy, the capacity to build solidarity and love across communities united to act for justice and democracy while respecting and honoring different values and cultures. Positive populists may not win over white workers if they do not reject their own forms of political correctness and cancel culture that alienate workers who would otherwise support their anti-corporate and pro-worker agenda. But the deepening economic crises and looming recession caused by Trump's tariff, budget and immigration policies will almost certainly bring many of the workers who voted for Trump into a new positive populist camp, since their problems of keeping a job or paying their rent or grocery bills will, as in the New Deal, create deeper anger and rejection of the corporate oligarchy. Personal economic anger and moral revulsion at Trump's politics of hate will lead many Trump voters to support the positive populist movement genuinely seeking to defeat corporate oligarchy and Trump's rising police state.

2 At the heart of resistance and renewal is social connection. Isolation is the recipe for depression and paralysis. People find the motivation, support and power to resist and rebuild most powerfully through solidarity with others in a positive populist movement. A focus on coming together, providing emotional support and building stronger ties among fellow activists is the key to positive populism. This has long been the central idea of labor unions and workers in positive populist struggles, beginning with the Populist unions like the Knights of Labor and the Industrial Workers

of the World (IWW) in the first Gilded Age. Their slogan became *an injury to one is an injury to all.*

Ideas, strategies and movements depend almost completely on the strength of solidarity. In the face of catastrophe, movements need to offer exceptional emotional solidarity, allowing people to cry with each other and express despair together. The best medicine they can offer initially is simple affirmation of each other's grief. Emotional support will tend to build more interdependence and belief in the possibility of future collective action, as bonds of trust and care grow stronger. Activists will gain belief in possibilities mainly by interacting with friends and fellow activists who are showing their own resistance and belief in the need to act – and to act together.

While the neoliberal and Trumpist oligarchies have worked tirelessly to break down our social relations, the resistance is helping rebuild social relationships in an atomized America. This is the hidden social and cultural work of positive populist movements that can only defeat Trump and the oligarchy not by protesting and going home, but by coming back to work after week, month after month and year after year. The warmth and joy of rallying on the streets, in workplaces or in town halls are the glue that keeps the resistance alive. It builds spontaneous protests into an enduring movement building organizational and political capacities. When people are finding new friends, relations and music together, binding them together in a culture of commitment to a long-term struggle, they are creating the only struggle that can win. In her chronicle of labor populism in the Great Depression, Vivian Gornick described in her book, *The Romance of American Communism*, how the Left and labor activists became friends, married, had kids and sent them to summer camp, where they learned the songs and strategies of a new community and a lifelong resistance. (Vivian Gornick, The Romance of American Communism. London: Verso, 2020)

Resistance emerges only when people and institutions under attack join together; the history of populist workers' struggles against oligarchy has helped make this the foundation of successful resistance for all movements. This involves not just creating new social relations and community but political strategies of coming together in common defense against oligarchic efforts to split and divide them. In his second term, Trump began to attack universities and law firms, one by one. And one by one they surrendered.

But on April 14, 2025, when Harvard University pushed back, saying government cannot dictate the curricula, programs, scholarship and speech on campuses; it appeared to mark the beginning of a collective reaction. A few days later, Yale University faculty celebrated the Harvard resistance and urged Yale's top administrators to do the same. Yale and Princeton University presidents declared solidarity with Harvard in written public statements. Faculty senates in big public state universities, including Rutgers, Indiana University and the University of Minnesota, issued a statement celebrating Harvard's resistance and urging their universities to do the same. After Harvard sued Trump and intensified its resistance, many other universities around the country joined in; leaders of more than 180 colleges and universities, with at least 200 more joining them in the following days and weeks, sent a statement on April 18, 2025, lambasting Trump's "overreach" into academic and university affairs. (Sebastian Murdock, "More than 180 College Leaders Blast Trump's 'Unprecedented Government Overreach,'" Huffington Post, April 22, 2025, huffpost.com. See also Stephanie Saul and Alan Blinder, "Emerging From a Collective Silence, Universities Organize to Fight Trump," NY Times, April 29, 2025, nytimes.com) Even at besieged universities like Columbia, which capitulated, the Harvard resistance led Columbia faculty and students to call for more resistance on their own campuses by uniting with allies at Columbia and universities around the country. (Luke Broadwater, "Trump's Threats Force Institutions to Choose: Cut a Deal or Fight Back," NY Times, April 16, 2025, nytimes.com. See also Ashley Dawson, To Resist Trump's Academic Purge, Campuses Must Unite With Each Other, Truthout, April 16, 2025, truthout.org.)

On April 16, these and other universities began declaring "mutual defense pacts." Any attack on any one of them would be viewed as an attack on all. This illustrates powerfully the crucial importance of connection and solidarity in building the resistance to Far-Right authoritarianism, pioneered by Gilded Age populist workers and farmers. Autocratic regimes gain power by isolating their targets and opponents. When isolated and alone, fear takes over and individuals or institutions surrender. But in "mutual defense pacts," alliances become a source of courage and strength, as individuals and institutions have others with whom they can band and fight back. This building of mutual defense and strong coalitions is among the most important secrets of an effective resistance, and calls for a Mutual Defense Compact among all members of the Association of American Universities began to grow. University presidents began to be in regular conversation with each other, finding new strategies to cooperate against Trump's funding cuts and attacks on curricula, faculty and students. (Stephanie Saul and Alan Blinder, "Emerging From a Collective Silence, Universities Organize to Fight Trump," NY Times, April 29, 2025, nytimes.com. See also Ashley Dawson, To Resist Trump's Academic Purge, Campuses Must Unite With Each Other, Truthout, April 16, 2025, truthout.org.)

Law firms under attack urgently needed to learn the same lesson. Law firms caving to Trump also went one by one, their isolation and fear leading to capitulation. But within a few months, a few major firms and high-profile attorneys said enough was enough. Major law firms, such as Jenner & Block, Perkins Coie and WilmerHale, began coming together, sharing strategy and uniting in fighting Trump, going to court together to ask federal courts to bar any further Trump executive orders against them. (Erin Mulvaney, "The Lawyers With Trump Ties Who Are on Harvard's Side,"

Wall Street Journal, April 16, 2025, wsj.com) Again, coming together and building unified resistance was a central lesson.

The same dynamic even emerged under judges being threatened by Trump and his allies. Trump and some of his cabinet officials denounced justices ruling against him as villains or rogues who should be impeached. Wisconsin judge, Hannah Dugan, was arrested by the FBI for allegedly obstructing immigration officials, and Attorney General Pam Bondi threatened more judges:

> Bondi declares war on the courts: "What has happened to our judiciary is beyond me ... they are deranged ... we are sending a very strong message today ... we will come after you and we will prosecute you. We will find you."[12]

Judges began coming together and issuing joint statements about the extreme constitutional dangers the Trump Administration was creating. (Marina Dunbar and Maya Lang, FBI arrests Wisconsin judge and accuses her of obstructing immigration officials, the Guardian, April 25, 2025, theguardian.com) The need for judges to take these extraordinary steps and speak publicly was among the most powerful signs of the constitutional crisis that Trump's Far-Right war on democracy was reaching a breaking point. (Tierney Sneed, "'Breathtaking in its audacity' Trump's conflict with judges has escalated to new heights," CNN, April 1, 2025, cnn.com)

All of these various institutions joining "mutual defenses" were learning the basic rule of positive populist movements, long understood by working people. In the New Deal, workers learned the only way to gain power and challenge the corporate regime was to come together in unions and build countervailing power to big money through labor solidarity and power; this proved essential to turning the Democratic Party from its big money donors to ordinary and desperate Americans. This happened during the New Deal, and it is now the central test of the resistance to Trump and his ruling oligarchy, especially as Trumpism moves the economy toward a new Great Recession, destroying the lives of millions of working people. We need now not only a rebuilding of the labor movement, which is a crucial element of the anti-Trump positive populist resistance but also a spreading of the principle of solidarity and collective struggle among all of America's most basic institutions and communities. When you fight alone, you lose; when you fight together, you win.

3 While it will seem almost unbelievable in a country voting to re-elect Trump, you represent the majority in terms of your views about the corporate Establishment and the rights of ordinary people to gather, organize for power and speak out. Remember, there is a hidden bipartisan majority of Americans who disapprove of big corporations and support unions and worker rights. It is a lot easier to build confidence in yourself and your

political movements when you recognize that you share key basic values with the majority, including some of those voting for Trump. When you realize you represent the majority, you not only gain rightful confidence in possibilities of change but also build a sense of solidarity with people who thought you could only hate. This breaks down barriers and expands activist possibilities with unexpected allies.

The "Fight Oligarchy" tour in the first few months of Trump's second term perfectly illustrated this principle. Leading positive populist politicians, Bernie Sanders and AOC, as noted above, took their outrage and anti-Establishment views to Red states and conservative voters. With tens of thousands of people coming out to see them, it was clear they were speaking to and for the general public. But in doing so, they were not softening their message or moving away from their Left anti-oligarchy view. To the contrary, their tour was all about highlighting the threat of oligarchic rule, a threat becoming more obvious and threatening to ordinary workers as they faced the very hard times and looming recession or even depression that could be created by Trump's tariff and budgetary war against American workers at home and in Europe, Canada and Mexico, all also targets of Trump's "America First" punitive tariffs and trade wars.

The very reason that Sanders and AOC "Fight Oligarchy" tour attracted so many people was that they spoke to the populist anti-corporate views already dominant in the US public, as shown in the data presented earlier. The public was hungry to hear politicians who spoke the truth, moving beyond the scripts of high-paid political consultants. Sanders and AOC showed that the way a populist resistance builds power is with political leaders moving outside of Washington and speaking directly to the pain of the public, with their unvarnished positive populism resonating powerfully across partisan lines and urging the public to fight furiously for their own rights and needs. They were the politicians most clearly speaking to the hidden populist bipartisan majority – and were making it clear that the Democratic Party could only defeat Trump by embracing their own positive populism resonating so strongly with the public.

Remember Sanders and AOC were already resonating with millions of ordinary Americans even before the full force of Trump's economically devastating tariff, trade, budget and immigration policies had time to hit most workers. When they fully hit, most workers, including many Trump voters already finding it hard to pay their bills, will find it harder and harder to survive. The current economic crisis, marked by the division of America into the billionaire class with 800 billionaires who have more wealth than all the rest of Americans combined, has already created the bipartisan populist majority of Americans disapproving of corporations and supporting workers and unions. As Trump's tariffs and budget savage the working population far more deeply in coming downturns or recessions, positive populism will emerge as the only real solution for working Americans trying to survive in the coming very hard times.

Successful social movements build a "collective identity" that unites millions of diverse people around shared values and a common vision. We have seen both in the surveys of American voters' political views and their rallies on the streets that they are coming together in the name of fighting a billionaire oligarchy and creating democracy. This essential collective identity will grow and increasingly take a class-based form as the capitalist economy further destabilizes and moves ordinary workers into personal crises of survival, unable to pay for their health care, housing and food. This personalizes and universalizes resistance – and offers the best chance of both defeating Trump and building sustainable economic and political democracy.

4 While you can only defeat Trump and Far-Right populism with a big coalition – building a very broad bipartisan coalition is crucially important to victory – it doesn't mean you have to tone down your values or end your fight for major change. What you share with the hidden populist majority is anger at the power of a small super-wealthy elite who are using their power to rip off the rest of the country. That is a view now held by an American majority. So do not moderate your values or hold back on your radicalism. What you share with the majority is, in fact, the radicalism of populism – the feeling that the system is corrupt and needs desperate change. The more you communicate that radicalism, the more you'll pick up support. You will build a winning coalition by being more anti-Establishment, not by caving into it.

This was a lesson slowly being absorbed by more and more Democratic Party officials and leaders. On April 19, 2025, Connecticut Senator Chris Murphy, a leading Democratic Party populist and possible presidential candidate, declared on the Senate Floor that it was time for "civil disobedience," an almost unprecedented view voiced by a US senator. Murphy declared an emergency, with democracy now dying in legally cloaked degradations of people's rights and dissent. ("Murphy: Trump is Dismantling Our Democracy," YouTube, April 11, 2025, youtube.com) Murphy was sending a radical populist message echoing non-violent civil rights strategies of Democratic hero, Democratic Congressman, John Lewis, who was almost beaten to death by Southern racists when he marched against the Jim Crow regime in 1960s Alabama. Murphy was also echoing the broader 1960s movements of Martin Luther King and of populist students, who he argued were the real target of Trump's war on the universities, fearful of the new generation's search for freedom, truth and activism on their campuses.

The new Chair and Vice-Chair of the Democratic National Committee, Ken Martin, a Minnesota labor-populist and David Hogg, an anti-gun youthful populist, both spoke of the need to transform the Democratic Party in the spirit of transformative change for and by working people and young people all over the country. Hogg was soon pushed out of his DNC post, but he continued to claim that the new DNC would have to back more "left-wing" and younger challengers in 2026 Democratic primaries against "asleep-at-the-wheel Democrats in deep blue states." (Elena Schneider, "In unprecedented move, DNC official to spend big to take down fellow Democrats," Politico, April 15, 2025, politico.com) The large Progressive Caucus in Congress also called for and participated on the streets in pro-democracy and pro-worker rallies all over the country. At the same time, they sponsored anti-oligarchic populist legislation, including laws and constitutional amendments to end Citizens United and the right of the billionaire class to give hundreds of millions of dollars to candidates. But many progressive populists remained concerned that Martin, the DNC and the Democratic Party were not embracing populism more deeply:

> *To shed its well-earned reputation for elitism, the DNC should stop running away from populism and instead embrace it – not by making peace with Trumpism, but by moving toward genuine progressive populism. That means showing that the party actually means business about siding with the interests of low- and middle-income Americans against the rapacious effects of unfettered corporate power – from systematic price gouging to regressive tax rates to runaway military spending – at the expense of programs that meet human needs.*[13]

A leading Left populist activist, Robert Borosage, was more specific:

> *"largely absent from the debate … is what progressives consider to be a fundamental question: What will the new chair do to curb the role of outside, dark money in Democratic Party primaries? This is increasingly an existential question for progressives – and for the party, if it is in fact to revive its commitment to working people."*[14]

As the economy further destabilizes in the wake of Trump's tariff, trade and immigration wars, and his budget transferring even more money to billionaire oligarchs from economically insecure workers, it will become hard for the Democratic Party – and most voters – not to see the urgency of a more transformative positive populist Democratic Party and resistance movement. As the economy moves into deeper crisis, it will become obvious that the Democratic Party must move to embrace some version of the positive populism of Bernie Sanders and AOC. Even before the recession or depression that Trump's policies will likely deliver, their "Fight Oligarchy" tour spectacularly resonated – and showed the kind of outspoken and unapologetic populist assault on the oligarchy that can speak to ordinary Democrats, Independents and Republicans, as well as the 80 million mainly poor and working Americans who don't vote.

The "Fight Oligarchy" tour success, massively increasing the size of the resistance, was the clearest demonstration of what will lead millions of more non-college working people to back a new Democratic Party against Trumpism, especially as the economy suffers increasing shock from Trump's policies and moves toward high prices, fewer jobs and recession ravaging the very workers who voted for Trump. While moderate Democrats fear culturally conservative workers will reject this populist "radicalism," it can succeed when its economic populism is essential and supportive of all workers in deep economic distress and is couched in a larger cultural message tolerant of many different positions on divisive issues in the "culture wars." Moreover, the workers who voted for Trump's own claims of populism will have to find a new populist agenda. Trump became the new Establishment and could no longer credibly claim to fight the ruling corporate oligarchy that he would save them from.

5 The fact that your radicalism is essential to building your winning coalition doesn't mean there is no need for pragmatism or compromise. You share with the majority of Americans disapproval of the big corporate, monied Establishment. You also share the majority support for unions and the power of ordinary working people. But you also are likely to have major cultural differences with many of the people who share your dislike of big money and its corrupting political power. Political success will come by finding the common ground of anti-Establishment economics and politics among allies across the partisan board – including those who don't vote. But your coalition won't work without genuine respect for cultural differences. Many of your unexpected populist allies will be likely to have different religious beliefs, different favorite novels and different ideas about gender or affirmative action, not to mention political party. Populist political success can happen when you can come together on shared economic and class-based values while agreeing to differ on a wide array of cultural values.

Keep in mind that Trump won because of the way that Democrats and identity party leaders among liberals and the Left played into Trump's hands. As Thomas Frank has highlighted, they embraced an elitist doctrine hostile to non-college-educated people, a majority of whom were white non-college workers. Many liberals excoriated them, following Hillary Clinton's misguided example, as "deplorables" who were racist. They pushed working people away with political correctness, cancel culture and purist language. They charged them with "white privilege." Positive populism means finding empathic means of uniting across shared anti-Establishment, anti-oligarchic values with people who do not share your cultural or educational backgrounds or cultural beliefs. Uniting around shared economic pain will become easier as Trump's policies bring deeper economic unraveling and growing prospects of recession or even depression.

6 You are now fighting a multifront battle that has to be waged in different ways at different levels of governance. Trump is going to command power at the national majority and, at least until 2026, in Congress and national politics. But positive populists have control of about 20 states, where anti-Trumpists include the Governor, the Attorney General and, in some cases, both houses of the state legislature. This includes major states like California, New York and Illinois. Anti-Trumpists will also hold power in hundreds of cities and small towns. Resistance will be waged powerfully at the state and local levels, such as in the Northwest and New England, where regional state coalitions are not just resisting Trump's national environmental agenda but are building new climate protections and green investments across their states and regions. Cities and states are building public banks that will invest in worker and environmental needs being rejected by Trump at the national level. They are putting abortion and gay marriage protections in their constitutions. They are protecting the integrity of voting in their own states.

7 Attorneys Generals in more than twenty states are suing in their state courts to challenge Trump's deportations and his use of the military to round up immigrants and control anti-ICE protesters in LA and other cities, his abolition of entire government agencies like the Department of Labor and Department of Education, his Musk-led massive cuts of social security and Medicaid and other mandated Congressional legislation and funding authority, his effort to jail international students from Columbia to Tufts to Harvard, putting crucial legal and political authority of the states and the Democratic Party in alliance and coalition with the mass protestors on the streets. They are also suing to guarantee an end to local and state racial discrimination as well as to maintain the constitutionality and power of labor unions. And they are mobilizing to fight fire with fire by creating their own partisan redistricting to counter Trump's order to Texas and other Red States to gerrymander their own electoral maps to deny Democrats any chance of winning.

This means there is clearly room for aggressive and radical moves at local, state and regional levels for popular positive new laws and government programs, even as the main task at the national level will be ever more fierce and radical resistance, shutting down business as usual. Every small step that slows the work of autocratic and oligarchic forces creates time for others to join and add another body to the rally or activism, unsettling the authoritarian movement; thousands of small steps make autocrats take notice that ordinary people are watching them, often outraged.

Moreover, each step you take, big or small, is a form of courage that will spread to others.

While autocrats are spreading fear to keep people quiet, courage is contagious, inspiring others in your family, neighborhood, workplace, town, state and nation to join you. Remember that there are big populist majorities who disapprove of big companies and support workers and their unions. They are horrified at the blatant corruption that oligarchs use to buy favor from Trump for their own projects and cancel crucial public agencies and programs, transferring government funds to their own companies like Musk's SpaceX and Bezos's Kuiper statellite company. Public small acts of resistance – multiplied in thousands of rallies on scores of crucial issues of defunding, corruption, cruelty, constitutionalism and greed – will open doors for larger and stronger resistance at every level of government in every state; this is the path to all successful resistance, as documented by Chenowitz and Stephan, in Why Civil Resistance Works (Chenowitz and Stephan, op cit in Chapter 6). Massive resistance grew quickly in Trump's second term, coalescing in different large national movements called Hands Off or 50-50-1, meaning in some accounts 50 protests in 50 states in one movement. In April 2025, 100 days into Trump's second term, mass positive populist rallies around the country were erupting almost every week.

8 Global resistance is also important. As Americans fight Trump, anti-Far-Right populists are fighting for their political life across most of Europe, including in France, Germany and Italy, as well as Hungary and Poland. In Europe itself, there are growing Left-populist movements within and across European countries to protect democracy and defeat Far-Right populists aligned with Trump. Far-Right populism is a global movement in which Far-Right leaders are aligned with Trump and other like-minded leaders, not only in Europe but in much of the Global South. Resistance will require alliances with Left positive populists wherever they are emerging in the world. This is a fight that is global with enormous worldwide consequences. What happens in America – and its ability to align with like-minded activists across the world – will determine humanity's future.

Trump and MAGA openly built alliances with Far-Right oligarchs and authoritarian leaders around the world. Trump met with Bukele, El Salvador's Far-Right dictator, even as masses of Americans were insisting that Trump follow the order of the Supreme Court to facilitate Kilmar Abrego Gacia's return to America's from Salvador's worst prison. Trump and Musk openly embraced Far-Right regimes of Orban in Hungary, Milei in Argentina, and Putin in Russia, inviting foreign Far-Right leaders to speak with Trump in the Oval Office or to give major speeches at Trumpist rallies. They were making clear that their authoritarian movement was global, reflecting the global character of the oligarchy and billionaire class they represented.

The resistance was slower to develop these global connections. But its success depends on "mutual defense pacts" with their peers who were fighting oligarchy and Far-Right regimes everywhere in the world. Left parties in major European countries such as France and Germany are building coalitions to fight their own Far-Right oligarchic threats. They are following in the example of the Czech Republic, which successfully ousted its own Trump-like authoritarian leader in 2021. (Robert Tait, "Anti-Trump protesters in the US night look to the Czech Republic: We are an Example," The Guardian, April 20, 2025, theguardian.com) The same is true in many countries of the Global South, such as Lula's pro-democracy partisans against Bolsonaro in Brazil. Since oligarchy is global, positive populist movements must also be global.

Since the economy and oligarchy are global, any genuine populist movement must build global solidarity as well. Trump's tariff and trade policies are creating massive economic crises not only for US workers and the American economy but also for workers and economies all over the world. Trump's tariff and trade policies are simultaneously a war on workers in Canada, Mexico, Europe and Southeast Asia as well as on American workers. Trump is thus unwittingly creating the foundations of a global positive populist resistance uniting working people in America who suffer from the same oligarchic and autocratic Trump policies as working people around the world.

Indeed, such global resistance has already begun. Across Europe and much of the world, people horrified by Trump's policies are protesting Trump in their own streets in solidarity with the American protests. As social media helped globalize images of the huge American "No Kings" protest, Euronews reported that protesters in France, the Netherlands and many other European towns rallied in solidarity against Trump on their own streets:

> *The national and international protests against President Donald Trump took place in towns and cities across the US and Europe in a coordinated event titled "No Kings."*[15]

The underlying principle of resistance – building strong connections and vast coalitions that overcome the isolation and fear that corporate regimes and Far-Right nationalism exploits – does not stop at the nation's borders. Positive populism can win when it unites its partisans across the globe, since they face a shared global oligarchic and authoritarian deathly threat. Solidarity forever is a global rallying cry for positive populists everywhere.

Positive Populism Is Not "Back to Normal": Successful Resistance Means Regime Change at Home

When threatened with authoritarian Far-right catastrophe, it is tempting to view resistance as simply ending the extreme danger and returning to the "normalcy" preceding Trumpism. But that was not a normal or democratic era. It was a neoliberal, oligarchic period so destructive to working people and the nation that they turned to Trump as their only agent of change. He has failed them, but a new Trump or Far-Right populist will emerge unless the resistance not only ousts Trump but also dismantles the disastrous oligarchic class and rule – and its assault on workers that led them to Trump in the first place.

This makes clear a central principle of positive populism. Resistance is not a return to "normalcy." It is a recognition of the power of the US corporate regime that created the very possibility of a Far-Right authoritarian and billionaire like Trump. Going back will open the door to another Trump. Resistance, then, means moving the nation forward to a transformed economic and political order that genuinely serves the interests of working people – and the broader environmental and justice agendas they desperately need. That, in turn, means a positive populism seeking to finally move America beyond oligarchic rule. While it seems impossible in a Far-Right oligarchic era, we have already seen that the majorities of Americans are searching for genuinely populist change to protect and empower working people and end the ruling power of corporate elites. That positive populism will inevitably grow stronger as Trump's policies further destabilize the economy, enriching billionaires and subjecting workers who voted for him to far harder economic times and more exploited by the billionaire class; they thought Trump would ally with them to defeat oligarchy.

We have already hinted at what a post-oligarchic agenda for America will look like. Its two main components are, first, to curb the wealth and power of the uber-wealthy and corporations and, second, to offer a social democratic agenda for working people that meets their desperate needs for secure jobs and broader environmental and social justice. History offers hope; we have seen that the New Deal regime embodied positive populism and an early anti-oligarchic model in the mid-20th century. Moreover, it is hardly utopian; much of this social democratic agenda has been successfully enacted in prosperous European nations during much of the late 20th and 21st centuries.

My book, *Regime Change at Home*, discusses US history as a series of domestic regimes (Charles Derber, *Regime Change Begins at Home*, SF: Berrett Koehler, 2004). The 1890s Gilded Age created the Robber Baron America that I call the "First Corporate Regime." It was our first modern corporate oligarchic system. From 1932, with the election of FDR, to the Reagan Revolution in 1980, we voted in and supported a "New Deal Regime," the nation's most important era of countervailing power for working people, challenging the rule of the oligarchs. It created, as discussed above, an early version of social and economic democracy for and by workers. The Reagan era created the neoliberal revolution, sweeping away the New Deal and creating a Second Corporate Regime. It empowered and enriched a new class of oligarchs even more powerful than the original Robber Barons. It led toward the Far-Right populism of Trump and MAGA, exploiting the absence of a populist Democratic Party challenge to the new second corporate regime.

The resistance today has the simultaneous challenge of destroying Trump while creating a new post-oligarchic nation. A positive populist resistance will succeed only if it offers a positive, credible regime change at home. This means ending the wealth and power of corporations and disempowering today's robber baron class, while creatively empowering something entirely new: a 21st-century New Deal regime based on economic and political democracy.

I briefly conclude by outlining steps to take down the oligarchs with regime change resistance. This requires at least three major key populist changes creating a post-oligarchic America: forcing the corporate elites to pay the enormous taxes they owe, ending their system that allows them to pour billions of dollars to buy candidates and lobby to write the legislation they want, and changing the charter of the corporation to create an institution serving and accountable to the public.

The fact that we don't have a tax on billionaires' wealth seems a form of lunacy, particularly when so much of their money comes from the largely hidden system of corporate welfare and corruption that creates their wealth. Along with populist politicians like Bernie Sanders and AOC, a growing number of leading economists and analysts of inequality, including Thomas Piketty and Chuck Collins, have been calling for a wealth tax on billionaires, with Collins also promoting a steeper inheritance tax on the very rich that will stop the rise of new dynasties of intergenerational privilege and uber-wealth aristocracy, an aim crucial to positive populism. In his books, *The Wealth Hoarders* and *Burnt by Billionaires*, Collins outlines simple and straightforward ways to tax the super-wealthy, showing how they have built a system of trusts, philanthropic foundations, lawyers and accountants to hide and shelter their billions; it allows them to pay, as Warren Buffet has acknowledged, lower tax rates than their secretaries.

Meanwhile, Trump's top gift to the oligarchy in his first term was to lower income taxes paid by the rich; he is using tariffs in his second term, as discussed already, to eliminate income taxes altogether as well as prevent wealth taxes, putting the entire tax burden on working people paying a sales tax as consumers on tariffed goods. Moreover, since corporations get so much money from a corporate welfare system, doled out through tax write-offs, subsidies, giveaways of public lands and resources, and trade and militarist policies, their wealth has ultimately come from taxpayers and should go back to them as a top priority of positive populist movements. As discussed in the first chapter, polls show that a supermajority of Americans blame the rich for not paying taxes and support far higher taxes on corporations and the rich; a tax revolution helped found America and can help create a new one.

Tied to this positive populist tax revolution, we must, second, end the system of oligarchs buying politicians and government that was put in place by the Robber Barons in the first Gilded Age. Since then, it has been massively oiled and greased to permit billions of dollars to buy elections in the current Second Corporate Regime. The Supreme Court played a major role in wiring this new oligarchic purchase of government and politics, writing the 2010 Citizens United decision that treats money as speech and curbs on big corporate donations as infringements of free speech. Later decisions, such as the 2014 McCutcheon decision, allowed far greater contributions to groups and superPACs and untraceable "dark money" that led to over $2 billion spent in the 2024 presidential election cycle and unprecedented control of Washington by billionaires. Overthrowing Citizens United and moving toward a public system of campaign finance is positive populist common sense; it has been enacted in many European nations. The data described in Chapter 1 show that the majority of Americans support curbing dark money; they see huge corporate campaign donations and lobbying as shredding American democracy. They want to stop it.

Third, creating new "public" corporations is a central positive populist goal. As shown in Chapter 1, super-majorities of Americans – more than 70% – disapprove of big corporations and banks, making clear that a positive populist agenda curbing and rewiring corporations can gain majority support. It may appear to go against the grain of American history, but corporations before the Civil War in the US were legally defined as public rather than private entities, created by the people and accountable to them and public interests. If early corporations and banks could not demonstrate that they were serving the public interest to state legislatures, their charters could be revoked. (Charles Derber, Corporation Nation, NY: St. Martins Press, 2000)

An oligarchic revolution, aided by the Supreme Court and the Robber Barons, transformed the corporate mission and charter after the Civil War. In the 1876 Santa Clara Act, the Supreme Court issued a statement of corporate personhood, viewing the corporation as akin legally to a private citizen with private interests. Legal scholars, like Harvard's Morton Horowitz, declared this a revolution, moving from the public corporation to the "privatized" one. This was a regime change, creating an entity chartered by private investors to serve profit interests and to be governed by and for the investors rather than the public.

Rechartering the corporation to serve the public is thus a return to the original American idea of the corporation. Early Americans feared that big banks and companies could threaten and destroy ordinary American freedoms and democracy, as British companies had. Companies today embracing "ESG" – or environmental, social and governance criteria – are beginning to recognize that some movement toward certifiable public and environmental standards are first step for their own public legitimacy. Rechartering the corporation as a public entity, accountable to workers and the public as well as investors is common sense, and a part of the history of US efforts for democratic rule. In a period of deepening economic inequality and stagflation or recession, climate change and militarism, the positive populist effort to bring corporations back to control by the people is now not only a condition for worker security and democracy but also for survival of the planet.

As highlighted throughout this chapter and book, conditions for regime change, already ripe given the existing economic crises of class and oligarchic inequality, and growing riper as the economy destabilizes and suffers more severe downturns and recessions as Trump's tariffs, trade and budgets sink in, will increase the urgency and resonance of a resistance fighting for regime change. Regime change in an economy breaking down and creating unprecedented divisions between billionaires and everyone else will become common sense.

The corporate regime giving rise to Trump will give rise to a post-Trump oligarchy without a resistance focusing on regime change. As recession and possible depression emerge, the need to change the regime that created Trump in the first place will become more urgent and more obvious. The anti-corporate and pro-labor American populist majority that elected Trump will become even more anti-corporate and pro-labor will become even more populist as economic crises deepen. But Trump, now the Establishment, can no longer offer his Far-Right populist rhetoric as a solution. Anti-Trumpists can and must take up the positive populist mantle both to show the lies and deceptions of Trump's populism and to create the transformative anti-corporate regime change that Trump's base thought he would deliver. It is now clear that the only anti-oligarchic America will come from the anti-Trump resistance that is firmly committed to destroying the corporate oligarchy that ruled America long before Trump.

Beyond destroying the oligarchic regime and ending the billionaire class wealth dynasties through these steps, positive populist regime change at home must be affirmative and positive, constructing a radically new form of American economic and social democracy. Such a post-oligarchic America must offer working people deep economic as well as political participation and control. This means creating the populist worker power and access to universal social welfare programs now common in many prosperous European nations; such populism began to emerge in the US New Deal. We have already documented the key elements of populist labor transformations in the New Deal that supplanted Robber Baron rule with countervailing power exercised by unions and New Deal labor and social reforms movements. Positive populists today are calling for a new system that is radically innovative and creates a new positive and loving social system, drawing on New Deal roots.

The three most important elements of such affirmative and creative regime change are rebuilding the labor movement to help workers run the economy, creating a positive populist Democratic Party politically enshrining worker rather than oligarchic power, and building a universal social welfare system ensuring safety nets for ordinary Americans. All of these got traction in the first New Deal, and can gain far more power in the second, based on the super-majorities of Americans with positive populist attitudes supporting workers, union power and social democracy.

Despite the Trumpist effort to eliminate unions, the rise of a new labor movement is now supported by 70% of Americans. This is hardly surprising, as the majority of Americans live "paycheck to paycheck," with only 6% of Americans unionized. In contrast, more than 70% of workers are unionized in European nations like Denmark and Sweden, which have far higher wages and social benefits than American workers. Moreover, more than 40% of Americans were unionized in the New Deal, demonstrating that when workers are allied with a positive populist Democratic Party, unions can thrive and fight oligarchy by delivering real benefits to Americans. In the post-World War II era of the 1950s and 1960s, Americans thrived as unions became powerful. It was so threatening to oligarchs that their top priority was to destroy unions. Reagan's first major official act was to destroy PATCO, the air traffic controllers' union.

In earlier chapters, we documented the new labor movement, led by positive populist industrial union leaders like Sean Fain, and a new generation of rising service and public sector unions. Fain is organizing for a national strike in 2028 to take down oligarchic rule. It aims to sustain the 2023 "summer of labor," which led to more annual strikes and union drives than in 50 years. New unions in the service and public sectors, which are the most highly unionized and dominant economic sectors, are increasingly led by women and people of color, who have new labor agendas. The very mission of unions is beginning to change from narrow collective bargaining to larger change in their communities and national regime change for economic democracy and social justice. Workers must help run their companies and the local and national economy.

A new alliance between positive populist labor movements and a populist Democratic Party is central to regime change at home. Before Trump, we had two corporate parties, often dubbed Bush and Bush-lite. The latter was the Democratic Party, which was taken over by corporations, as already described in the Clinton era. In Europe, where labor parties have ruled for decades, social democratic unions and parties require companies to pay higher wages and grant more job training and security to their workers. A new populist Democratic Party, aligned closely with workers and unions, will move the US toward its own worker-friendly, anti-oligarchic system, a form of social democratic regime change with workers in charge.

In the new regime, rather than simply bargaining for higher wages for their own members, unions must partner with each other and the Democratic Party to create system-wide change to end oligarchic rule. Labor and labor parties will move to democratize the companies and the nation. In the New Deal, government created millions of jobs and took over industries when necessary to drive system-wide change out of depression. From its current oligarchic form, a new form of ESG – with system-wide high wages, job security and environmental sustainability – will emerge. It will no longer be a reformist initiative by individual firms and oligarchs but a systemic imperative driven together by government and workers co-managing the economy across the entire nation.

In Germany, companies with over 500 employees must give 50% of their corporate board seats to representatives elected by workers. This anti-oligarchic systemic regime change, called "codetermination," is viewed as part of economic democracy. Such codetermination is positive populist change and is paired with elected worker councils in every corporate department that rule together with managers and independent unions. Such worker power in the company is increased by national negotiations over every aspect of wages and economic life in which workers and labor parties have a major decision-making role. A Green New Deal in the US, sponsored by AOC and Senator Markey of Massachusetts, seeks many of the same worker and public investments, not only to secure workers' jobs and influence but also a larger social compact to save the environment; this means taxing oligarchs for major public investment in renewable energy, public transit, affordable public housing and other major public goods. The regime moves from a system of commodity production for profits toward a public goods economy.

Universal social welfare is also key to creative and positive populist regime change. While Trump is slashing Social Security, Medicare and Medicaid, undermining the survival needs of many who voted for him, American majorities will move, if only for their own survival, toward a positive populist social welfare model ensuring health care, education, child care, elder care, public transit, and public services for ordinary citizens. Such measures all got initial legal foundations and support in the New Deal and grew stronger in LBJ's Great Society. While Reagan and Trump aligned with the oligarchy to destroy New Deal social safety nets, persevering and expanding them are now a high priority for the millions of Americans out on the streets.

Europeans have built universal social welfare, ensuring free or inexpensive health care, higher education, child and elder care and many other universal public goods and services that even Far-Right movements in Europe today do not dare challenge. They have become too essential and popular in their publics to destroy or challenge. As Trump used Musk to begin to destroy the more limited American social welfare system while redirecting billions into Musk's and his fellow oligarch's corporate welfare system, the public passion for public safety nets and essential services will grow, much as it did in the New Deal and has taken strong root in Europe today.

Resisting Trumpism is taking down American oligarchy while creating social democracy, American-style. The New Deal is the historical precedent; another new one, likely Green, will follow. Such regime change at home will emerge from the catastrophic failures and disasters of Trumpism. The notion that crisis is opportunity is never truer than in the US today. Our survival requires making good on that promise.

Notes

1 Chris McGreal, "Voters who backed Trump identity new swamp to drain: Corporate power," *The Guardian*, Jan. 17, 2025, theguardian.com

2 Steven Greenhouse, "He's brazenly anti-worker:' US marks the first Labor Day under Trump 2.0" the Guardian, Sept. 1, 2025, theguardian.com

3 Conor Murray, "Over 1,000 'Workers Over Billionaires' Protests Planned for Labor Day," What to Know," Forbes, Sept. 1, 2025, forbes.com

4 By Robert ChiaritoAbigail GeigerSean Piccoli and J. David Goodman, "Labor Day Protests Denounce Trump While Supporting Workers," *New York Times*, Sept 1, 2025 nytimes.com

5 Wendy Weiser. The President's Executive Order on Elections, Explained, April 15, 2025, brennancenter.org

6 Latosha Brown, cited in Charles Derber, 1964's Freedom Summer Offers a Model of the Voting Rights Work We Need to Do," Truthout, April 21, 2024, truthout.org

7 Paul Blumenthal, "Donald Trump Targets Democratic Party Fundraising Platform ActBlue," Huffpost, April 24, 2025, huffpost.com

8 Robert Kuttner, "Trump's Ultimate Cure for an Unpopular Budget," Kutttner on Tap, American Prospect, July 7, 2025, info@prospect.org

9 We should all be very, very afraid." (Erwin Chemerinsky and Laurence Tribe, "We Should All be Very, Very Afraid," *NY Times*, April 9, 2025, nytimes.com

10 Morgan Lee, "Thousands Across the US Protest Trump Policies," pbs.org Feb. 5, 2025, pbs.org

11 Morgan Lee, "Thousands Across the US Protest Trump Policies," pbs.org Feb. 5, 2025, pbs.org

12 Lydia O'Connor, "Pam Bondi Hints At More Judge Arrests In Bone-Chilling Interview," HuffPost, April 25,2025, huppost.com

13 Norman Soloman, "New DNC Chair Ken Martin must embrace genuine populism," *The Hill*, Feb. 6, 2025, thehill.com

14 Robert Borosage, cited in Norman Soloman, "New DNC Chair Ken Martin must embrace genuine populism," *The Hill*, Feb. 6, 2025, thehill.com

15 Euronews English, Euronews English's post, facebook.com

Afterword
The Ten Commandments of Positive Populism

All political transformative movements must live by principled ideals. This requires courage and hope in the face of brutal and often violent repression. But holding on to hope and high ideals is crucial for positive populists. I have drawn these "ten commandments" from my own experience in these movements, including multiracial voter registration and voting in the Deep South in 1965, where all activists faced life or death. Martin Luther King inspired many of these ideals, and he both faced the ultimate consequences for living up to them and left a legacy still vital and nourishing for positive populists today.

1 Be nonviolent, even when you face violent militias, inside and outside agitators, or militarized police.
2 Model the democracy you fight for – and always fight for democracy. Don't let the bullies and authoritarians take over your own space, organizations and communities.
3 Use your media and social media skills to demolish the propaganda and power of the ruling elites. Educate the public and listen to them the way they should listen to you. Advance a positive populist agenda against corporate oligarchy and for democracy – an agenda that the polls show is supported by the majority of Americans.
4 Build solidarity with the mainstream as you call for universal human rights. You are the voice of working people across class, race and gender lines, fighting for their freedom and yours. Speak to the anti-big money anti-corporate oligarchy majority even when fascists are in power.
5 Avoid dogma, cancel culture and political correctness. Focus public attention on the issues, not on yourself.
6 Move beyond siloed identity politics as you unite and universalize across race, gender and religion against militarized capitalism and its poisoned fruit of fascism, climate catastrophe and war. There will be no justice – or survival – without you.
7 Organize for small-scale and large-scale system change to revolutionize the nation, but like Martin Luther King, embrace the best ideals of the country. You can't change what you hate; only what you love.

8 Counter and Destroy the Right-Wing Narrative about Protest and Law and Order. Trumpism has destroyed Law and Order – and the country increasingly sees him as trampling on basic rights and the Constitution.

9 Align with progressive politicians and support voting rights in the face of Trumpist election denialism. Run movement candidates for office, including yourself, who speak truth to power and wed revolution to pragmatism. Model courage that everyone now needs to see and embrace.

10 Model also the caring community you are fighting for. Be the love that sustains the movement and yourself for the long run. Bring the movement's music, poetry, comradeship and activism into your life's work and family – and don't join a revolution you can't dance in.

Index

Note: Page numbers in *italics* refer to figures.

For Product Safety Concerns and Information please contact our EU
representative GPSR@taylorandfrancis.com
Taylor & Francis Verlag GmbH, Kaufingerstraße 24, 80331 München, Germany

www.ingramcontent.com/pod-product-compliance
Lightning Source LLC
Chambersburg PA
CBHW070324270326
41926CB00017B/3751

9 781041 119975